Creating a Balanced Scorecard for a Financial Services Organization

Creating a Balanced Scorecard for a Financial Services Organization

NARESH MAKHIJANI AND
JAMES CREELMAN

WILEY

John Wiley & Sons (Asia) Pte. Ltd.

Other Wiley Editorial Offices

John Wiley & Sons, 111 River Street, Hoboken, NJ 07030, USA
John Wiley & Sons, The Atrium, Southern Gate, Chichester, West Sussex, P019 8SQ, United
    Kingdom
John Wiley & Sons (Canada) Ltd., 5353 Dundas Street West, Suite 400, Toronto, Ontario,
    M9B 6HB, Canada
John Wiley & Sons Australia Ltd., 42 McDougall Street, Milton, Queensland 4064, Australia
Wiley-VCH, Boschstrasse 12, D-69469 Weinheim, Germany

Library of Congress Cataloging-in-Publication Data
ISBN 978–0–470–83030–7 (Hardcover)
ISBN 978–0–470–83032–1 (ePDF)
ISBN 978–0–470–83031–4 (Mobi)
ISBN 978–0–470–83033–8 (ePub)

Typeset in 10/12pt Sabon-Roman by Thomson Digital, Noida
Printed in Singapore by Toppan Security Printing Pte. Ltd.
10 9 8 7 6 5 4 3 2 1

From James Creelman

*With hands big as shovels and a heart full of love . . .
my Father, my Father.*

To the memory of Robert Murray Creelman:
1933–2009.

From Naresh Makhijani

*To my brother, Rajesh Makhijani, nothing is impossible
and miracles will happen.*

Contents

Introduction

The seeds of this book were sown in 2008 when the world became all too aware of that hitherto obscure term "credit crunch." As we watched financial institutions crumble and witnessed the devastating effect of the economic tsunami that ripped its way through global economies, a number of things became abundantly clear. That the world would likely spend many years recovering from what proved to be a "near depression," and that financial institutions, most notably the banking sector, would need to go through a radical overhaul to be "fit for purpose," for the new post-credit crunch economy.

What being "fit for purpose," would look like also began to become clear as the credit crunch unfolded. And as researchers, analysts and economists told the story (or at least the early versions; the *actual* story has perhaps yet to be told), certain words and terms began to be regularly applied. Financial institutions would, it was repeatedly argued, need to become much more "accountable," for their performance. Their day-to-day working practices and decision-making processes would need to be far more "transparent," than had hitherto been the case, and there would have to be a greater understanding of the risks that were inherent in the products being sold and, of course, the strategic choices that were being made.

Moreover, organizations would need to better understand, and communicate to shareholders and other stakeholder groups the non-financial drivers of future financial performance and must be at least as much concerned with managing for the longer-term as driving short-term performance and demonstrate this. And perhaps imbued with the greatest emotions (especially from the general public, who is experiencing most of the fallout from the credit crunch in terms of job losses throughout the economy and massive cutbacks in public services), compensation systems would need to be overhauled to be more reflective of actual performance and the sustainable value that is built.

As we thought about a roadmap for recovery that could contend with these challenges, our thoughts continually anchored back to the Balanced Scorecard. Since its original launch in the early 1990s (and confirmed through our consulting and research experiences) the scorecard has repeatedly proven to help organizations from various sectors and industries to overcome the myriad trials that financial institutions face.

In writing this book, and in our description of the Balanced Scorecard, we have been fully and constantly cognizant of the huge task facing the leaders of financial institutions (most notably of course from the banking sector) over the coming years and the intense scrutiny that will be under from a raft of stakeholder groups, such as shareholders, legislators, regulators and the general public. All will need a lot of convincing before they replace their trust in the beleaguered sector.

Sprinkled with case examples and advice from scorecard experts, this book provides a complete picture of how to build and implement the Balanced Scorecard within a financial services organization. Written as a practitioner's step-by-step guide the book explains how to build a causal Strategy Map of strategic objectives and select Key Performance Indicators, targets and strategic initiatives from one financial and three non-financial perspectives of customer, internal process and learning and growth, (the core components of a Balanced Scorecard) at both the strategic business unit and devolved levels. In addition to being a framework that enables the balancing of long-term performance stewardship while optimizing short-term efforts, a Balanced Scorecard also drives performance accountability and transparency deep inside the organization.

The following chapters also outline how to put in place the appropriate culture for managing with the Balanced Scorecard (particularly important as we make "risk management," an integral part of the strategic management process) and how to select the appropriate technology for strategy management (very important for making performance fully visible and transparent). Moreover, we also explain how to rework an incentive-compensation system so it reflects the drivers of future value creation as well as historic financial performance (the most emotive of the change requirements). And we also show how to link the Balanced Scorecard framework and methodology with other key management processes such as the annual budget and other planning processes, how to link strategic and operational processes and how to reengineer management (operational, strategic and boards of directors) review meetings to drive greater clarity, focus and relevance into performance assessments. We also explain how to build the internal capability (through an Office of Strategy Management) that will inculcate the capabilities to manage with a Balanced Scorecard and to make strategy "everyone's every day job."

This work reflects the many years experience and field observations of the two authors but would not have been possible without the involvement of others, which we here fully acknowledge. We would like to thank the case study companies that we profiled, and in particular the three from

Indonesia and their representatives: Dyah Nastiti Kusumowardani,'s Director of Strategy Planning, Bank Indonesia, Wahyu Eko Wardon, Head of Corporate Strategy, Bank CIMB Niaga and Falk Archibald Kemur, Head of the President's Office, ADIRA Finance. We would like to thank present and past OTI staff for contributing their knowledge and experience and all present and past OTI clients, who have continually shown enthusiasm for the Balanced Scorecard approach, have benefited from the results and enriched our understanding of how best to apply this framework and methodology within diverse sector settings.

We also acknowledge the thought leadership of people such as Andrew Smart of the U.K.-based management consultancy Manigent and Nigel Penny of the Singapore-based ClaritasAsia who were especially useful in shaping our understanding of how to integrate risk management with strategy management within the scorecard framework. Finally we would like to thank Professor Robert Kaplan and Dr. David Norton for their work in developing and evolving the Balanced Scorecard. We truly stand on the shoulders of giants.

CHAPTER 1

The Curse of Living in "Interesting Times," The Credit Crunch, and Other Challenges

EXECUTIVE SUMMARY

1. The 2008 collapse of the financial markets that triggered the commonly termed "credit crunch" had a catastrophic impact on the financial services industry.
2. According to the Association of Chartered Certified Accountants, the principal cause of the credit crunch was a failure in corporate governance at banks, resulting in short-term thinking and blindness to risk.
3. We explain that the introduction of a properly architected Balanced Scorecard system can help overcome these failings.
4. Many of the "lessons" now being learnt by Western organizations as a result of the credit crunch were already understood in Southeast Asia as a result of the region's 1997 currency crisis.
5. Deregulation, the globalization of markets, and breathtaking advancements in information and communication technologies are also transforming financial services.
6. With many experts claiming that customer loyalty is essentially "dead" in financial services, it is interesting that some organizations from the sector are using the Balanced Scorecard to drive loyalty.
7. A case report on Canada's Scotiabank shows how it continues to succeed through using the Balanced Scorecard.
8. We provide a snapshot of the scorecard successes of the early pioneering financial services organizations: Chemical Bank and CIGNA Property & Casualty division.

INTRODUCTION

An ancient Chinese adage states that it is a curse to live in interesting times. If that is true then those working in the financial services industry (most notably the banking sector) have been "cursed" over the past few years. Without question they have lived in "interesting" times.

THE IMPACT OF THE CREDIT CRUNCH

The 2008 collapse of the subprime mortgage market that triggered the commonly termed "credit crunch" had a catastrophic impact on the financial services industry. In the middle of the first decade of this century, it would have been unthinkable that venerable and long-established organizations such as Lehman Brothers would be out of business before the end of the decade and that Merrill Lynch would survive only thanks to being taken over by the Bank of America. It would have been equally unimaginable that "darlings of the stock markets" such as the U.K.-headquartered Royal Bank of Scotland would only survive the decade thanks to massive bailouts from national governments.

The fallout from the collapse of banks and other financial institutions has had a profound and debilitating impact on all industries and sectors. As the full extent of the credit crunch took hold, many economists and other experts feared that we are entering a recession that might be as deep and long lasting as the great depression of the 1930s—itself essentially triggered by a collapse of confidence in the banking industry. Although, largely thanks to government bailouts as well as massive spending to get economies moving, we managed to avoid "depression," the financial services sector will likely never be the same again and it will probably take many years before public, and perhaps more importantly, customer confidence is fully restored.

Even before the credit crunch, customer confidence in the financial services sector had badly eroded because of the uncovering of long-term issues caused by the systematic misselling of pensions and mortgages. Customer anger has been further stoked because to pay for the banking bailouts and the spending to avoid "depression," there will be massive cuts in public sector in many countries (the U.K. being a prime example where for some years there will be severe cuts across government departments and public services. Many public sector workers will lose their jobs—and guess who they're blaming?)

The Causes of the Credit Crunch

Let's consider what caused the financial disaster that was the credit crunch. It is obvious that widescale inappropriate lending to people with poor credit ratings had a dramatic impact on those who had invested in these securities. According to the global body of professional accountants, the Association of Chartered Certified Accountants (ACCA), the principal cause of the credit crunch was a failure in corporate governance at banks, resulting in short-term thinking and blindness to risk.

Before looking in more depth at the ACCA findings, note that "blindness to risk," which has been noted by most experts as a key cause of the credit crunch (or perhaps more accurately a reckless attitude to risk management) has long been a cause for concern in financial services, especially banking. Indeed, as early as 2004, Alan Greenspan, chairman of the U.S. Federal Reserve noted that:

> *It would be a mistake to conclude that the only way to succeed in banking is through ever-greater size and diversity. Indeed, better risk management may be the only truly necessary element of success in banking.*

Even earlier, in 2001, the influential Risk Management Group of the Basel Committee on Banking Supervision defined risk as: "the risk of loss resulting from inadequate or failed processes, people, and systems or from external events."[1]

ACCA's policy paper, *Climbing Out of the Credit Crunch*,[2] examined five key areas of banking performance: corporate governance; remuneration and incentives; risk identification and management; management accounting and financial reporting; and regulation.

Within its wide-ranging and damning report, the failures identified for the first three of these areas are particularly interesting when considered through the lens of this book.

Corporate Governance   "A fundamental role of the board is to provide oversight, direction and control but also to challenge where necessary. This does not appear to have happened in many of the banks," the ACCA paper noted. "No doubt this is partly owing to a lack of understanding of the complexities of the business, but more training is probably only part of the solution . . . [but] what inhibited boards and managers from asking the right questions and understanding the risks that were being run on their watch?"

As we explain in this book, one of the key strengths of the Balanced Scorecard system is that it inculcates performance transparency and accountability into organizations: from the very top down to team and even individual levels.

The existence of a well-thought-out enterprise-level Strategy Map and accompanying scorecard of metrics, targets, and initiatives provides corporate boards with an excellent and concise view of corporate financial performance and the nonfinancial drivers of that performance. As a governance tool this is clearly much more useful to corporate boards than the weighty and overly detailed board packs that they typically receive before board meetings.

Moreover, as we explain in chapter 2, it is possible to build strategy maps and scorecards for the corporate board and their constituent oversight committees (such as those for remuneration and incentives). This board scorecard system can have a powerful and positive impact on how a board discharges its corporate governance responsibilities.

Remuneration and Incentives In the paper, ACCA stated that although executive remuneration arrangements should promote organizational performance, the existing incentive and career structures of banks meant enormous rewards reinforced short-term thinking. "If not addressed, remuneration issues will continue to frustrate other attempts for reform," the paper noted. "Risk management and remuneration and incentive systems must be linked. Executive payments should be deferred (e.g. held in an escrow account) until profits have been realized, cash received and accounting transactions cannot be reversed."

Sukhend Pal, managing partner at the U.K.'s Centrix Consulting made an interesting observation on the role of incentive compensation and product complexity in the cause of the credit crunch in an article that appeared in a June edition of *Raconteur* (a supplement distributed within the U.K.'s *Times* newspaper).[3] "The role of structured products created by derivatives specialists as investment, such as collateralized debt obligations, has been the root cause of the financial crisis," he said. "Many [Centrix] clients have been seriously beguiled by the structure of these products that were expensive, highly complex and simply not appropriate. Yet, investment bankers sold them for their personal gain and sky high bonuses."

In chapter 10 of this book, we describe how remuneration and incentives can be hardwired to performance against the Balanced Scorecard system. If a risk management theme is included within the scorecard (and it most likely will be for those involved in financial services), then how this affects present and future financial results should be a key determinant of remuneration and incentive payouts.

Risk Identification and Management The ACCA paper notes that:

> Banks have highly sophisticated risk management functions yet recent events have tested them and found many wanting . . . In early 2007, few senior managers thought they were betting on

the viability of their banks. It appears they did not understand the risks and were using risk assessment with tools which were inappropriate. Boards may not have expended the necessary time and energy, and/or lacked the expertise to ask the right questions.

In chapter 3, we explain the importance of strategic risk management as part of, or at least aligned to, the scorecard system, while in chapter 4 we consider key risk indicators. Andrew Smart, a performance and risk management expert with the U.K.-based consultancy Manigent, says: "Simply, the credit crisis arose because financial services organizations failed to develop and execute sustainable strategies that fully considered their risk environment, and they neglected to embed risk management at the heart of their strategic and operational processes."[4]

The Southeast Asia Currency Crisis

As financial institutions begin to put in place the strategic risk and control tools to help them emerge from the credit crunch (and ensure that it doesn't happen again), we should reflect on the fact that although most of the world is witnessing a once-in-a-lifetime restructuring of banking and related industries, this is not the case in Southeast Asia. The banking industry in this region, and most profoundly Indonesia, went through massive transformation after the Asia currency crisis of 1997, precipitated when the Korean company Hanbo Steel collapsed with $6 billion of debts. As a result, Asian banks faced massive problems with nonpayments of loans, while Asian currencies sharply fell in value.

In Indonesia, the repercussion for the banking sector was dramatic, with the closure of almost 50 percent of the country's 250-plus banks. Those that survived were placed under government supervision through the Indonesian Banking Restructuring Agency (IBRA). As a result, banking became essentially state controlled while it was being reorganized.

Understood in relation to the present global financial sector meltdown, it might be telling that the sector in Indonesia is relatively unscathed. Indeed, while most of the world's banks were restructuring and downsizing to survive the fallout from the credit crunch, one of the case studies within this book—the Jakarta-headquartered Bank CIMB Niaga—spent 2008 aggressively growing its business and planting the seeds of future growth. That Bank CIMB Niaga found itself in this position is partly thanks to the excellent work done since the currency crisis by Bank Indonesia, which is the nation's independent and autonomous central bank. Bank Indonesia is another case study within this book.

It is likely that after the 1997 currency crisis, banks in Indonesia learnt the governance and other lessons that most of the rest of the world is, with great pain, learning today.

Although the aftermath of the credit crunch is the most pressing challenge facing the financial services sector today, it is not the only one: further proving the adage that the sector is living in "interesting times." Over recent years, other powerful influences have been profoundly reshaping how the sector operates, goes to market and relates to customers.

DEREGULATION, GLOBALIZATION, AND TECHNOLOGY

Deregulation, the opening up of global markets and breathtaking advancements in information and communications technologies, has affected all organizations to some degree. But, as with the credit crunch, it is something of a struggle to identify another industry in which the effect has been as pervasive and transformational as in financial services.

Online Market Channels

For example, consider the revolutionary impact on the industry of online market channels. Today, individuals can source all of their financial products and services from the comfort of their own home, and at a click of a button can instantly compare prices and product characteristics for many hundreds of suppliers. It is a sobering thought that when the remote bank Banking 365, another case study in this book, opened its lines for business in 1996, such operations were virtually unknown.

THE COLLAPSE OF CUSTOMER LOYALTY

Financial services was once a sector (across the spectrum from banking to insurance through financing to investing) in which competitive advantage was largely the outcome of the quality and depth of personal relationships. Think, for example, of the historic relationships between a homeowner and an insurance salesman, or an individual investor and a broker, or even a bank employee and people who live in the neighborhood and had all their banking needs catered to by one branch.

Today, personal relationships play a substantially smaller part in the financial services supplier and customer dynamic. Naturally, this has had a profound impact on levels of customer loyalty. For example, most people find it much easier to sever links with a bank that they experience mainly through a customer contact center or on the internet than it is to "leave" a local bank manager that they have known and been friends with for many years.

Customer Loyalty Research

Not surprisingly, therefore, customer loyalty and retention have become growing concerns for most financial services organizations. Consider, for instance, the retail banking sector. A European report by the U.K.-based *Datamonitor* found that customer loyalty is decreasing year on year. Branch managers surveyed revealed that they believed that an increase in consumer awareness of financial services products and the growth in online banking are the principal reasons for the decrease in loyalty.[5] Interestingly, Banking 365 set out with a mission that through remote channels it would *improve* the then low levels of customer satisfaction—and consequently loyalty.

The *Datamonitor* researchers claim that customers are increasingly looking at their financial services providers not as lifelong partners, but as providers for a short time. Moreover, their research finds that the customer loyalty issue looks set to worsen for lenders in the long run, as competition intensifies and deregulation continues.

Since this research was conducted before the financial services industry was hit by the credit crunch, we can reasonably assume that the massive erosion of customer confidence has further reduced loyalty tendencies. Indeed, banks—and most firmly their senior managers—are treated with at best deep suspicion and at worst downright hatred.

Using the Balanced Scorecard to Create a Customer Experience

That said, we would argue that through using the Balanced Scorecard, financial services companies are better able to predict and plan for customer defection, leading to much higher retention rates and, on doing so, gradually rebuilding the trust that customers have in banks and their senior employees.

Banks can do this by modeling how to configure people competencies and customer-facing internal processes so that the customer receives the type of service and experience that encourage them to continue the relationship with the supplier.

Case Example: Scotiabank   An exemplary example is the Canadian bank Scotiabank. In-depth research on its customer database at the turn of the century suggested that upcoming issues across the banking world would seriously affect loyalty and therefore profitability. Among these was the commoditization of financial services products, which meant that product differentiation would likely no longer provide competitive advantage for any length of time. Consequently, in 2001 Scotiabank introduced the Balanced Scorecard to support a new vision to "to be the best at helping its customers become financially better off, by providing relevant solutions to their unique needs." By delivering that experience, Scotiabank believed it would retain (and also win) customers in fiercely competitive markets.

Has Scotiabank delivered on this vision? Fast forward to March 2007 and the address to the annual general meeting made by Richard E. Waugh, the corporation's president and CEO.

> *Our objective is to achieve the highest levels of customer satisfaction and loyalty. We want to deepen our relationships with our existing customers. And we want to continue to acquire new customers.*

He continued that its research had found that its vision resonated with customers. "In fact, it's a proposition that translates into a tremendous level of customer loyalty," said Waugh. "[And] compared to the other Canadian banks, Scotiabank customers report very high levels of customer loyalty. This higher level of commitment means that our customers are more likely to recommend our services to others. And it means they'll trust us with more of their business."

As for 2007 success, the 60,000-employee-strong Scotiabank reported net income available to common shareholders of C$3,994 million and return on equity of 22 percent. Dividends increased by 16 percent. The total return to shareholders (share price appreciation plus dividends reinvested) was 12 percent—resulting in 13 consecutive years of positive returns to shareholders of the bank. The compound annual return of the bank's shares over the past five years has averaged 22 percent.

In the same presentation Waugh also referenced the important role of the Balanced Scorecard. "[W]hen we look at our performance as an organization, we look at more than just our financials," he said. "We use a Balanced Scorecard [which] means financial performance [but] also means meeting our customer goals. It means operational success and, of course, it means our people."

Of course, this presentation predates the credit crunch. So let's fast forward to the speech made by Waugh at the 2009 annual general meeting, after the credit crunch tsunami had hit the world.[6] He said:

> *Scotiabank is a strong bank. We have performed well relative to our global peers. And we are facing the challenges of this difficult environment head on. I have confidence in our ability to do so because of our Bank's culture . . . a culture with clear strengths—diversification, risk management and cost control. And a culture that manages in a balanced way—thinking about the people our decisions impact—our stakeholders—our employees, our customers, our communities and our shareholders.*

Despite the credit crunch, Waugh has kept his faith in managing in a "balanced" way; a faith strengthened by the bank performing much better than most in the challenging and interesting times of 2008.

SCORECARD PIONEERS

Scotiabank was far from the first financial services organization to introduce, and demonstrate stunning successes through the Balanced Scorecard. From the inception of the Balanced Scorecard framework and methodology back in 1992 (see chapter 2 for the history of the scorecard), financial services organizations have been among the most prolific adopters. Early success stories included the following.

Chemical Bank (Later Part of Chase Manhattan)

At the turn of the 1990s, the retail bank division of Chemical Bank faced declining margins and increased competition in its credit and deposit gathering and processing business. It decided to implement a new strategy to become a preferred financial service provider to targeted customer groups. In 1993 the division adopted the Balanced Scorecard to clarify and communicate the new strategy and to identify the key drivers for strategic success. By 1996, the results of the new strategy were becoming apparent. In the space of three years, profitability had increased by a factor of 20.

CIGNA Property & Casualty Insurance

In 1993, the Property & Casualty (P&C) division of the insurance firm CIGNA lost nearly $275 million. Although this poor performance was due in part to a few major catastrophes, most lines of business were marginal. In the opinion of the new management team brought in to turn the situation around, the division had lost control of the underwriting process—the process by which risks were evaluated and priced. The management team believed that CIGNA was pursuing an obsolete "generalist" strategy, trying to be all things to all people; therefore, a new strategy was developed. CIGNA would be a "specialist," focusing on niches where it had comparative advantage. The division would make underwriting an asset instead of a liability. If the strategy succeeded, CIGNA would become a "top quartile" performer. The strategy was rolled out to 20 business units in 1993. The Balanced Scorecard was used as the core management process.

Again the results were rapid and dramatic. Within two years, CIGNA had returned to profitability. This performance has been sustained for four consecutive years. In 1998, the company's performance placed it in the top quartile of its industry. At the end of 1998, the parent company spun off the P&C division for a price of $3.45 billion. The Balanced Scorecard was core component of this success story.

We talk more about the CIGNA P&C success story in the following chapters. One of the authors of this books spent some time in the late 1990s uncovering the inside secrets of the CIGNA P&C scorecard success story.

OTHER SCORECARD-USING FINANCIAL SERVICES COMPANIES

If Chemical Bank and CIGNA P&C were scorecard pioneers, other financial services organizations followed suit, a sample of which is listed in figure 1.1.

Adira Finance; AllFirst Bank; Artesian Banking Corporation; Astra Insurance; BMW Financial Services; Bank of England; Bank Indonesia, Bank CIMB Niaga; Bank Universal (now merged into PermataBank) Bank of Tokyo-Mitsubishi; Banking 365—Bank of Ireland; Barclays; Bristol & West; Chemical Bank (later part of Chase Manhattan); CIGNA Property & Casualty Division; Depository Trust & Clearing Corporation; First Commonwealth Financial Corporation; First Union (now part of Wachovia); JP Morgan Investor Services; KeyCorp; Kiwibank; Nationwide Bank (U.S.); Nationwide Building Society (U.K.); NatWest Bank; Nordea Bank; Pentagon Credit Union; Scotiabank; Skandia; State Street Corporation's Alternative Investment Solutions (AIS) unit, and UNUM Corporation.

FIGURE 1.1 Sample financial services organizations that have successfully used a Balanced Scorecard

CONCLUSION

We profile many of these organizations within this book. We will explain how the Balanced Scorecard has helped them win in challenging markets and how it will continue to do so going forward. Some of the successes have been truly spectacular which we will explain later. Chapter 4 is where we begin the process of providing a practical description of how to build and implement the Balanced Scorecard. In the next chapter, however, we will explain how the Balanced Scorecard has evolved to become a truly enterprisewide strategy management system and will provide a robust description of a Balanced Scorecard framework. Getting this basic understanding in place makes it easier to succeed in the scorecard building and deployment phases.

ENDNOTES

1. Quoted from G. J. G. Lawrie, D. C. Kalff, and H. V. Andersen, *Integrating Risk Management with Existing Methods of Corporate Governance* (U.K.: 2GC, 2003). See www.2gc.co.uk.
2. Association of Chartered Certified Accountants, *Climbing Out of the Credit Crunch*, policy paper, 2008.
3. Simon Brooke, "Can Lean and Six Sigma Help Revive Financial Services? Or Was Their Usage Partly to Blame for Current Turmoil?", *Raconteur Media*, June 8, 2010.
4. Andrew Smart, *Aligning Risk Management and Exposure: The New Paradigm of Strategic Execution* (London: Manigent, 2009).
5. *Datamonitor, Trends in Customer Loyalty and Acquisition Strategies in Europe*, 2007.
6. Presentation made by Richard E. Waugh, President and CEO, Scotiabank, to the Scotiabank annual general meeting, March, 2009.

CHAPTER 2

Describing the Balanced Scorecard

EXECUTIVE SUMMARY

1. By the late 1980s, it had become clear that financial measures had become inadequate for assessing performance. The Balanced Scorecard evolved out of this recognition.
2. Recent research suggests that 66 percent of large companies use the Balanced Scorecard.
3. The scorecard was originally positioned as a balanced measurement system that mainly focused on using nonfinancial metrics to support financials.
4. The scorecard took a major step forward with the creation of a Strategy Map that shows the cause and effect relationship between strategic objectives.
5. A Balanced Scorecard framework includes a Strategy Map and accompanying scorecard of metrics, targets, and initiatives. Balanced scorecards are typically collocated to four perspectives: financial, customer, internal process, and learning and growth, though such a collocation is not mandated.
6. The next evolution saw the development of the idea of the strategy-focused organization.
7. Next came the idea of aligning the extended enterprise through strategy maps and balanced scorecards.
8. The idea of an Office of Strategy Management has evolved from the scorecard, which might have far-reaching implications for how work is managed in the knowledge era.
9. The Execution Premium Model is a powerful mechanism for aligning strategy with operations through the Balanced Scorecard.

INTRODUCTION

Two decades have passed since consultant Dr. David P. Norton and Harvard Business School Professor Dr. Robert S. Kaplan launched their proposition for the Balanced Scorecard in a *Harvard Business Review* article. The proposition emerged from a simple argument: that the financial model of business alone as the primary means of managing performance was no longer adequate. The financial model was useful, they said, for providing detail on what happened yesterday, but was of little use in managing the development of the business.

Their argument, and their proposal that the solution was found in the Balanced Scorecard, were further elaborated in a series of agenda-setting *Harvard Business Review* articles and books.[1]

Organizations readily accepted Kaplan and Norton's argument and solution. In many ways it was the right idea at the right time, because in the later 1980s there was a growing movement to promote the importance of "balancing" nonfinancial performance information with financial data; largely thanks to the surge of interest in Total Quality Management that followed the Japanese taking large chunks of various Western markets.

Indeed, the *Harvard Business Review* says that of all management ideas in the last 75 years of the twentieth century, the Balanced Scorecard has had one of the greatest impacts on business.[2] Its enduring appeal into this century is shown in the 2007 research by the consultancy Bain & Company, which found that 66 percent of large organizations used the Balanced Scorecard: the highest percentage since Bain began its survey in 1993.[3]

According to the Bain study, Asia-Pacific is presently the fastest-growing region of scorecard users.

THE SCORECARD'S ORIGINS

As background to the creation of the scorecard idea and methodology, in 1990, Kaplan and Norton led a study of about 10 companies including CIGNA, Apple Computer, and Hewlett Packard, that set out to look into the growing awareness amongst corporate leaders of the inadequacy of financial metrics.

As part of this review, Kaplan and Norton received a presentation from Analog Devices. The company's then vice-president of quality improvement and productivity, Art Schneiderman, explained to the study group how Analog Devices was successfully using what it called "a corporate scorecard" to monitor its performance. This scorecard included performance measures relating to customer delivery times, quality, and cycle times for manufacturing processes, and effectiveness of new product development, as well as financial measures.

The study group considered Analog's approach a promising start for a new balanced measurement system, and adopted the term scorecard. Consequently, on the basis of this research program, Kaplan and Norton formulated the first-generation Balanced Scorecard.

A BALANCED MEASUREMENT SYSTEM

Positioned at this stage as a measurement system, the classic Balanced Scorecard set out to capture performance from four perspectives: one financial and three nonfinancial: customer, internal process, and learning and innovation (subsequently redefined as learning and growth when Kaplan and Norton realized that innovation correctly belonged within the internal process perspective). Figure 2.1 shows a schematic of the Balanced Scorecard, illustrating how it supports a central vision and strategy. Around this hub is built the four perspectives with their own strategic objectives, measures, targets, and initiatives.

THE EMERGENCE OF THE STRATEGY MAP

Although organizations gained substantial value from the first-generation Balanced Scorecard, some early adopters, including CIGNA Property & Casualty and Mobil Oil, found that the Balanced Scorecard worked best not when used simply as an extension of the financial measurement system, but when it was hardwired to strategy and deployed as a strategic implementation system.

What they found to be missing was a mechanism for showing the cause-and-effect relationship among the strategic objectives from the four perspectives. Thus was born the idea of strategy maps (which would eventually become the topic of Kaplan and Norton's third book).[4] Originally, the maps were generally referred to as linkage models. Figure 2.2 shows a generic banking Strategy Map.

Case Example: CIGNA Property & Casualty

As mentioned in chapter 1, an early adopter was the Philadelphia-based CIGNA Property & Casualty (P&C) division.

In 1996, CIGNA P&C achieved a profit of $80 million on revenues of $3.5 billion. Although on first take this might not seem that impressive, it actually amounted to an astonishing turnaround since 1992. That year it posted losses of about $300 million, which was the third year of major losses, with a cumulative loss of about $1 billion over that period.

Transformation began in March 1993 when Gerry Isom was appointed as CIGNA P&C's divisional president. Isom faced several fundamental

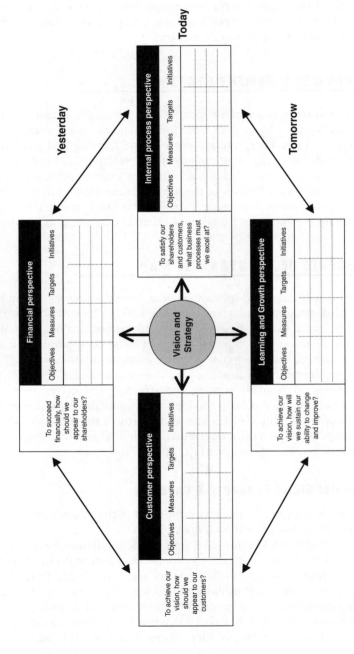

FIGURE 2.1 A schematic of the Balanced Scorecard

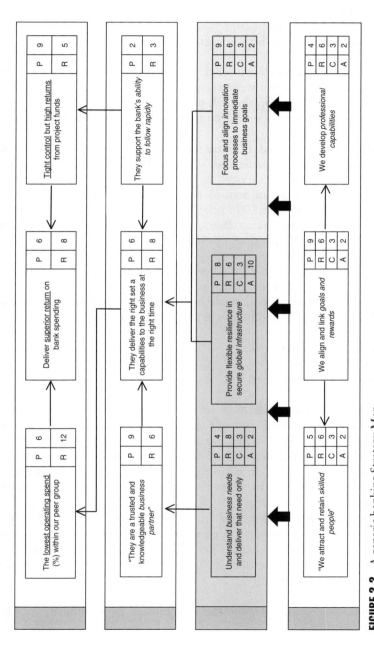

FIGURE 2.2 A generic banking Strategy Map
Source: Manigent, *The New Paradigm of Strategic Execution,* 2009.

challenges that he recognized had to be overcome if the organization was to return to profitability. Note that the division was in the "last chance saloon." The parent organization had intentions of closing down the division if it did not achieve turnaround quickly.

- First, the company had lost its critical underwriting discipline: the quality of underwriting directly correlates with payouts on losses; a problem compounded by deteriorating relations with agents and brokers—who worked with customers on selecting policies and assessing risks—was deteriorating.
- Second, the division had an outdated business strategy. CIGNA P&C was positioned as a "generalist" insurer at a time when customers required more specialist services.
- Isom and his top team undertook a search 10-week business analysis. This included more than 100 in-depth interviews with employees while talking to and surveying customers, field staff, agents, and brokers. The key question was, "How does this business work?"

Armed with the information gleaned, Isom articulated a goal to transform CIGNA P&C from a generalist to a specialist insurer.

Isom's vision was that P&C would be a top-quartile performer in each of its specialist markets. The company was reorganized into three profit centers:

- Specialty Insurance Services
- Special Risk Facility
- Commercial Insurance Services.

Isom recruited Tom Valerio as senior vice president, transformation. Valerio decided to use the Balanced Scorecard to align the division behind the specialist strategy. Valerio had already experienced the scorecard in his work with the consultancy from which he was recruited by Isom.

The scorecard was introduced in the fourth quarter of 1993, and what followed was an 18-month program to develop a common framework for the division's Balanced Scorecard.

Through in-depth workshop sessions with business leaders, the first step was to create a common set of strategic objectives that would, in essence, be the same at divisional, profit center, and business unit levels (thus enabling strategic "line of sight"). These 14 objectives were grouped within the four perspectives of:

- financial: shareholder expectations, operating performance, growth, and shareholder risk
- external: producer relations, policyholder relations, and regulators

- internal: business growth, underwriting profitability, claims management, and operating productivity
- learning and growth: upgrading competencies, information technology support, and organizational alignment.

In support of the divisional scorecard, each profit center and business unit had to consider what top-quartile performance looked like in its own area, assess its current position, and devise a roadmap for closing the gap. Recalls Valerio:

In planning we had always focused on the financial outcomes we wanted to achieve. However, we didn't really understand the key nonfinancial performance indicators which would drive the financial results. By developing this balanced planning process, leaders could focus on how and in which direction they should be moving forward, allowing them to select their top three-to-five specific initiatives.

According to Valerio, the most profound impact on building and implementing a Balanced Scorecard was in organizational learning. He says:

If you can create a learning loop, where you're constantly creating and accessing individual knowledge, and if you have the right infrastructure, you're creating organizational know-how. As the individual's knowledge improves, so does his performance.

He also states that the division had to unlearn before it began to improve, admitting that for many the shift from generalist to specialist insurer was at first difficult to understand. "After all, we were telling people to turn business down, which may sound strange for a company in financial trouble.

"[But] once we got people to understand why and how they had do things differently, how we would support them to develop new skills, and how all this change was paying off, and then everybody in the division became focused on driving the strategy forward."

THE STRATEGY-FOCUSED ORGANIZATION

With the Balance Scorecard being gradually repositioned during the 1990s as strategy—as opposed to measurement—focused, Kaplan and Norton's second scorecard book, published in early 2000, set out a step-by-step process for creating a strategy-focused organization.[5]

The authors specified five principles for creating a strategy-focused organization. These principles emerged from their observation of the

FIGURE 2.3   Principles of a strategy-focused organization

interventions deployed by the most successful scorecard adopters, such as CIGNA P&C. Figure 2.3 shows the principles.

Principle 1: Mobilize Change Through Executive Leadership

Kaplan and Norton emphasize the make-or-break influence of top management: "If those at the top are not energetic leaders of the process, change will not take place." Figure 2.4 illustrates principle 1.

A successful balanced scorecard program starts with a recognition that it is not a "metrics" project; it's a "change" process.

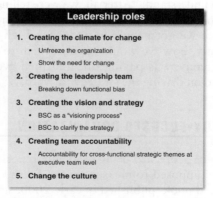

FIGURE 2.4   Principle 1: Mobilize change through executive leadership
Source: Balanced Scorecard Collaborative materials

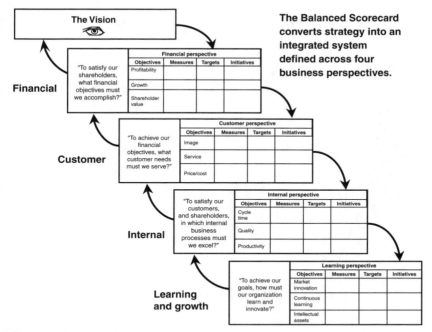

FIGURE 2.5 Principle 2: Translate the strategy into operational terms
Source: Balanced Scorecard Collaborative materials

Indeed, in just about every successful Balanced Scorecard implementation, the support of the most senior executives (in particular the CEO) had been central to that success, as demonstrated by the case studies in this book.

Principle 2: Translate the Strategy to Operational Terms

It is by translating strategy into the logical architecture of a Strategy Map and a Balanced Scorecard that organizations create a common, understandable point of reference for everyone (see figure 2.5).

Principle 3: Align the Organization to the Strategy

Synergy is the overarching goal of organization design. Organizations consist of numerous sectors, business units and specialized departments, each with its own strategy. For organizational performance to become more than the sum of its parts, individual strategies must be linked and integrated (see figure 2.6).

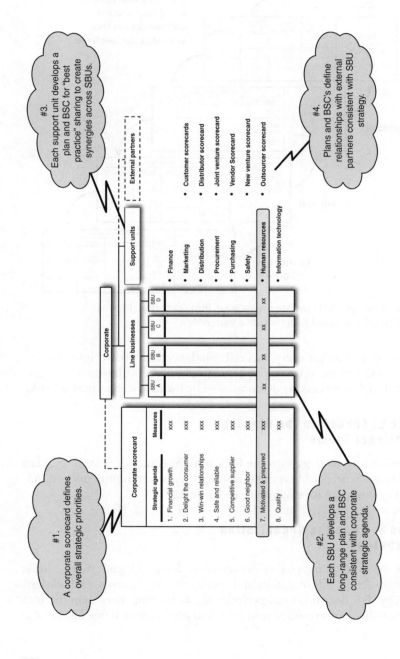

Strategies are executed through business units. *the strategies of the business units must be integrated if organization purpose and synergies are to be achieved.*

FIGURE 2.6 Principle 3: Align the organization to the strategy

FIGURE 2.7   Principle 4: Make strategy everyone's everyday job
Source: Robert S. Kaplan and David P. Norton,*The Strategy-Focused Organization*
(Cambridge, Mass., Harvard Business Press, 2000).

Alignment is typically secured through a process of creating devolved scorecards, which often sees the creation of a "family" of scorecards that cascades from enterprise level, through business unit, function, and team levels.

Principle 4: Make Strategy Everyone's Everyday Job

Strategy must be moved out of the boardroom and into the office and shop-floor so that it is "everyone's everyday job". Strategy must become a living, dynamic process that everybody in the organization comprehends and moves towards implementing (see figure 2.7).

Principle 5: Make Strategy a Continual Process

Putting the Balanced Scorecard at the heart of the organization's management system involves creating links from strategy to budgets and calls for a robust learning process.

From the outset, the Strategy Map and Balanced Scorecard represent no more than a hypothesis about the cause-and-effect linkages that will deliver the strategy. This hypothesis must be tested and amended over time.

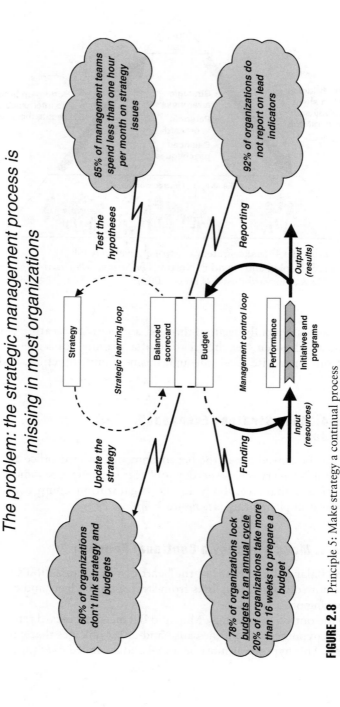

The problem: the strategic management process is missing in most organizations

85% of management teams spend less than one hour per month on strategy issues

92% of organizations do not report on lead indicators

Test the hypotheses

Reporting

Strategy

Strategic learning loop

Balanced scorecard

Budget

Management control loop

Performance

Initiatives and programs

Output (results)

Input (resources)

Update the strategy

Funding

60% of organizations don't link strategy and budgets

78% of organizations lock budgets to an annual cycle 20% of organizations take more than 16 weeks to prepare a budget

FIGURE 2.8 Principle 5: Make strategy a continual process
Source: Balanced Scorecard Collaborative materials

24

Many companies now make the Balanced Scorecard central to their management meetings. An important subcomponent of this principle is "analytics and information systems" (see figure 2.8).

We consider these principles in depth as we progress through the book.

ENTERPRISEWIDE ALIGNMENT

Kaplan and Norton's fourth book *Alignment: Using the Balanced Scorecard to Create Corporate Synergies*[6] took the scorecard concept to a new level. They presented the idea of a Corporate Strategy Map and Balanced Scorecard that sits atop more common scorecards at strategic business unit (SBU) level and devolved levels.

Alignment Checkpoints

The vision is that whole enterprise can be aligned from the corporate level down and out to board of directors and customers and vendors. This organizational alignment is described through eight alignment checkpoints (see figure 2.9).

1. Enterprise (or corporate) strategy: most of the alignment process flows from here.
2. Align the enterprise Strategy Map with the board of directors' Strategy Map.
3. Align the enterprise Strategy Map with corporate functional strategy maps.
4. Align enterprise strategy update with SBU strategy update.
5. Align SBU strategy update with support unit strategy update.
6. Align SBU strategy updates with customers.
7. Align SBU strategy updates with vendors and alliances.
8. Align corporate functional strategy update with SBU support unit updates.

The corporate scorecard depicts how the organization creates value through synergy. The focus on synergy signals a crucial difference from a conventional SBU scorecard in that the corporate scorecard does not include a perspective that is concerned with how success looks in the eyes of the customer. Indeed, it *owns* the business units.

Sources of enterprise synergy

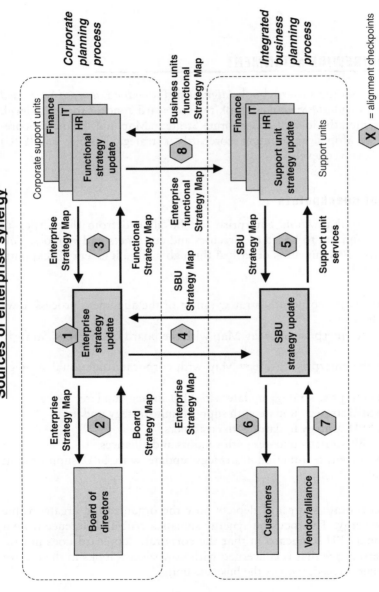

FIGURE 2.9 Alignment checkpoints
Source: David P. Norton and Robert S. Kaplan, *Alignment: Using the Balanced Scorecard to Create Corporate Synergies* (Cambridge, Mass., Harvard Business Press, 2005).

TABLE 2.1 The corporate role in creating synergies

The enterprise scorecard	Source of enterprise-derived value (Strategic themes)
Financial synergies "How do we increase the shareholder value of our SBU portfolio?"	Internal capital management: Create synergy through effective management of internal capital and labour markets. Corporate brand: Integrate a diverse set of businesses around a single brand, promoting common values and themes.
Customer synergies "How can we share the customer interface to increase total customer value?"	Cross-selling: Create value by cross-selling a broad range of products and services from several business units. Common value proposition: Create a consistent buying experience, conforming to corporate standards at multiple outlets.
Internal process synergies "How can we manage SBU processes to achieve economies of scale or value-chain integration?"	Shared services: Create economies of scale by sharing the systems, facilities, and personnel in critical support processes. Value-chain integration: Create value by integrating contiguous processes in the industry value chain.
Learning and growth synergies "How can we develop and share our intangible assets?"	Intangible assets: Share competency in the development of human, information and organization capital.

Descriptively the corporate scorecard might recast its perspectives as synergies. Kaplan and Norton provide the example, shown in table 2.1 and figure 2.10.

CREATING A BOARD SCORECARD SYSTEM

Given that in chapter 1 we reported research that strongly suggests that a failure of the oversight duties of corporate boards was a primary cause of the credit crunch, alignment checkpoint 3: "Align the enterprise Strategy Map with the board of directors' Strategy Map" might be of particular interest for those working within financial services.

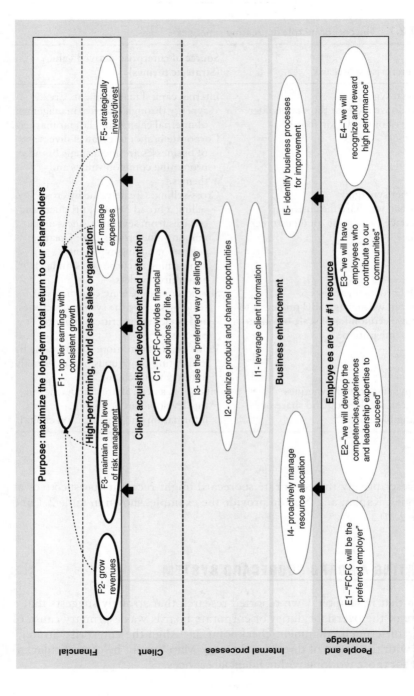

Purpose: maximize the long-term total return to our shareholders

"High-performing, world class sales organization:

Client acquisition, development and retention

Business enhancement

Employe es are our #1 resource

Financial
- F5- strategically invest/divest
- F4- manage expenses
- F1- top tier earnings with consistent growth
- F3- maintain a high level of risk management
- F2- grow revenues

Client
- C1- "FCFC-provides financial solutions. for life."

Internal processes
- I3- use the "preferred way of selling"®
- I2- optimize product and channel opportunities
- I1- leverage client information
- I5- Identify business processes for improvement
- I4- proactively manage resource allocation

People and knowledge
- E4-"we will recognize and reward high performance"
- E3-"we will have employees who contribute to our communities"
- E2-"we will develop the competencies,experiences and leadership expertise to succeed"
- E1-"FCFC will be the preferred employer"

FIGURE 2.10 The corporate role in creating synergies

28

There are several key reasons for using the Balanced Scorecard as a governance tool. These include:

- *Clarity:* The scorecard describes how an organization will create value and provides a way to manage and monitor the delivery of this value.
- *Accountability:* It clarifies the role of the board, the executive management team, and individual executives.
- *Information:* The scorecard isolates and delivers the essential information which board members and executives require to fulfill their responsibilities.
- *Visibility:* It enables a shift from reliance on financials to examination of the nonfinancial indicators that drive value creation.
- *Composition:* The scorecard provides a way to clarify the strategic skills required by the board.
- *Compensation:* It provides a way to clarify and assess the strategic contributions of an executive.

A Board Scorecard System

Note that when we speak of a board Balanced Scorecard it has to be understood within the context of the board scorecard system, which has three mutually reinforcing components:

- the enterprise scorecard
- the board scorecard
- the executive scorecard.

The Enterprise Scorecard   The enterprise scorecard is the corporate scorecard, which describes how value will be created for shareholders. Indeed, if executive management teams just use the enterprise Strategy Map and Balanced Scorecard to communicate with their boards (without building a board scorecard), it will still signal a dramatic step forward from communicating through the impenetrable board packs that are too often typically distributed, which provide boards with a poor guide for assessing performance.

The Board Scorecard   As shown in figure 2.11, the board Strategy Map clarifies how the board contributes to the success of the corporation. The financial perspectives on the board and enterprise scorecards will be identical, as both share the same vision of creating value for shareholders. However, rather than use a traditional customer perspective, a board scorecard introduced a stakeholder perspective, reflecting the board's responsibilities to investors, regulators and communities. As a generic example, these can

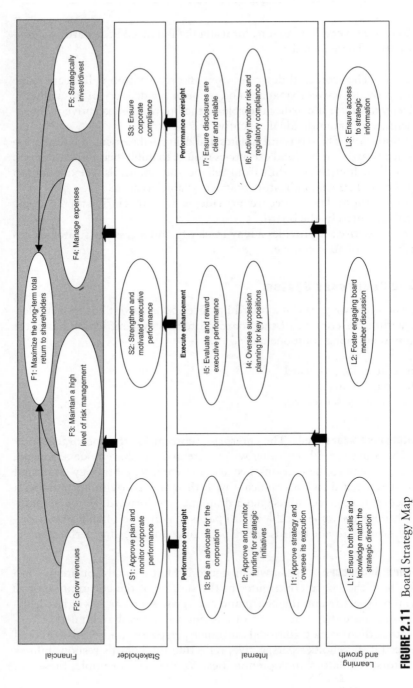

FIGURE 2.11 Board Strategy Map

Source: 2GC Limited, Integrating Risk Management with Existing Methods of Strategic Control.

30

be translated into the stakeholder objectives of "approve, plan, and monitor corporate performance," "strengthen and motivate executive performance," and "ensure corporate compliance."

Each of these three objectives then becomes a discrete theme within the board's internal perspective. For instance, the performance oversight theme will include an objective such as "approve strategy and oversee its execution."

Within the learning and growth perspective, the board will be ensuring that it has the skills, knowledge and information systems in place for it to judiciously dispatch its duties. A typical objective might be "ensure board skills and knowledge match the strategic direction."

Committee Scorecard Furthermore, given that boards of directors typically disaggregate into committees, themes can also be managed separately with ownership assigned. See the "executive enhancement" example in figure 2.12.

Executive Scorecard The final aspect of the board scorecard system is the executive scorecard. This describes the strategic contributions of each of the executive committee (including the CEO) and is drawn from the objectives within the enterprise scorecard, thus ensuring that the executive will take responsibility for the enterprise-level strategic objectives.

The executive scorecard becomes the performance contract between the executive and the board and is used to evaluate and reward senior executive performance. Moreover, an executive scorecard essentially serves as a job description for a senior role, so is equally valuable for selection or succession planning purposes. We discuss executive scorecards in more detail in chapter 9.

THE OFFICE OF STRATEGY MANAGEMENT

Although introduced in their fourth book, Kaplan and Norton's fifth book, *The Execution Premium: Linking Strategy to Operations for Competitive Advantage* fleshed out the idea of the Office of Strategy Management (OSM)[7] a scorecard evolution that might have far-reaching implications for how work is managed in the knowledge era. This book also introduced the idea of strategic expenditure (stratex) that might also have a significant impact on how organizations are managed going forward and which we discuss in later chapters.

Led by a chief strategy officer (or an official with these responsibilities) the theory has it that the OSM integrates and coordinates activities across functions and business units to align strategy with operations. Kaplan and

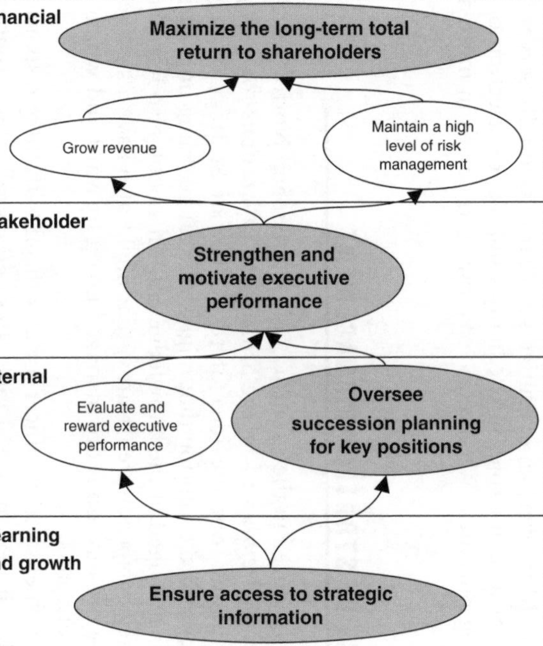

	Executive enhancement theme	Objective	Measure or measures	Target or targets	Owner
Financial	Maximize the long-term total return to shareholders / Maintain a high level of risk management / Grow revenue	▪ Maximize the long-term total return to shareholders	▪ REO relative to peers	▪ 2003 seventy-fifth percentile	▪ Executive management
Stakeholder	Strengthen and motivate executive performance	▪ Strengthen and motivate executive performance	▪ Are executive and affiliate CEOs on track with development plans?	▪ Yes	▪ Compensation committee
Internal	Oversee succession planning for key positions / Evaluate and reward executive performance	▪ Oversee succession planning for key solutions	▪ Share of executives with a current succession plan in place	▪ 75% Year 1 ▪ 100% Year 2	▪ Governance committee
Learning and growth	Ensure access to strategic information	▪ Ensure access to strategic information	▪ Board member survey on relevance of information presented	▪ Above-average year 1 ▪ Excellent year 2	▪ Full board

FIGURE 2.12 Executive enhancement theme example

Source: 2GC Limited, *Integrating Risk Management with Existing Methods of Strategic Control.*

Norton state that the OSM can be viewed as the designer of an intricate watch, keeping all the various planning, execution, and control processes synchronized despite their running at various frequencies. The OSM keeps all of the diverse organizational players—executive team, business units, regional units, support units (such as finance, human resources, procurement, and information technology), theme teams, departments, and ultimately the employees aligned, and executing the enterprise's strategy in unison, with each component playing its distinctive part.

Roles and Responsibilities

The OSM has 12 core roles and responsibilities, which can be described according to three dimensions: architect, process owner, and integrator.

Architect   The OSM ensures that all of the planning, execution, and feedback processes are in place.

Defining the strategy management framework and conventions   The OSM is the designer of the frameworks and processes for a single, integrated, closed-loop strategic and operational execution system. Its tasks include introducing the missing strategy execution processes and bringing order to what is otherwise a fragmented collection of management processes.

Designing the strategy management process   The OSM creates the design for the sequence and linkage of strategy execution processes, ensuring the business unit and support unit strategic cycles are aligned in support of that of the enterprise.

Process Owner   On an ongoing basis, the OSM should have primary ownership of the following strategy execution processes.

Developing the strategy   Typically, strategy development processes are the responsibilities of an existing strategic planning unit. But developing strategy should not be a one-time annual event. After all, performance measures, such as those supplied by the Balanced Scorecard, provide continual evidence about the validity of the assumptions underlying a company's strategy. The executive team, at its strategy review meetings, discuss the assumptions and can fine tune the strategy, strategic measures, or strategic initiatives as required.

Rather than put an artificial distinction between strategy development and strategy execution, it is recommended that processes for developing strategy and executing strategy be performed within one group in the organization: the OSM. This will typically be an expansion of the strategic planning department into a more comprehensive OSM that has responsibility for facilitating both strategy development and its execution.

Planning the strategy   By owning the scorecard process, the OSM ensures that any changes made at the annual strategy planning meeting are translated into the company's Strategy Map and Balanced Scorecard. Once the executive team has approved the objectives and measures for the subsequent year, the OSM coaches the team in selecting performance targets on the scorecard measures and identifying the strategic initiatives required to achieve them. The OSM also standardizes the terminology and measurement definitions throughout the organization, selects and manages the scorecard reporting system, and monitors the integrity of the scorecard data. The OSM also serves as the central scorecard resource, consulting with units on their scorecard development projects and conducting training and education on building strategy maps and scorecards.

Aligning the organization   The OSM oversees the processes to cascade strategies and scorecards vertically and horizontally throughout the organization. It validates whether the strategies and scorecards proposed by business and support units are linked to each other and to the corporate strategy. In this role, the OSM helps the enterprise realize the gains from corporate synergies.

Reviewing and adapting the strategy   At the strategy review meeting, the executive team reviews strategic performance and adjusts the strategy and its execution. Managing this meeting is a core function of the OSM. It briefs the CEO in advance about the strategic issues identified in the most recent scorecard review. Therefore the agenda can focus on strategy review and learning, rather than on short-term financial performance review and crisis management.

The OSM, at the beginning of the meeting, provides a brief report on the progress of each action plan recommended at earlier meetings, records all the recommended action plans, and follows up with the assigned manager or department to ensure that the actions are carried out. The leadership team tests and adapts the strategy. The meeting requires a new input into the annual strategy meeting in addition to the traditional external and competitor analysis produced by the planning department. The company's internal competitor analysis should now include analytic studies of the existing strategy's performance. These studies use tools such as activity-based cost analysis of product line, customer, channel, and regional profitability, and statistical analysis that estimates and tests a Strategy Map's causal linkages.

Integrator A variety of existing management processes must be informed by and aligned with the strategy, such as budgeting and operational planning and those to do with human resources and information technology.

Linking strategy to financial resource planning and budgeting The OSM integrates with finance to ensure that business unit profit plans, resource capacity planning, and performance targets are aligned with strategic objectives. In addition to business and functional unit budgets, the corporate financial plan needs to incorporate the authorized spending (stratex) for crossfunctional strategic initiatives.

Aligning plans and resources of important functional support departments In addition to coordinating the linkage between strategy planning and finance, the OSM ensures that the plans for other functional departments are consistent with executing the strategy. The OSM plays a consulting and integrating role with these functional departments to help them align their strategies and plans with enterprise and business unit strategies.

Communicating the strategy The OSM actively promotes understanding of the company's strategy and the scorecard to all business unit and support functions. If the strategy communication task is assigned to an existing internal communication department, the OSM plays an editorial role, reviewing the message to see that they communicate the strategy correctly. If a corporate communications group does not exist or if the group has little knowledge of or focus on strategy, the OSM becomes the process owner for communicating both strategy and the scorecard to employees.

Managing strategic initiatives When the organization uses theme owners and theme teams to manage selection and management of strategic initiatives, the OSM monitors the process, soliciting information about initiative status and performance and reporting this information to the executive team in advance of the strategy management review meeting.

For organizations that do not use theme owners and theme teams, the OSM is the default mechanism for running the team process to select and rationalize strategic initiatives. The OSM assigns responsibility to an appropriate unit or function for those initiatives that already have a natural home. The OSM manages initiatives that cross unit and functional lines, ensuring that they get the financial and human resources they need.

Linking strategy to key operating processes Strategy is also executed through business processes. The Strategy Map identifies the processes that are most important to the strategy and that must be analyzed, redesigned, and managed. The OSM works with the theme teams, local line management, and the quality management department to see that necessary resources and organizational support have been provided to improve the performance of the strategic process.

Sharing best practices   The OSM needs to ensure that knowledge management focuses on sharing the best practices that will be most beneficial to the strategy. At some companies, learning and knowledge sharing are already the responsibility of a chief knowledge or learning officer; in those cases, the OSM needs to coordinate with that person's office. But if such a function does not exist, the OSM must take the lead in transferring ideas and best practices throughout the organization.

Case Example: Bank Indonesia

Bank Indonesia, which is an independent state institution, with the authority to issue policy rules and regulations that are binding to the public-at-large, is one organization that is in the process of developing an OSM. A Strategic Planning Unit (SPU) under the Office of Governor presently carries out the roles and responsibilities of the OSM. The OSM has day-to-day responsibility for the Balanced Scorecard and related strategic activities.

Currently, the SPU has nine full-time officials and three support staff. The main responsibilities of the team are to make sure that every step of the strategic planning, monitoring and evaluating is done properly and effectively. This includes identifying issues and risks and understanding and communicating their implications, developing action plan and reporting progress to the board. In addition, the SPU facilitates a quarterly strategic review meeting.

"The team oversees the creation of Bank Indonesia's Strategy Map and accompanying scorecard of measures, targets and action programs," says Dyah Nastiti Kusumowardani, Bank Indonesia's director of strategy planning. "It then guides the process of translating and aligning the bank's highest-level Strategy Map into maps at the unit level."

Furthermore, the unit trains those employees throughout the bank who have responsibility for local scorecard performance or are designated owners of specific Key Performance Indicators.

Case Example: Kiwibank

As a further example, consider New Zealand's 915-employee-strong Kiwibank, which was inducted into Palladium's Balanced Scorecard's Hall of Fame in 2009 (becoming the first inductee from that country).

The organization introduced the Balanced Scorecard in 2007, five years after its formation. Kiwibank introduced an OSM, which played a key role in the Balanced Scorecard implementation. Today, it acts as the steward of enterprise portfolio management, and coordinates and oversees strategic initiatives. The OSM evaluates all strategy-related investments, ensuring a comprehensive overview of initiative performance and delivery, the allocation of adequate resources and a balance of initiatives across its four themes of Excellence in Business Processes, Sales and Service Leadership, Sustainable Growth, and Learning and Growth. As stated in Palladium's *Balanced Scorecard Hall of Fame Report 2010,*[8] more recently the OSM has assumed an expanded role, helping to ensure continued organizational agility as the bank continued to implement more advanced systems. Moreover, the OSM runs the Kiwibank Strategy Network, through which best practice sharing is facilitated in formal monthly meetings and informal brainstorming sessions across business and support units.

"Since 2008 the OSM has been situated within the business transformation team, alongside the business improvement (Six Sigma) team," the report notes. "The arrangement embeds process improvement and operational excellence in the bank's DNA. The head of strategy execution reports directly to the general manager of business transformation. [Moreover] the Project Management Office was moved to the business transformation team to ensure further integration of project selection and delivery. This structure creates valuable synergies because the business transformation team supports the OSM in implementing key projects; a Six Sigma Black Belt, for instance, is leading the projects for developing a system for employee performance reviews."

Impressively, in just 18 months Kiwibank recorded a resounding improvement in financial, market share, and customer performance and in employee satisfaction (and this coinciding with the worst period of the credit crunch!). From June 2007 to June 2009 revenues increased by 55 percent to NZ$311 million and net profit before taxes (NPBT) grew 86 percent to NZ$72 million. The bank's market share of customers whom it serves at their primary bank—a main goal—rose from 5.1 percent to 6.9 percent. Staff turnover (many staff work in call centers) fell from 25.7 percent to 14 percent. Staff engagement scores rose from 2007–09 from 70.7 to 75.7 (on a 100-point scale).

Very impressively the bank also made large strides in mitigating risk, as the Hall of Fame report noted. "For example, seeing signs of the economic downturn early on, executives anticipated the need for improved service alongside customers' needs for financial help. After translating this anticipated need into a strategic objective, a theme team designed a series of initiatives. Today, Kiwibank is outperforming its competitors in customer service. In addition the [Balanced Scorecard's] troubleshooting capability prompted the bank to introduce more effective programs for managing operational risk. The result? A considerably lower level of impaired assets compared with other banks."

THE EXECUTION PREMIUM MODEL

As we can see, the OSM has an important role to play in aligning strategy with operations, a fact Kaplan and Norton made clear in their *The Execution Premium* book. To secure this alignment, Kaplan and Norton suggested in that book a six-step Execution Premium Model that would link strategy with operations. Shown in figure 2.13, the steps are as follows.

Stage 1: Develop the Strategy

At this stage, organizational leaders answer three questions.

- *What business are we in and why (clarify mission, values, and vision)?* The MVV statements establish guidelines for formulating and executing the strategy.
- *What are the key issues (conduct strategic analysis)?* Managers review the situation on their competitive and operating environments since they last crafted their strategy.
- *How can we best compete (formulate the strategy)?* This considers areas such as the customer value proposition, key processes required to create the differentiation in the strategy and human capital, and technological requirements to enable the delivery of the strategy.

Stage 2: Plan the Strategy

In this stage, managers plan the strategy by developing strategic objectives, measures, targets, initiatives, and budgets that guide action and resource allocation. Companies typically answer five questions at this stage.

- *How do we describe our strategy (create Strategy Maps)?* This describes the objectives required to deliver to the strategy. It is now common for organizations to cluster related objectives according to perhaps five or six strategic themes. This makes it easier for managers to separately plan and manage each of the key components of the strategy but still have them operate coherently.
- *How do we measure our plan (select measures and targets)?* In this stage, managers convert the objectives defined in the Strategy Map into a Balanced Scorecard of measures, targets, and gaps (that must be closed over the lifetime of the plan).

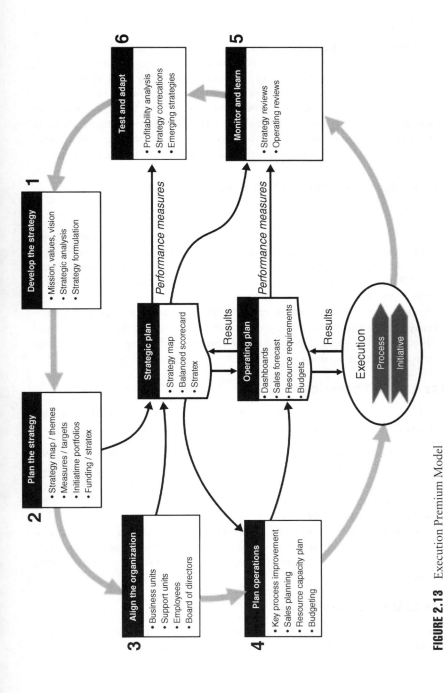

FIGURE 2.13 Execution Premium Model

Source: Robert S. Kaplan and David P. Norton, The Execution Premium: Linking Strategy to Operations for Competitive Advantage (Cambridge, Mass.: Harvard Business Press, 2008).

- *What action programs does our strategy need (choose strategic initiatives)?* The initiatives and action programs aimed at achieving targeted performance for the Strategy Map objectives.
- *How do we fund our initiatives?* Executing strategy required that the portfolio of initiatives be executed simultaneously in a coordinated manner. This requires explicit funding for the portfolio of initiatives.
- *Who will lead the execution of strategy (create theme teams)?* Companies are introducing a new accountability structure for executing strategy through strategic themes. Theme owners and teams provide accountability for and feedback on the execution of the strategy within each theme.

Stage 3: Align the Organization with the Strategy

At this stage, managers ask three key questions.

- *How do we ensure that all organizational units are on the same page?* This is about devolving the scorecard to lower level business units.
- *How do we align support units with business unit and corporate strategies?* This is about creating strategy maps and scorecards for support units such as HR and finance, as two examples.
- *How do we motivate employees to help is execute the strategy?* Essentially this is about proper communication and the linking of personal objectives and (more common in the commercial sector) incentive compensation to the scorecard.

Stage 4: Plan Operations

Companies need to align process improvement activities with strategic priorities. At this stage managers focus on two key questions.

- *What business process improvements are most critical for executing the strategy?* Companies must focus on Six Sigma, reengineering, and other efforts on improving performance to a strategic objective. Moreover, they should create customized dashboards consisting of key indicators for local process performance.
- *How do we link strategy with operating plans and budgets?* The process improvement plans and the high-level strategic measures and targets on the Balanced Scorecard must be converted into an operating plan for the year.

Stage 5: Monitor and Learn

This is where the organization monitors the execution of its strategic and operating plans and learns from experience. To do these things, it holds two meetings—an operational review meeting and a strategy review meeting—which answer two questions.

- *Are our operations under control (operational review meetings)?* Companies hold these meetings to review short-term performance and respond to recently identified problems that need immediate attention.
- *Are we executing our strategy well (strategy review meetings)?* These meetings review the progress of the strategy, identify problems and order remedial action.

Step 6: Test and Adapt the Strategy

This is where organizations question whether their fundamental strategic assumptions remain valid.

Managers ask one question.

- *Is our strategy working (hold a strategy testing and adapting meeting)?* Periodically, the senior team meets to question and challenge the strategy and, if necessary, to adapt it.

It is clear to see how the Execution Premium Model evolved out of the five strategy-focused organization principles that Kaplan and Norton introduced in an earlier book.

Case Example: Bank Indonesia (2)

The Execution Premium Model is central to how Bank Indonesia has managed going forward. "In the future, the six-stage Execution Premium Model of the Balanced Scorecard will be more widely used," says Dyah Nastiti Kusumowardani, Director of Strategic Planning. "We recognize that we have to take a more holistic view of performance, including linking the strategy into daily operations. Also, the model provides a double-loop process using test and adapt the strategy and monitor and learn."

CONCLUSION

As we can see from this chapter, the Balanced Scorecard methodology and framework have come a long way since they first entered the corporate lexicon in the early 1990s. What was once positioned as essentially a balanced performance measurement system has undergone several evolutionary steps, including the rise in importance of the Strategy Map; placing the scorecard system at the heart of a strategy-focused organization; to enabling the alignment of an enterprisewide value chain; to its triggering the creation of a dedicated function, the OSM to manage the whole strategic management process, from strategic planning, through implementation to learning. The scorecard system has also evolved to being a core tool for aligning strategy with operations.

In the next chapter, we discuss the important concept of where risk sits within the Balanced Scorecard methodology. Understanding the relationship between strategy and risk will enable organizations to move into the practicalities of building and implementing the Balanced Scorecard, which we begin to look at in chapter 4.

ENDNOTES

1. The series of books and articles began with the article Robert S. Kaplan and David P. Norton, "The Balanced Scorecard: Measures that Drive Performance", *Harvard Business Review*, January–February 1992.
2. *Harvard Business Review*, 75th Anniversary Issue, September 1999.
3. Bain & Company, *Management Tools and Techniques*, survey, 2007.
4. Robert S. Kaplan and David P. Norton, *Strategy Maps: Converting Intangible Assets Into Tangible Outcomes* (Cambridge, Mass.: Harvard Business Press, 2005).
5. Robert S. Kaplan and David P. Norton, *Creating the Strategy-Focused Organization* (Cambridge, Mass.: Harvard Business Press, 2001).
6. Robert S. Kaplan and David P. Norton, *Alignment: Using the Balanced Scorecard to Create Corporate Synergies* (Cambridge, Mass.: Harvard Business Press, 2005).
7. Robert S. Kaplan and David P. Norton, *The Execution Premium: Linking Strategy to Operations for Competitive Advantage* (Cambridge, Mass.: Harvard Business Press, 2008).
8. Palladium, *Strategy Execution Champions, The Palladium Balanced Scorecard Hall of Fame Report, 2010* (Cambridge, Mass: Harvard Business Publishing/Palladium, 2010).

CHAPTER 3

The Balanced Scorecard and Risk Management

EXECUTIVE SUMMARY

1. The credit crunch led to questions regarding the continued validity of the Balanced Scorecard.
2. Balanced Scorecard co-creator Professor Robert Kaplan suggested that risk management was a missing driver of shareholder value for many organizations.
3. Although a central concern to senior executives today, the arguments for linking risk management to strategy date back more than a decade.
4. The U.K.-headquartered Balanced Scorecard consultancy 2GC proposes a nine-step process for aligning risk management to strategy.
5. Strategic risk management has to become a core competency for organizations.
6. We describe a three-tier hierarchy of risks as described by Professor Kaplan.
7. A new framework for aligning performance with risk management called Risk-Based Performance is introduced.
8. Also introduced is the concept of a Risk Balanced Scorecard.
9. We explain the five principles of strategic risk management, which are closely aligned to the five principles of the strategy-focused organization.

INTRODUCTION

Among the various lines of questioning that followed the onset of the credit crunch, some people looked at, and queried, the continued validity of the Balanced Scorecard. After all, as we illustrated in chapter 1, since the introduction of the scorecard financial services companies have been among the heaviest users—banks in particular. Indeed, one of the authors of this book penned an in-depth research report on creating a Balanced Scorecard for financial services companies as early as 2001, drawing on the then already large number of sector scorecard users.[1]

The question that many asked was why did so many apparently success-ful scorecard users not see the credit crunch coming? After all, a key prom-ise of the Balanced Scorecard system is that it provides some visibility into the future—that is, how by understanding nonfinancial performance dimen-sions we gain insights into likely future financial performance. Something obviously had gone terribly wrong; Professor Kaplan perhaps put his finger on the problem in a blog entry in December 2008.

> *The high-level objective in a Balanced Scorecard's financial per-spective is growing and sustaining shareholder value. Traditionally, we have advocated two methods to drive shareholder value: reve-nue growth and productivity improvements. The third method for sustaining shareholder value, missing in many companies' strate-gies, should be risk management.*

After the credit crunch, Palladium (the U.S.-headquartered management consultancy which merged with BSCOL-which was founded by the co-creator of the Balanced Scorecard Dr. Norton) was quick to begin the process of integrating risk management into the Balanced Scorecard system, as we will explain in a moment.

LINKING STRATEGY MANAGEMENT WITH RISK MANAGEMENT: A HISTORY

But we should highlight that Kaplan and Norton were far from the first to suggest a formal process for integrating risk management within a wider strategy management framework. Indeed back in 1997, the In-dian consultant R. Muralidharan recommended the following approach within an article that appeared in the magazine *Long Range Planning*.[2]

- Agree unambiguous descriptions of a set of strategic goals, the achievement of which are likely to achieve the long-term vision of the organization.
- Agree the actions necessary to achieve these goals (causes) and the results they are expected to produce (effects).
- Monitor the implementation of the plan using indicators chosen and tailored to suit this particular purpose and subsequently use the

information produced to inform management discussion and decisions about possible corrective actions.

- Monitor changes in the external environment, for example new or changed policy directives, sudden changes in the economy and update the plan on the basis of a) changes in external planning assumptions, b) learning about the management team's cause and effect assumptions, identifying the need to change these when relevant.
- Involve staff in the decision-making process, developing ownership and building on the combined operational insight of the organization.

Muralidharan highlights the need for this process to be continuous so that emerging strategic threats and opportunities trigger timely changes to strategy.

2GC Research

Moreover, in a 2003 conference paper, the U.K.-headquartered management consultancy 2GC suggested a nine-step framework for integrating risk management and strategic control processes (so once again, well before the credit crunch).[3] Shown diagrammatically in figure 3.1, the first five steps relate to the strategic control process, while the final four relate to the risk management process.

1. Agree strategic goals.
2. Identify required actions and likely effects.
3. Monitor implementation of actions.

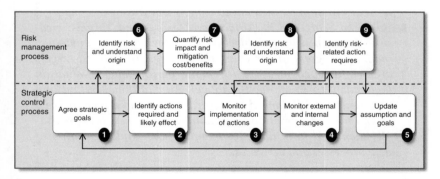

FIGURE 3.1 2GC's suggested nine-step framework for integrating risk management and strategic control processes
Source: 2GC Limited, *Integrating Risk Management with Existing Methods of Strategic Control*, 2009.

4. Monitor external and internal changes.
5. Update assumptions and goals.
6. Identify risks and understand origins.
7. Quantify risk impact and mitigation cost/benefit.
8. Agree acceptable risk levels.
9. Identify risk related actions required.

2GC (which is headed by Gavin Lawrie, who worked for Kaplan and Norton in the Renaissance consultancy that preceded the Balanced Scorecard Collaborative and Palladium) stated in the paper that the strategic control framework selected is not itself important; but it must meet the requirements outlined by Muralidharan. Although the Balanced Scorecard as described by Kaplan and Norton could obviously serve as the strategy framework, 2GC suggests its own version, which is known as a Third-Generation Balanced Scorecard. This, it says, "provides a good example of a proven framework for strategic control into which risk management sub-processes can readily be incorporated."

The paper authors state that components of the Third-Generation Balanced Scorecard design process match components 1–3 of the Strategic Control process:

- *Destination Statements: long-term goals describing in some degree of detail what the organization should look like at some point of time in the future (equivalent to component 1 above)*
- *Strategic Objectives: activities and their expected outcomes defining what needs to happen to ensure achievement of the long-term goals and intermediate goals on the way to the long-term destination (equivalent to component 2 above)*
- *Balanced Scorecard Performance Measures and Targets: measures for each strategic objective are chosen to inform management of progress in achieving the strategic objectives; targets are set for each measure to enable performance evaluation (equivalent to component 3 above). An additional output of a well-structured Balanced Scorecard design and review process is a number of discretionary initiatives or projects that are usually identified to initiate, for example, the implementation of new processes and activities.*

The 2GC authors continue that using the Balanced Scorecard/Strategic Control components 1 and 2 as input to the risk assessment process, it is possible to identify risks to: a) the achievement of agreed strategic objectives and goals, and b) the successful completion of actions necessary to deliver these goals (components 1 and 2). Thereafter the risk assessment activities of component 7 (quantify risk impact and mitigation cost/benefit) can be conducted, typically by specialists rather than generalist senior managers.

> *With this understanding of the organization's risk profile and the costs and benefits of various risk mitigation options, senior managers are then able to make decisions about the levels of risk they are prepared to accept (component 8), allowing them to then agree the actions required (component 9), generally in discussion with line management, the people who will be responsible for completing these actions. This agreed list of actions should now be used to update the strategic goals/objectives where these risk mitigation activities are significant enough to warrant inclusion in the organization's strategic goals.*

They go on to advise that senior management should regularly review progress in the implementation of activities chosen to deliver the organization's goals, including the activities selected as part of the risk review (component 3). Also recommended is that they should periodically assess changes to their original assumptions about the business model, including their assumptions about the organization's risk profile (component 4). "Any significant changes that are identified will then drive changes to both risk mitigation requirements and the organizations higher level goals. This is a cycle of planning, acting, and reviewing can be embedded, allowing senior management to manage risk within the strategic control framework."

Strategy, Risk, and Financial Services: Advanced Performance Institute Research

Also before the credit crunch, in his research report *Managing Strategic Performance in Banks and Financial Services*,[4] management consultant and academic Bernard Marr of the U.K.-based Advanced Performance Institute (of which one of the authors of this book is a fellow) observed that only effective way to manage risk strategically is to align risk management with strategic performance management, ensuring that cause-and-effect factors are considered, and that conclusions are relevant and have an optimal impact on the business.

Marr recommends that financial services organizations should integrate risk management with strategic performance management (SPM), because they are in fact different sides of the same coin. SPM, Marr observes, looks at value generation, whereas risk management looks at value loss prevention. "Banks and financial services firms should align their performance and risk management and ensure that all critical areas of performance also have associated risk indicators," he says.

Marr also states that having identified components such as reputation, talent management, IT systems, or customer relationships as key drivers of future performance, it is critical that any potential risk surrounding these areas be controlled and assessed.

By starting with a clear understanding of the components of their business that deliver value, firms can start to identify potential threats to each of those components. By identifying potential focus areas for their risk mitigation strategies, they are able to manage these much more comprehensively. Risks associated with these enablers or drivers of performance can take various forms. Some common, but sometimes overlooked risks include:

- *Human resource risk:* An important risk that is regularly overlooked in organizations is risk related to their staff and to the ongoing cultivation of the knowledge they possess.
- *Structural resource risks:* These include threats to organizational processes and routines, especially those posed by losing database contents and software because of hackers and viruses, or by intellectual property theft.
- *Relational resources risks:* In today's networked economy, relationships are crucial. Reputations take years to develop, but can be destroyed very rapidly indeed. If a company fails to live up to its declared values, the consequences can be catastrophic.

One bank participating in Marr's research program commented: "Whereas our strategic performance management approach focused on the value-creation strategies, our risk management focused on the value loss prevention strategies—once we realized that these were two sides of the same coin we started to integrate them into one management framework."

About BSC — Reasons

STRATEGIC RISK MANAGEMENT: THE NEW CORE COMPETENCY

More recently (that is, after the credit crunch), the importance of aligning risk with strategy has become a burning hot topic. Indeed, within the Balanced Scorecard community of practitioners, consultants, and academics there is no subject that is generating as much debate or interest. "Strategic Risk Management: the New Core Competency"—an article that appeared in the January/February 2009 edition of Palladium's *Balanced Scorecard Report,*[5] made the need to link risk with strategy very clear.

ROI

The author opened the article by saying: "As recent developments throughout the world's financial community show, risk management done badly can be as devastating as no risk management at all . . . in focusing on their upside (their ROI) [return on investment] banks ignored the business risk that was built into their strategy—a fatal error."

The article explained that after the corporate accounting scandals at the turn of the decade enterprise risk management (ERM) became a hot topic in organizations. However, as more recent events have shown, ERM has not been fully effective, largely the consequence of it not being aligned and connected to strategy. This, the article explained, is where SRM comes in, which the author defines as:

ERM

> *the process of identifying, assessing and managing the risk in the organization's business strategy—including taking swift action when risks are actually realized. SRM involves evaluating how a wide range of possible events and scenarios will affect the strategy and its execution and the ultimate impact on the company's value. "Risk" is all inclusive, including everything from product innovation risk and market risk to supply chain risk and reputational risk . . . SRM requires an organization to define tolerable levels of risk as a guide for strategic decision making. It is a continual process that is embedded in strategy setting and strategy execution.*

The Balanced Scorecard can be a powerful mechanism for embedding SRM into strategy setting and execution, as the author explained: "Holistic performance management frameworks such as the Balanced Scorecard give organizations an unprecedented opportunity to align strategy and performance measures with risk management—and to achieve integrated, strategic risk management.

> *SRM should be a continual process that uses metrics to continuously monitor and manage risk. As organizations' key risk indicators and metrics should link to the potential impact of risk on shareholder value. . . . With its focus on strategy and accountability the [Balanced Scorecard] can help foster a continuous process for risk assessment and risk management. Strategy Maps can also provide a useful way to understand the cause and effect relationships in critical risk scenarios and can suggest metrics that would be useful in effective risk management.*

The author also gave examples of how SRM dovetails with the six-stage Execution Premium Model (as described within the previous chapter).

> *Stage 1: Develop the Strategy, companies would conduct strategic risk assessments and formulate strategic risk management plans as part of their strategy. In Stage 2: Translate the Strategy, they would identify strategic risk management objectives and measures that could be included in the Balanced Scorecard; they would also use Strategy Maps to identify the cause-and-effect linkages and root causes of strategic risks. In Stage 5, Monitor and Learn, management teams would hold strategic risk management reviews. And in Stage 6, Test and Adapt, management would conduct strategic risk analysis.*

Risk Management and the Strategy Execution System

The importance of risk management within the Balanced Scorecard community was shown by Palladium's November/December 2009 edition of *Balanced Scorecard Report* being wholly dedicated to the role of risk management within the Balanced Scorecard.[6] Within one of the articles (we highlight another later) Professor Kaplan introduced the concepts of a three-level hierarchy of risk (a risk management framework).

A Risk Management Framework
Level 3: Routine Operational and Compliance Risks

> *At the bottom of the risk hierarchy, Level 3 risks arise from errors in routine, standardized, and predictable processes that expose the firm to substantial loss . . . Examples of Level 3 vital processes are maintaining and updating the financial accounting and tax systems (such as posting entries to the general ledger and the accounts receivables and accounts payables ledgers; and paying and receiving cash), protecting assets and information, and ensuring information security, privacy, backup, and disaster recovery. They also include the internal control processes that protect the firm from fraud, negligence, legal, and other potential regulatory liabilities.*
>
> *Any breakdown in a Level 3 process could expose the company to significant financial and information losses and expensive regulatory and litigation procedures.*

In short, Level 3 risks are known and avoidable. Risk management of these processes strives to achieve 100 percent compliance and zero defects.

But even when these processes are performed perfectly, the company could still fail in its strategy execution.

Level 2: Strategy Risks Kaplan pointed out that companies select strategies that they hope will create and sustain a competitive advantage that leads to superior financial returns. But, he explained, earning superior returns requires companies to accept some risk.

Strategy risk can be straightforward and easily quantifiable, as when a company accepts the risk of default when extending credit to customers; or it can be more speculative, as when a company invests in developing an entirely new product line or entering a new geographic market.

To manage its various Level 2 risks, a company should identify the major plausible risks inherent in the strategy, attempt to mitigate and manage those risks, and then continually monitor the risk exposure it has accepted to earn superior returns.

The risk management literature identifies a long laundry list of possible strategy risks, such as financial risk; customer, brand, and reputation risk; supply chain risk; innovation risk; environmental risk; human resources risk; and information technology risk. Such a list implies a complex risk management process perhaps specific to each type of risk.

Kaplan continues that the Strategy Map and Balanced Scorecard already contain all of an entity's strategic objectives and the interrelationships among them: the learning and growth perspective contains objectives for people and technology; the internal process perspective has objectives for managing operations, customers, innovation, and environmental, regulatory, and social processes; the customer perspective shows those linked to the customer value proposition and customer outcomes; and the financial perspective depicts those related to revenue, price, and margin objectives. "The Strategy Map thus provides a natural framework for identifying, mitigating, and systematically managing the risks to a company's strategic objectives in an integrated and comprehensive manner," he says.

He went on to explain that some companies, particularly those in financial services such as Bank of Tokyo-Mitsubishi UFJ and SwissRe, already incorporate a risk management strategic theme into their Strategy Maps. "Defining a risk management strategic theme highlights risk management as a key component of the company's strategy and makes it visible for resource allocation, monitoring, and discussion at strategy review meetings," Kaplan said. "I have tentatively concluded, however, that measuring and managing risk differs so substantially from measuring and managing strategy that it may be preferable to develop a completely separate risk scorecard. Strategy is about moving the company forward toward achieving breakthrough performance. The Strategy Map and scorecard provide the roadmap to guide this strategic journey. Risk management, in contrast, is about identifying, avoiding, and overcoming the hurdles that the strategy may encounter along the way. Avoiding risk does not advance the strategy; but risk management can reduce obstacles and barriers that would otherwise prevent the organization from progressing to its strategic destination."

Level 1: Global Enterprise Risks   Kaplan explained that Level 2 risk management tackles the known unknowns. "But the failures of many companies are triggered by the 'unknown unknowns': the unpredictable, unprecedented occurrences that create existential risk . . . the VaR models used by many financial institutions (and the risk models used by credit rating agencies) . . . were based on data going back several decades during which there was no nationwide decline in housing prices," he wrote. "Senior managers at many financial institutions apparently believed that such an across-the-board decline was an extremely unlikely event, outside the 99% confidence interval of their VaR models. As a result, they had no alternative or complementary process for assessing or mitigating their exposure to rare events."

> . . . Companies need to consider what unlikely event or combination of events could lead to their demise . . . Some companies do their Level 1 risk planning by conducting active discussions of unlikely events and their consequences. Goldman Sachs and JP Morgan Chase hold regular tail-risk meetings of senior management where they discuss the consequences of unlikely external events. (They are called tail-risk meetings because the likelihood of the events are in the "tail" of the probability distribution.)
>
> As the chief risk officer of JP Morgan Chase told me, "Most of the events we discuss at these meetings never occur, thank God; but a few of them have happened, and we have either already mitigated their consequences or, because of our prior contingency planning, acted rapidly to minimize the damage."
>
> Following the Kaplan/Norton Strategy Execution model, managers can address these Level 1 enterprise risks during their deliberations in Stage Six of the strategy execution system, Test and Adapt

the Strategy. The CEO could lead a discussion around "the three things that would cause our strategy to fail." The leadership team could engage in scenario planning, war-gaming, and tail-risk stress-testing to learn the sensitivity of the company's strategy to events that occur outside normal business operations that they cannot control . . .

Risk management requires predicting events, particularly unlikely ones that have never occurred. But despite the difficulty of risk management, senior executives who avoid, deemphasize, or delegate it do so at their peril.

RISK-BASED PERFORMANCE

Andrew Smart is the founder of the U.K.-headquartered Manigent, a specialist performance and risk management consultancy delivering integrated business and technology solutions. Manigent has developed a methodology for fully integrating performance with what it calls "Risk-Based Performance," which is a strategic execution methodology that integrates and aligns performance and risk management processes, improving strategic execution through improved management discussions, decision making, and action taking. The methodology builds on the Balanced Scorecard and COSO frameworks, so it has both strategy and risk themes.

As a brief explanation, the COSO internal control framework consists of five interrelated components derived from how management runs a business.

- *Control environment:* Control environment factors include the integrity, ethical values, management's operating style, and delegation of authority systems, as well as the processes for managing and developing people in the organization.
- *Risk assessment:* A precondition to risk assessment is establishment of objectives, so risk assessment is the identification and analysis of relevant risks to the achievement of assigned objectives. Risk assessment is a prerequisite for determining how the risks should be managed.
- *Control activities:* Control activities are the policies and procedures that help ensure management directives are carried out. They include a range of activities as diverse as approvals, authorizations, verifications, reconciliations, reviews of operating performance, security of assets, and segregation of duties.
- *Information and communication:* Information systems play a key role in internal control systems as they produce reports, including

operational, financial, and compliance-related information, that make it possible to run and control the business.

■ *Monitoring:* Internal control systems need to be monitored—a process that assesses the quality of the system's performance over time. This is accomplished through ongoing monitoring activities or separate evaluations.

In his white paper *"Aligning Risk Management and Exposure, the New Paradigm of Strategic Execution,"* Smart argues that historically performance and risk management have been essentially siloed disciplines, which is no longer acceptable.[7] Indeed, recall that in chapter 1 we reported his statement that: " . . . the credit crisis arose because financial services organizations failed to develop and execute sustainable strategies that fully considered their risk environment, and they neglected to embed risk management at the heart of their strategic and operational processes."

Within the paper, he says that organizations should look for an approach that integrates risk within the context of their strategic objectives.

> . . . *successful strategy execution, in a post credit crunch world, will be built on the foundation of balancing risk appetite and exposure within the context of clear strategic objectives. Embracing the new paradigm will enable organizations to answer three critical questions:*
>
> 1. *What are we trying to achieve, i.e., what are our strategic objectives.*
> 2. *What level of risk is acceptable to achieve those objectives, i.e., what is our risk appetite?*
> 3. *What is our current level of risk, i.e., what is our risk exposure?*

In the paper Smart states that he believes that the Strategy Map is one of the most powerful management tools of the past 15 years or so and can deliver many benefits to organizations. But he goes on to say that although the development and benefits of the Strategy Map are well understood from a performance management perspective, less obvious is the fundamental role it has with relation to risk management. "It is well documented in risk frameworks such as COSO Enterprise Risk Framework [which was launched in 2004) and BS31100, and it is widely accepted within the risk community, that the starting point for an enterprise-wide risk management initiative must be strategy and strategic objectives.

"Without a clear strategy and set of strategic objectives, it is too easy to take a measure everything approach. This often leads to risk frameworks that attempt to manage thousands of risks, resulting in unwieldy, unsustainable situations, which sap energy, buy-in and support for the risk initiative and does not generate promised benefits."

However, Smart argues that rather than just distilling strategy into a set of objectives and key performance indicators (KPIs), they should take an additional step of evaluating the level of risk they are willing to take to achieve those objectives. Smart provided a client example. "After developing a risk appetite based on a number of 'dimensions,' such as capital, cash-flow, reputation, etc., the organization considered questions such as: 'To achieve this objective, how much capital are we willing to put at risk?' 'What potential impact on cash-flow can we expect?' and 'How much of a hit on our reputation can we afford?'"

In the white paper, Smart argues that the next step is to identify the "key risks." These are the critical few risks that could have the most significant impact on the successful achievement of strategic objectives. He continues that many organizations choose to review their risk appetite in light of the insights and understanding gained through the process of identifying key risks. And he makes the important point that key risks have both a downside, such as the potential to wipe out the year's profit and an upside, the realizing of opportunities.

Smart goes on to say that in this integrated performance and risk management approach organizations should then complete a risk assessment. "Risk assessments at this strategic level are often conducted on a quarterly, bi-annual or even annual basis. Between assessments indicators can be used to monitor changes in risk profiles (Key Risk Indicators) and changes in control effectiveness (Key Control Indicators)."

To visualize the alignment of risk exposure to risk appetite, Manigent created a simple but useful Risk Exposure and Risk Appetite Matrix (see figure 3.2). The matrix presents the level of risk appetite along the horizontal axis and the level of risk exposure vertically. Smart states that the matrix often points to areas where the level of risk was *not* high enough. "Organizations are often surprised to discover areas in which they are not taking enough risk and therefore not developing the capabilities to respond to—or position themselves for—opportunities in the market."

He continues that risk exposure can be expressed in the same terms used to express appetite, such as extreme, high, moderate, or low.

A RISK-BALANCED SCORECARD

Nigel Penny, managing director of the Singapore-headquartered management consultancy ClaritasAsia, has also been doing much innovative and groundbreaking thinking on how best to integrate risk management

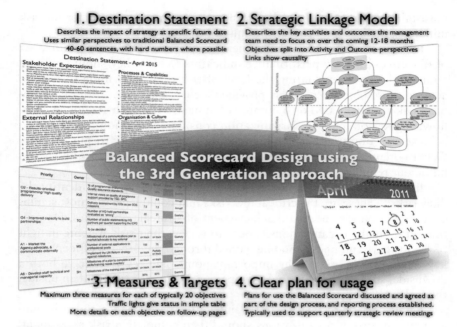

FIGURE 3.2 Risk Exposure and Risk Appetite Matrix

with strategy management. He would agree with Smart that risk and performance should not be separate processes and that their being so is a major cause of organization problems. "Historically organizations have assessed risk and their response to it, in a large standalone process, reviewed separately from normal business performance reviews," he says. "On one side we have a set of financial results which reflect an 'after the event' statement of financial performance. On the other hand we have a set of identified risks prioritized as to overall seriousness per risk. Nothing seems to integrate these two approaches, so management is left to 'second guess' the impact of realized risks on business results."

This, Penny says, leads to four undesirable outcomes:

- Senior executives do not have the access to the information that they need to manage the business.
- Information focus is largely financial and historical.
- There is little concept of issues-based reporting.
- It is easy to miss big items affecting the organization's survival.

To rectify these problems, Penny (as did Smart) looks to the Balanced Scorecard as a "start point" in the quest for integrating performance and risk. However, in Penny's approach, risk is managed through the Balanced Scorecard format. "But in its original form it does not explicitly address risk issues," he says. "So we must understand how to expand it into an integrated performance and risk management system."

Penny is well qualified to speak of the strengths and weaknesses of the conventional Balanced Scorecard. He was previously executive vice-president for Asia of the Balanced Scorecard Collaborative, which was headed by Dr. Norton and has since merged into Palladium.

To bring performance and risk together, Penny has created what he calls a Risk Balanced Scorecard. An indicative Strategy Map of a Risk Balanced Scorecard for an IT outsourcer is shown in figure 3.3. As we can see, the Strategy Map is collocated according to the conventional four-perspective model as described by Kaplan and Norton. However, what is new and innovative here is that the map comprises three themes (which Penny also refers to as "macro strategic waves"), Survive, Execute, Capitalize. Penny explains: "The Survive wave provides insight into changing underlying assumptions (internal and external) on which strategic plans have been built. The Execute wave monitors progress against the chosen strategic plan. The Capitalize wave ensures windfall opportunities are identified and progressed."

We'll now provide a breakdown of the role of each macro strategic wave.

Survive   The Survive wave:

- identifies critical parameters that could affect business success, for example, oil price fluctuations for an airline business or market availability of staff for an IT outsourcing business
- covers areas that could be related to external shifts in the business environment or to internal issues encountered when executing our strategy
- defines, for each identified parameter, what is the critical KPI that we need to keep in view
- sets tolerance thresholds for critical event monitoring for each critical KPI
- establishes, in advance, likely action plans to be deployed for the occurrence of each critical event.

Execute   The Execute wave:

- keeps focus on an organization's long-term strategy by monitoring progress against strategic objectives and their associated KPIs
- checks the need for readjustment in key areas such as resource allocation

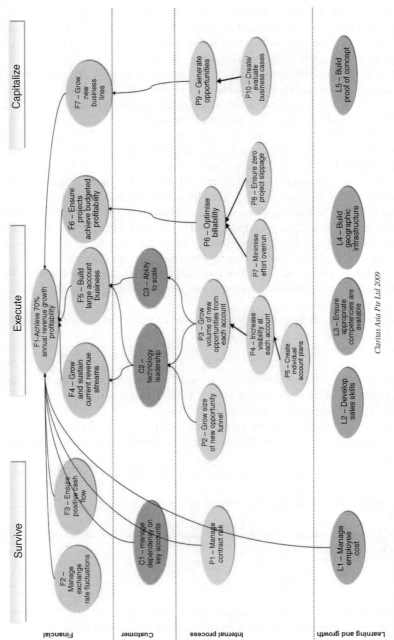

FIGURE 3.3 Risk-Balanced Scorecard for an IT outsourcer

Claritas Asia Pte Ltd 2009

- monitors implementation of key strategic projects and initiatives
- checks ongoing validity of strategy based on emerging business results.

Capitalize   The Capitalize wave:

- recognizes problems presented by competitor problems
- understands requirements for new internal capabilities
- tracks results from new opportunities.

"The Risk-Balanced Scorecard is a new approach using core Balanced Scorecard thinking to give you a new way to create management information that is relevant to managing in today's volatile business environment," says Penny, who adds the very important statement that, "Risk management is not about eliminating risk; it is about managing risk. Organizations must continue to aggressively drive their strategy forward but without losing sight of emerging dangers."

Stratagility Example

Mark Ranford, CEO of the strategy consultancy Stratagility, is another who's been busily considering how best to integrate risk management with strategy management through the Balanced Scorecard. "The management of risk should focus the organization around best achieving its strategic objectives by explicitly recognizing and even undertaking risks that may be deemed necessary to achieve the objectives, while also avoiding risks that are deemed unacceptable to the organization, its mission, values, vision and strategic objectives," he says.

Within one Palladium Hall of Fame-winning organization in the Middle East (not a financial services organization), Ranford led a program to integrate strategy management and risk management through combing the Balanced Scorecard with the ISO 31000: 2009 risk management standard.[8] "We adopted 'Effect of uncertainty on objectives' (from the ISO 31000:2009 standard) as the definition of risk for this organization," explains Ranford. "This definition clearly relates risks to the things that will affect the achievement of organization objectives and hence puts strategy at the center of risk management."

Following are the principles of risk management that the organization adopted (adapted from the ISO standard):

Risk management:

- creates and protects value
- is an integral part of all organizational processes

- is part of decision making
- explicitly addresses uncertainty
- is systematic, structured, and timely
- is based on the best available information
- is tailored
- takes human and cultural factors into account
- is transparent and inclusive
- is dynamic, iterative, and responsive to change
- facilitates continual improvement of the organization.

"Integrating the ISO standard for risk management into the Balanced Scorecard framework was a fairly straightforward effort as the two methodologies complement each other very well," says Ranford. "The efforts to integrate these have been documented in a new combined strategy and risk management framework within the organization."

He goes on to say that the Balanced Scorecard provides the strategic context within which risk is identified and managed. "A very powerful aspect of managing risk within the Balanced Scorecard framework is that the perspectives used for the strategy in the Balanced Scorecard framework provide the strategic context for the risk; in fact, the perspectives provide a very clear representation for the universe of risk," he says.

So financial risks can be placed under a shareholder perspective; customer risk (such as brands) are covered under the customer perspective, process and project risks are under the internal process perspective, and risks relating to knowledge, people, culture and infrastructures are under learning and growth. "The perspectives were very helpful to guide us in identifying and classifying risks," says Ranford.

THE FIVE PRINCIPLES OF SRM

Case Example: State Street Corporation's Alternative Investment Solutions Unit

To conclude the chapter on the Balanced Scorecard and risk, we will look at an interesting spin on the description of a strategy-focused organization (described fully in the previous chapter). It uses the five principles of SRM, which broadly follow the five principles of the strategy-focused organization (see previous chapter). Shown in figure 3.4, these are:

- executive leadership
- measurement

FIGURE 3.4   Five principles of SRM

- alignment
- engagement
- governance.

How the U.S.-headquartered State Street Corporation's Alternative Investment Solutions (AIS) Unit (which provides fund accounting, fund administration, and risk services for approximately $400 billion in alternative assets, including hedge funds, private equity funds, and offshore funds) put the framework into practice was highlighted in a November/December 2009 issue of *Balanced Scorecard Report*.[9] Note that AIS was already a scorecard user.

1. Executive Leadership

The article stated that first and foremost, senior management, and not only the chief risk officer (CRO) or the risk management group, should be responsible for risk management. "A leader's enlarged role in risk management . . . does not mean that the CRO's role is reduced," the article noted. "In fact, the CRO must work with the businesses and manage the 'escalation procedures'—all the steps involved in a risk mitigation effort. The CRO's independence ensures that senior managers aren't tempted to unduly influence or compromise any standards and that they balance responsibility with authority."

Within AIS the organization leader, Jack Klinck sets the appetite for and approach to risk, clarifying the strategic direction and path to getting there. As one example, the leading private equity administration business that State Street AIS acquired in 2007 had been growing at a rate of 35 percent a year. Therefore, establishing a risk management infrastructure and culture from the start was critical. "We aligned the private equity unit's strategic objectives to AIS priorities and collaborated on devising client acquisition criteria," said Klinck. The leadership team, Klinck added, also provides the model for values and behavior. "That includes cultivating not only risk-mindedness but also team members' willingness to be candid in assessing performance, rather than sugarcoating the picture for the boss"

Because State Street AIS grew through several acquisitions, it was particularly important that the unit understood the way each of its three groups affects the others. "Besides recognizing the need to create a coordinated approach to marketing and client service (to minimize client confusion) and the need for an integrated approach to technology (to ensure seamless client servicing), senior management saw the need to develop coherent standards for risk management among the acquired units. For example, the leadership team strenuously debated managing client acquisition risk: How can the company achieve business growth targets while avoiding clients that don't match the organization's strategic risk profile?"

Klinck notes that few organizations allow such debate, but, he added, "We're convinced that when the financial crisis hit, AIS was in a much stronger position than many of our competitors."

2. Measurement

The same Balanced Scorecard measures that provide an early indication of strategic performance success or failure also serve as key risk indicators when analyzed from a 360-degree perspective. The article stated that: "The red/amber/green 'traffic light' assessment on the strategic objectives, measures, and initiatives shows—in the context of the whole Strategy Map—how subpar performance puts other goals at risk."

This assessment gives managers the ability to respond rapidly with corrective action. The color coding provides in effect a "heat map" of key strategic issues, showing their connection with other indicators and helping the organization identify trends and gain insights. For example, an amber rating on a sales win/loss analysis metric would suggest not only that sales losses are in line with projections but also that wins may be declining—a risk that would need to be investigated.

3. Alignment

The article continued that the Strategy Map and strategic themes provide the structure for aligning businesses, teams, and individuals to the organization's common goals. Alignment also encompasses risk. "We look at our themes and objectives to ask, 'Will they promote the right behaviors—or create conflicts?'" commented Klinck. For example, "Are our incentives to grow promoting undue risk taking? Are we investing in the right places in product development to meet the latest marketplace requirements for transparency?" The Strategy Map thus serves equally as a "shared risk agenda."

4. Engagement

An organization's staff are, the article stated, probably the most effective leading risk indicator. "We try to engage staff as much as possible and to listen carefully to people throughout the organization," noted Klinck. Indeed, well before the financial crisis, State Street AIS already had in place a culture that encouraged employee dissent and candor in discussing strategic issues. Developing the business unit strategy maps generated awareness and ownership of AIS's strategic priorities and of the role each business has in contributing to them. Its theme teams bring together a broader group of people involved in strategy implementation.

Yet another group is developing initiative teams. Every quarter, the executive team holds a town hall meeting at a key location to provide a forum for open discussion with local leaders.

5. Governance

Traditionally, the article explained, governance in financial services firms occurs mainly through the business units, resulting in a siloed approach to managing risk and strategy. A solid governance structure can help emphasize the mutual impacts of different groups or performance drivers, at the same time ensuring that dialog occurs horizontally and at multiple levels, the article noted.

The article went on to say that strategy review meetings are as critical to risk management as they are to strategy review itself. "At AIS's monthly strategy review meetings, the strategy map is assessed as a whole. Klinck and his team review the heat map of red/amber/green ratings of performance against objectives, examining the ratings' implications and ramifications. Then they explore a given strategic theme in detail. Each strategic theme owner leads a discussion on the assessment results, looking at their impact on strategic outcomes, both negative and positive.

"'We actively debate the risks and implications—focusing on the horizon, not the past,' said Klinck. 'This approach allows us to manage strategic risk even in the absence of perfect measures.'"

Crucially, the article pointed out that to be robust, an SRM approach must embed risk management into the organization in good times as well as bad. It must treat risk holistically, as an integral part of strategy and performance management. In this way, organizations can adapt to change—even rapid change—with speed and agility. "We hope," said Klinck, that "by recognizing the importance of a proactive, holistic approach, the entire financial services industry will emerge from this crisis stronger."

CONCLUSION

Risk management is not only of concern to financial services but, given the horrors of the credit crunch, it is perhaps of particular interest to this sector. What we have made clear in this chapter is that risk must be understood in the context of the strategic goals of the organization and aligned accordingly.

With an understanding of strategy and associated risks, we can then move into the creation of a Balanced Scorecard Strategy Map. This is the most important part of creating the Balanced Scorecard framework and is the subject of the next chapter.

ENDNOTES

1. James Creelman, *Creating a Balanced Scorecard* (London: Lafferty Publications, 2001).
2. R. Muralidharan, "Strategic Control for Fast-moving Markets: Updating the Strategy and Updating the Performance," *Long Range Planning*, vol. 30, pp. 64–73, 1997.
3. G. J. G. Lawrie, D. C. Kalff, H. V. Andersen, *Integrating Risk Management with Existing Methods of Strategic Control* (U.K.: 2GC, 2003). See www.2gc.co.uk.
4. Bernard Marr, *Managing Strategic Performance in Banks and Financial Services Firms: from Going through the Motions to Best Practice* (Cranfield, U.K.: Cranfield School of Management, 2007).

5. Mark L. Frigo, "Strategic Risk Management, The New Core Competency," *Balanced Scorecard Report*, January/February, 2009.

6. Harvard Business School Publishing, *Balanced Scorecard Report*, November/December 2009.

7. Andrew Smart, *Aligning Risk Management and Exposure: The New Paradigm of Strategic Execution* (London: Manigent, 2009).

8. See www.iso.org.

9. Harvard Business School Publishing, *Balanced Scorecard Report*, November/December 2009.

CHAPTER 4

Building a Strategy Map

EXECUTIVE SUMMARY

1. Strategy mapping is the most important task in building a Balanced Scorecard system.
2. Because the senior team owns the strategy, it follows that it should own the process of creating the map.
3. Creating the Strategy Map requires the senior team to agree on the core drivers of strategic success—achieving such consensus is a major benefit of the scorecard system.
4. The initial Strategy Map is a hypothesis that has to be tested in practice. It can then be amended based on field learnings.
5. It is important to keep the number of strategic objectives to the critical few—perhaps 15 to 20.
6. A Strategy Map is just that—a Strategy Map—it is not an operational map or an organizational map.
7. About 40 percent of objectives should appear in the internal process perspective, because this is where the real work of the organization gets done.
8. Use strategic themes to organize objectives that focus on a specific outcome.
9. A Value Creation Map is an alternative to the classic Kaplan and Norton Strategy Map.
10. Risk maps can be used alongside strategy maps to integrate risk management into the Balanced Scorecard system better.

INTRODUCTION

As we explained in the chapter 2, the idea of a Strategy Map that shows the cause and effect relationship between, and within, perspectives evolved after the original concept of the Balanced Scorecard as a balanced measurement system. Despite being an "afterthought," strategy mapping (the process of creating the map) was soon recognized as the most important task in building a Balanced Scorecard system. Get the map right, it emerged, and it becomes much simpler to select meaningful measures, targets and initiatives. Indeed, Professor Robert Kaplan has said that, ideally, *Strategy Maps*, the third in the sequence of books he wrote with Dr. David Norton, should have been the first. It is fair to say that the Balanced Scorecard education and training industry has been somewhat hampered by many people (including some consultants) believing that the first book is all they need to read to glean a full understanding of the Balanced Scorecard concept and methodology. This has to lead to innumerable poor scorecard implementations.

From a risk management viewpoint, the Strategy Map has a key role to play when attempting to align risk and performance by ensuring that the organizational strategy and strategic context are clear and well understood. This ensures that only the "vital few" objectives, risks, controls, indicators, and so on are incorporated into the overall risk and performance framework, enabling the management discussion to remain focused on the right things.

Starting with objectives and remaining very focused on them ensures that the often seen and very costly "measure everything" approach is avoided, thus significantly increasing information quality, which leads to better, more informed decision making.

START WITH THE STRATEGY

As demonstrated through the CIGNA P&C division case study in chapter 1, a scorecard design process starts from when the strategy, oftentimes captured in a compelling vision or mission statement, is agreed. Consider these two examples from Indonesia.

Case Example: Bank Indonesia

Before the 2002 introduction of the Balanced Scorecard, there were several major occurrences that affected Bank Indonesia negatively. The most notable is the Southeast Asian currency crisis, which led to a massive devaluation of the Indonesian rupiah and a collapse of the nation's economy (see chapter 1).

Consequently, the Indonesian Government enacted the Central Banking Act No. 23 of 1999, which granted Business Indonesia full independence (autonomy) in performing its tasks. The independence in turn obliged the bank to be more transparent in its activities and to be fully accountable to the public.

In 1999, Bank Indonesia launched a large-scale transformation program to develop an integrated tool that could improve its planning, budgeting, and performance evaluation processes. The previous systems were disjoined and did not provide a balanced view of processes and results. There was also no linkage between the organization's mission and vision and the strategic objectives of each directorate.

After a wide review of available methodologies, the Balanced Scorecard was identified as the most promising for closing the identified performance shortcomings and especially for the delivery of a "balanced" view.

On the launch of the scorecard program, there was strong resistance from some managers at each management level. Dyah Nastiti Kusumowardani, Bank Indonesia's director of strategy planning, explains how overcoming this resistance required strong and committed leadership from the top. "It was through the passionate leadership and commitment of the deputy governor that the necessary buy-in from other board members was secured," she says. "With the board of governors onside, systematic and open communications were deployed to secure buy-in at each of the other managerial levels and throughout the organization."

Indeed, she adds that the first principle of strategy-focused organization, "Mobilize change through executive leadership," is the most critical of all scorecard success factors. "It was crucial to get the involvement of the top management level (board of governors), the head of directorates, and Balanced Scorecard managers in each of the working units."

Bank Indonesia's Balanced Scorecard system is in support of its vision and mission statements. Its vision is "to be recognized, domestically and internationally, as a credible central bank through the strength of our values and achievement of low, stable rates of inflation." The mission is "To achieve and maintain Rupiah stability by maintaining monetary stability and by promoting financial system stability for Indonesia's long-term sustainable development." It also has five strategic values: Competency—Integrity—Transparency—Accountability—Cohesiveness.

The bank's Strategy Map has four perspectives: at the highest level, there is a "stakeholders' expectation" perspective, which is supported by "main business processes," "financial" and "organization, HR, and information management" (essentially learning and growth). "The stakeholder perspective is placed at the top of the Strategy Map as that defines the ultimate goal of the organization," explains Dyah Nastiti Kusumowardani. "Cause-and-effect is correlated through a process and outcome relationships."

The Strategy Map of the organization is formulated using the following steps:

1. Refer to the mission that defines the reasons for existence and the overall strategy to achieve the mission.
2. Identify what results in terms of products and services that the mission is set to accomplish, to fulfill customer and stakeholder expectation.
3. Identify which work processes must be excelled in to provide the highest-quality products and services.
4. Identify what kind of resources are needed to support the work processes in terms of budget, people, organization, and other intangible infrastructures.

It is also notable that destination statements are formulated to provide an intermediate target in the long journey to the reach the vision. For example, a destination statement describes what performance should look like at the end of year two of a five-year strategic plan.

Being a scorecard user for almost a decade, it is notable that Bank Indonesia has secured real benefits from the approach (the fact that the scorecard is still in place is itself a measure of its success). Benefits, according to Dyah Nastiti Kusumowardani, include:

- Alignment of the strategy throughout the organizational units creates focused efforts toward achieving the same objectives, thus creating a more effective and efficient organization.
- Balanced measurement among financial, customer, processes, and learning and growth perspectives provide a comprehensive view of the strategy, not only the short-term results, but also its sustainability in the long run.
- Increased value placed on the role of organization, people, and information system in driving strategy achievements.

Case Example: Bank CIMB Niaga

Another exemplary example from Indonesia is Bank CIMB Niaga. In early 2008, the bank, which offers a comprehensive suite of conventional and Islamic banking products and services from 255 branches in 47 cities in Indonesia, created a new vision for up to 2010: "To be Indonesia's Premier Universal Bank" ("universal" means integrally providing all banking products and services). This new vision was the result of Bank Niaga's merger with the Malaysia-headquartered financial service company CIMB Group. From the vision came these targets:

- premier universal bank in Indonesia
- national bank status
- overall market share of 5 percent, return on equity of 20 percent
- integrated regional operating model.

Supporting the targets were a set of core strategies:

- Be top three in the following:
  - affluent and mass affluent
  - *syariah* banking (investment banking as entry strategy).
- Be top five in the following:
  - credit card
  - corporate banking (including high-end commercial)
  - treasury (product manufacturer, FX, bonds, BSM, and so on).
- Strengthen market position and optimize profitability of:
  - mortgage (top three)
  - business banking
  - auto loan
  - UKM program lending.
- De-emphasize mass consumer and lower-middle segments.

Bank CIMB Niaga has been a scorecard user since 2003 (or at least under the Niaga brand) and has notched up some impressive results as a consequence, including:

- Bank Niaga improved its position from the eleventh-largest bank in 2003 to sixth in 2007 in terms of assets; loans grew by 26 percent; deposits grew by 15 percent.
- Niaga Mortgage Market share (as of 2007) was the second largest in the industry.
- It was the best *syariah* banking unit for asset category above RP500 billion, with loans growing by 92 percent in 2007.
- It was ranked second in the Indonesian Service Quality Awards for the category Priority Banking Service for All Multinational and Domestic Banks by CCSL in 2007.
- Credit card holders grew by 53 percent in 2007.
- Ranked first in the HR Excellence Award 2007 by SQA & LM FEUI.
- Ranked third in top 10 employer choice by SWA & Hay Group.

SENIOR MANAGEMENT MUST OWN THE STRATEGY MAP

Senior management responsibility.

Perhaps the biggest mistake in strategy mapping is the tendency for the senior management team to devolve responsibility for the process to a lower-level team. It follows that if the senior team is responsible for strategy, then it should be responsible for fashioning the enterprise-level Strategy Map and Balanced Scorecard. The former describes the strategy as agreed by the senior team, while the Balanced Scorecard shows how the senior team requires the strategy to be implemented. Consequently, ownership has to be accepted by those at the top.

One reason for this is that the process of building the enterprise-level scorecard framework can be as useful to the organization as the end product. Getting the top team focused on the same high-level performance perspective as shown on a Strategy Map is extremely useful in getting each senior manager to see clearly how the work of his or her own function relates to the work of others. Put another way, it helps leaders, who are otherwise departmentally focused in their day-to-day work, to see the bigger picture and their responsibility for strategy formulation as part of the senior executive team.

Case Example: Pentagon Federal Credit Union

This was recognized at the Virginia, U.S.-based Pentagon Federal Credit Union, when it built its scorecard system, as stated in the report: *Understanding the Balanced Scorecard: A HR Perspective*, which was penned by one of the authors of this book.[1] CEO Frank Pollack commented that he pulled his executive team together to debate, discuss and define the scorecard objectives, measures, targets, etc. Pollack stressed "What we didn't do was send each functional head back to their cubby-holes to build their own piece of the scorecard. We are trying to run the company as a group effort rather than as a group of siloed individuals."

Did this approach pay dividends? The results for 2001 (compared with the end of 1998) are shown in table 4.1.

TABLE 4.1   Pentagon Credit Union performance for 2001 compared to 1998

Member satisfaction had reached 8.54 (on a scale of 1–10).
Membership growth rate increased 103.5%.
Net income had increased 152.8%.
Net operating expenses were reduced 21.9%.
Loan loss rate had reduced 11.4%.
Return on assets had increased 27%.
Net income had increased 141.4%.

STRATEGY CLARIFICATION

At the very outset of the scorecard effort it is critical to clarify the strategy—to get agreement on the tangible deliverables. For example, market leadership or leadership in customer satisfaction can mean different things to different people, so it is important to clarify this in terms that are collectively understood and agreed.

The need to secure this agreement should be built into the scorecard design process. A typical process includes senior management interviews and workshops supported by work by lower-level managers or consultants who are facilitating the scorecard development process.

THE USE OF EXTERNAL FACILITATION

A question that most senior managers ask themselves before commencing the scorecard design and implementation effort is whether to engage an external consultant or use available in-house personnel and expertise. In most instances, we would recommend the use of external facilitation. However, the Balanced Scorecard consulting community is full of organizations with little real understanding of the scorecard, which peddle either KPI scorecards or Strategy Maps and scorecards that to an expert eye are clearly not fit for purpose. Others offer scorecard solutions that build upon existing HR or IT offerings, which might also lead to poorly designed systems—as well as being functionally biased. As with the appointment of any external facilitator, the buying organization should take care to research the expertise of scorecard consultants. This is very important in the scorecard community, which has no universally recognized system for accrediting those who call themselves "Balanced Scorecard consultants."

With that caveat, there are several key reasons we generally recommend external expert support.

■ A good external facilitator should contribute expertise, insights and knowledge gained from other successful implementations.

Someone who has successfully built a scorecard should know what works, what doesn't, and the pitfalls to avoid. This knowledge is extremely useful and prevents the organization from wasting significant amounts of time, energy, and money as its internal resources *learn* about the Balanced Scorecard.

Note for example the words of Pak Krisbayanto, who was vice president, human capital at Indonesia's Bank Universal (now merged into PermataBank) during its scorecard implementation, which used the Jakarta-based management consultancy OTI.

"The role of the consultancy is hugely important in the early stages," he says. "They can explain what the scorecard is, provide best practice information based on other corporate implementations, and they have the expertise to facilitate the scorecard design and implementation process. But their skills must be transferred to the company itself because it's the organization that must own this and manage the scorecard on an ongoing basis, and this skills transfer was provided by OTI." Krisbiyanto's comment is important because a core outcome of any engagement should be that the client is able to manage the scorecard on its own once the consultancy project comes to end. An in-depth case study on Bank Universal appears in the book *Mastering Business in Asia: Succeeding with the Balanced Scorecard*,[2] which was written by the authors of this book.

An external facilitator may not be required when the organization has an expert employee—such as a former consultant or someone who has successfully implemented a scorecard successfully elsewhere. For instance, although an early adopter, Cigna P&C's Tom Valerio had scorecard experience with a consultancy before leading Cigna's scorecard program.

■ A skilled external facilitator is able to bring together individual views without getting involved in politics or pushing his or her own agenda.

This is a point that should not be underestimated. It is rare for internal people to be able to remain completely outside the politics of the organization. They either do not have enough perceived authority to challenge the views of the senior team or they are seen to have their own strong interests or agendas—for example, a finance director might have the authority to lead a scorecard effort but might push his or her own agenda and make the scorecard too finance oriented (this is also true of IT or HR directors, as other examples). Conversely, performance analysts might have the independence but might not have the authority required to influence the scorecard design process or to challenge senior managers.

■ Provide a safe environment for everyone to express their honest views.

The external facilitator should conduct focused one-to-one interviews with each member of the senior management team and report the findings in an aggregated, anonymous format. This is important because it allows the senior team to express its views honestly and safely.

While the facilitator is completing the interviews, he or she should also review strategic plans and other strategic documents. With this knowledge, he or she can then prepare a draft Strategy Map for

TABLE 4.2 Workshop 1: Strategy Mapping

Workshop 1 tasks	Issues
Resolve senior management differences on interpretation of the core strategic goals of the enterprise.	Although the workshop is not a strategy formulation forum, it offers an opportunity to clarify differences of interpretation and establish a common view of strategy.
Surface and discuss any outstanding concerns relating to scorecard creation.	There will inevitably be outstanding concerns that need to be aired at this stage of scorecard development.
With the draft Strategy Map as a steer, agree a set of objectives to be incorporated in a Strategy Map, starting with financial through to learning and growth.	Apply concepts such as strategic theming to focus on the primary drivers of strategic performance.
Prepare a one- or two-line definition of each objective.	The high-level objective needs to be more broadly defined for ongoing usage. Although this more detailed definition will not appear on the Strategy Map, it will provide more clarity for the selection of KPIs.
Limit strategic objectives to about 15–20 in total.	Too many objectives make a Strategy Map and scorecard unmanageable.
Assign ownership for objectives.	Senior management ownership should be combined with accountability for the achievement of strategic objectives.
Be prepared for the challenges presented by agreeing strategic objectives.	The process of clarifying strategic objectives can present threats to existing power bases within the organization.

presentation, discussion, and amendment during the first workshop, which is focused on strategy mapping (see table 4.2). We look at the following workshops in later chapters.

A Hypothesis

At this stage the initial Strategy Map is no more than a hypothesis, a best guess as to the cause-and-effect linkages that will deliver the strategy. It is through use that the hypothesis can be proved or disproved: if the latter, then the Strategy Map should be amended appropriately. Indeed, one of the perhaps least-trumpeted benefits of the Balanced Scorecard system is that it will tell you when the strategy is not working as ably as it signals strategic success. Getting an early warning sign that there are fundamental weaknesses in the strategy can save an organization untold millions in investments and, of course, save the CEO from facing the wrath of shareholders.

Case Example: Banking 365   This was true at the Ireland-based remote bank Banking 365 when it launched its scorecard in the mid-1990s. Then CEO Cathal Muckian commented:

> *We believe that excellence in customer service is of paramount importance. Therefore our strategy was based on a person-to-person differentiated service—essentially ensuring that our operations delivered outstanding services to our customers, which they did consistently.*

Although this strategic focus led to extremely high levels of customer satisfaction, the downside was that cost became unacceptably high. There was a disconnection between customer satisfaction and financial success. So the leaders of Banking 365 faced a conundrum. How could they continue to achieve exceptionally high customer satisfaction scores while keeping costs to an acceptable level?

Banking 365 therefore introduced self-service options (very much in their infancy in the mid-1990s) for customers, who could still deal with an operator directly if they wished. Muckian commented:

> *The scorecard quickly showed us a problem with our strategy. Therefore we were able to introduce a different strategic approach early on and monitor its success.*

The Strategy Map consists of the four perspectives of financial, customer, internal, and people. Flowing through the map are the three strategic themes of "sales" (a revenue growth strategy), "operations efficiency" (a productivity strategy), and "service" (a quality strategy) (see figure 4.1).

Successfully getting the "this is a hypothesis" message across may go some way to moving this workshop to the point at which there is a general agreement as to the objectives on the Strategy Map, especially the non-financial objectives.

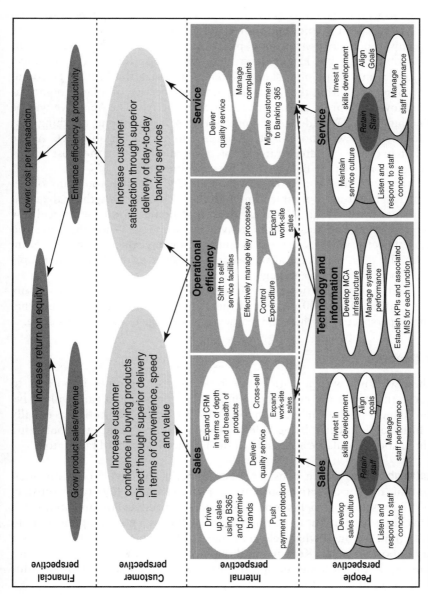

FIGURE 4.1 Banking 365 Strategy Map

77

CREATING OBJECTIVES

If organizations make mistakes in the process of mapping, they also often make mistakes in map design in itself. For instance, a common weakness of many (if not most) strategy maps is that many of the objectives are not really objectives, but rather describe a strategic initiative. For instance, "Create a multifunctional shared services organization" might be found as an objective within the internal process perspective of a large organization. However, this is an initiative, not an objective. The objective will be something like "World-class support services." Simply put, anything that includes a verb will more likely be an initiative than an objective. As we explain in chapter 6, after strategic objectives initiatives are the most important component of the Balanced Scorecard framework.

Another common weakness is the tendency to choose too many objectives. The result is an organization map that describes everything the company does, rather than a Strategy Map that homes in on the critical few objectives that will successfully deliver the strategy. When there are too many objectives, the scorecard becomes unmanageable and the program eventually dies, or if kept alive, becomes a lower priority because people find it too exhausting to manage.

From our observations, 15–20 objectives should be sufficient for any organization. About 40 percent of these should be located in the internal process perspective—where the real work in strategy execution gets done.

Be Specific

When working with a critical few objectives, it becomes important to choose those that are meaningful and highly focused and can really drive step changes in performance. Choosing 15–20 "vague" objectives is equally of little value. Indeed, being able to create a "simple" map, without being "simplistic," should be a key skill of the Balanced Scorecard facilitator.

Customer   For instance, consider the customer perspective. Too many organizations opt for objectives such as "Improve customer loyalty (or satisfaction)." By selecting such simple and generic objectives, organizations will derive little benefit, but more importantly will miss a golden opportunity to really think through what delivers value. And for this perspective, this is a very important point. Keep in mind that according to Kaplan and Norton's framework, the customer perspective represents outcomes that are of value "in the eyes of the customer."

Customers rarely procure a service or buy a product because they want to be satisfied (that's a given), and they certainly do not *want* to be loyal.

Going beyond satisfaction and loyalty means understanding the essence of that value proposition (which is typically something to do with brand and experience) and capturing it in specific objectives. This is a difficult task, so it is usually avoided. Those who accept the challenge reap substantial rewards. Of course, both satisfaction and loyalty might appear in an index of metrics to support a "value-focused" objective.

More than a Perspective: A Customer Theme   But truly understanding the customer cannot be a one-off exercise. Shaping permanent learning channels between the organization and its customers (and indeed stretching out to partners) is becoming a prerequisite for success in most industries. Most companies should capture this customer–organizational interface on their Strategy Map, maybe as a strategic theme that runs through the internal process and learning and growth perspectives.

Internal Process   Although objectives based on service, price, and quality are typically located in the internal process perspective, organizations need to ensure that objectives here support how the organization differentiates itself in the marketplace. For instance, objectives based on cost and quality may be more critical to an organization that competes from a standpoint of operational excellence than one that competes from a position of customer intimacy, whereas service will predominate for the latter. The organization should spend some time on defining the objectives for this perspective, for as cited about 40 percent of strategic objectives should be housed here. And along with the learning and growth perspective, internal process represents the enablers that deliver the customer and financial outcomes.

Learning and Growth   By some distance learning and growth is the least understood of all the perspectives. Typically, it is no more than an add-on, when the "real scorecard work" of populating the other three perspectives has been done. Usually, learning and growth contains objectives that focus on areas such as "a high-performing culture," "employee satisfaction," or "live the values." Again, these can be so generic as to be worthless and once more managers miss a golden opportunity—this time to really think through the key people objectives that must be developed and nurtured as a strategic necessity.

What's more, selecting an objective such as "a high-performance culture," is pointless unless it is recognized that for most organizations this is a huge undertaking that will require significant resourcing. Large-scale funding is never given to objectives that are no more than a passing thought. As a result, such objectives become essentially worthless because no real effort is focused on their achievement.

Financial And finally, there are sometimes mistakes with the financial, or shareholder, perspective (although it is by some distance the easiest of the perspectives). Although this seems a simple collocation of key financial outcomes, it might be sensible to ask shareholders to describe what they want from the organization. In some cases they will want more than short-term gains, and they may also have other concerns—about governance for instance. This input can be invaluable steers for scorecard creation. Of course, for many financial institutions, a need to ensure that there's a robust emphasis on longer-term shareholder benefits is certainly a key focus today.

For many in the financial services industry, risk has become a high-level stakeholder or financial objective within the Strategy Map. Figure 4.2 shows a Strategy Map for the pseudonymous Consumer National Bank, where this is the case. Note that this Strategy Map was created to contend with the pressures that emerged from the credit crunch. While focusing on the "3 Cs" of credit, cost, and capital (to meet short-term needs), the map is designed to protect the long term at the same time. One of the original tenets of the scorecard that it balances short-term and long-term needs still holds true.

Some commentators believe that such is the importance of risk management within financial services, it should become a perspective on its own, much as "environment" is often found as a separate perspective on the Strategy Map of an oil and gas organization (it is for instance the case at Balanced Scorecard Hall of Fame member, the giant StatoilHydro). Although the idea might be appealing, the fact is that the management of risk affects each of the four perspectives within a Strategy Map and it would therefore be difficult to create objectives within a dedicated "risk" perspective that do not duplicate objectives elsewhere. Because risk management requires a focus on both enablers and outcomes, it would be a challenge to figure where to place the "risk" perspective on a Strategy Map while maintaining robust and strategically meaningful cause-and-effect relationships and descriptions. Perhaps more useful is to make risk a strategic theme on the Strategy Map, which we now discuss.

STRATEGIC THEMES

Within a Strategy Map objectives should typically be collocated according to strategic themes. This is a way of organizing objectives (typically within the internal process and learning and growth perspectives but sometimes more broadly over all four perspectives) that must be focused on as a group to deliver the customer and financial outcomes. Note the sales, operational efficiency, and service themes within Banking 365's map.

What is different about managing in a recession?

Modify the strategy to focus on short-term while protecting the long-term:

One bank hunkered down to focus on "the three c's"

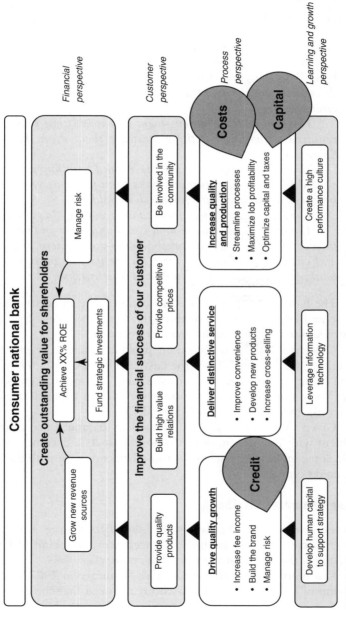

FIGURE 4.2 A Strategy Map for the Pseudonymous Consumer National Bank

Consider too the Indonesia-based Bank Universal (now merged into PermataBank). The starting point for Bank Universal's scorecard program was a review of its strategy and vision in the early years of this century. Mahdi Syahbuddin, the bank's then deputy president director, said:

> When we created our Balanced Scorecard, we started with our corporate vision, which is "To be the best Indonesian regional bank." In designing the scorecard, it forced us on an executive discussion around what we meant by best, given our own set of circumstances.
>
> The senior management team concurred that being the best required delivering on three strategic themes on the Balanced Scorecard.
>
> The first identified theme was around handling past problems caused by the nonperforming loans from previous years. The goal here was to minimize loss for the shareholders.
>
> The second theme was focused on becoming "a good bank."
>
> The third theme was around communication and building confidence in the eyes of our stakeholders—government, shareholders, and customers—that they were on the way to becoming a good bank, one that can be profitable and trustworthy.

The bank's Balanced Scorecard captures the three strategic themes in cause-and-effect relationships through the perspectives of people, process, customer satisfaction, and financial performance.

Objectives focused on becoming profitable include, from a financial perspective, "fee income," from the customer perspective, "effective selling," from an internal perspective, "cross selling," and from an employee perspective, "core mindset" (with measures including a product-knowledge index and a risk-management knowledge index).

Given that Bank Universal created its Balanced Scorecard system to content with the aftermath of the Southeast Asia currency crisis, it might hold some interesting lessons for those banks dealing with the aftermath of the credit crunch.[3]

Case Example: Kiwibank

Consider too New Zealand's 915-employee-strong Kiwibank, which was inducted into Palladium's Balanced Scorecard Hall of Fame in 2009 (becoming the first inductee from that country).

Kiwibank introduced the Balanced Scorecard in 2007, under the sponsorship of CEO Sam Knowles, who recognized that the organization had outgrown is original structure as a startup (it was founded in 2002). By mid-2008, scorecard systems were in place at the corporate level and at seven business and six support units.

As explained in the *Balanced Scorecard Hall of Fame Report 2010*,[4] an early learning within Kiwibank was that assigning individual executives to be "objective owners" simply perpetuated an already problematic silo mentality. As a result, Knowles created crossfunctional theme teams structured around the bank's four strategic themes: Excellence in Business Processes; Sales and Service Leadership; Sustainable Growth; Learning and Growth. "Every executive leader was assigned to at least one enterprise-level team," the reports noted. "About 150 people—17 percent of staff—were enlisted as theme team members, theme managers, business-unit strategy leads, objective champions, and measurement leads."

This is not to say that objective owners should not be assigned. Indeed, owners should be assigned for all themes, objectives, measures, and initiatives. Rather, objective owners should report to and have their work orchestrated and aligned by the theme owner: in this way avoiding the problems of silo management identified by Kiwibank. It should also be stressed that theme owners should liaise closely together to ensure that the themes are working in unison for the betterment of the organization: an easy trap to fall into is to become narrowly focused on a theme.

Risk Management

Of course, today it is likely that financial institutions will include a theme that focuses on risk management, ensuring that they understand customer and product risk and have the internal systems capabilities and people competencies for the identification, assessment, and management of risk indicators. Indeed, it is difficult to think of many financial services companies that would not include risk management as a strategic theme.

Now there are those who would disagree with the proposition that risk management should be a separate theme in a strategy. One such person is Mark Ranford, CEO of the consultancy Stratagility. "Organizations need to manage the risk associated with each objective," he says.

Indeed, within one Middle Eastern organization, Ranford has facilitated a process by which theme teams have been central to integrating risk management with strategy through the Balanced Scorecard.

"Following awareness and training sessions the next stage of the implementation was to incorporate the Risk process into the Annual Strategy Review process, and in particular the use of theme teams to drive the review and changes," says Ranford. "In the 2010 Theme Team workshops it was

FIGURE 4.3 Risk management process

agreed that the theme teams would predominantly focus on the incorporation of risk into the strategy."

The theme teams undertook the following steps, which essentially follow the generic process as outlined by the ISO 3100: 2009 standard for risk management (see figure 4.3).

In the first step, the theme teams considered the theme and the objectives of that strategic theme in relation to the perspective and the objective, its definition, and particularly its current and desired states establishing the landscape and context of the risks.

In the second step, the theme teams brainstormed and identified the risks that related to the theme objectives. After this, they analyzed the risks in more detail and then evaluated them, assigning likelihood and consequence scores and calculating the corresponding risk severity levels, which were then displayed on a heat map (see figure 4.4).

The theme teams then considered what kind of response and treatment types, if any, were appropriate and put together proposed treatment initiatives where required. "These outputs resulted in a strategy and business plan incorporating risk for all objectives, with identified risks, risk heat maps, and indicators, along with a proposed risk treatment plan," says Ranford.

These risks, the treatment plan, initiatives, and the controls to monitor and manage them are managed through the unified strategy and risk management system, with the objective owners taking responsibility for the

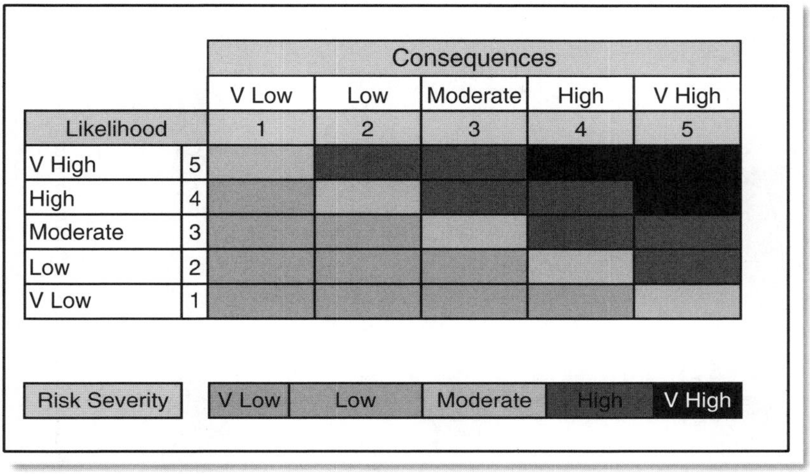

		Consequences				
		V Low	Low	Moderate	High	V High
Likelihood		1	2	3	4	5
V High	5					
High	4					
Moderate	3					
Low	2					
V Low	1					

Risk Severity	V Low	Low	Moderate	High	V High

FIGURE 4.4   Heat map

risks within their objective context, and reviewing these in the same quar-terly cycles and review meetings as strategy is reviewed and managed.

To assess the likelihoods of risks dynamically, the organization is using a tool called a "Prediction Market." This tool allows a broad range of partici-pants from across the organization provide input into the assessment of the likelihood of a particular risk occurring, commonly referred to as exploiting the "wisdom of the crowds" or the collective intelligence. A powerful aspect of employing this tool is that it allows the organization assessment of risk likeli-hood to be dynamic and always up to date for every quarterly review meeting.

RISK-BALANCED SCORECARD

In the previous chapter we introduced the innovative new concept of a Risk-Balanced Scorecard, within which the Strategy Map is built according to the classic Kaplan and Norton architecture but is collocated according to three themes of survive, execute, and capitalize (which the originator of the concept Nigel Penny, managing director of the Singapore-headquartered ClaritasAsia, also describes as "macro strategic waves"). An example Risk Balanced Scorecard Strategy Map is shown in figure 4.5.

In constructing the Strategy Map and Balanced Scorecard, Penny makes much use of value driver trees, (which enable the understanding of the inter-dependencies of measure that drive ultimate value) such as shareholder value for instance, see figure 4.6. A value driver tree is a well-established

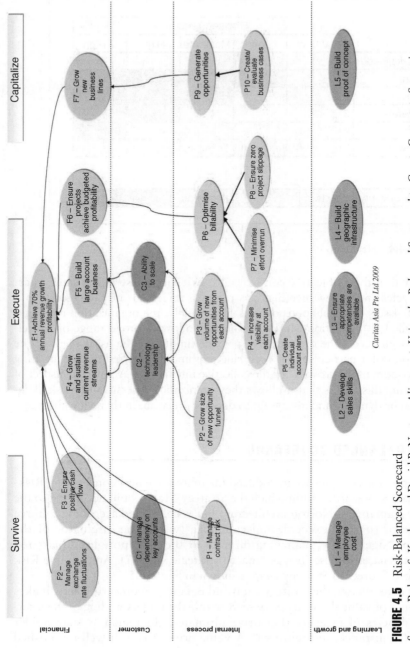

FIGURE 4.5 Risk-Balanced Scorecard

Source: Robert S. Kaplan and David P. Norton, *Alignment: Using the Balanced Scorecard to Create Corporate Synergies* (Cambridge, Mass.: Harvard Business Press, 2005).

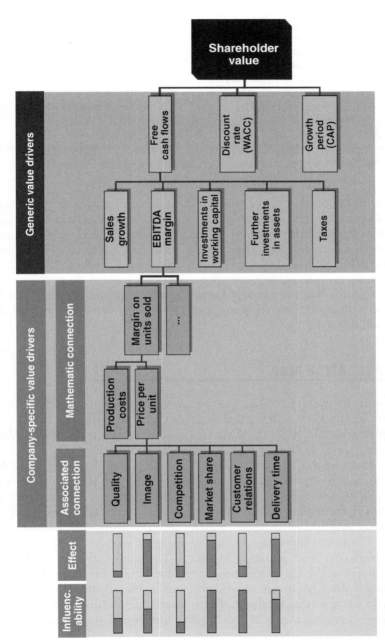

FIGURE 4.6 Risk management scorecard value driver

TABLE 4.3 Survival theme output from a value tree analysis

Perspective	Objectives	Measures
Financial	Managing cost of funding	Average cost of borrowing
Customer	Minimizing dependency on major customers	Percentage of total revenues from top 5% of customers
Internal	Securing continuous raw material funding	Percentage of key parts sourced from single supplier only
Learning and growth	Protecting key accounts	Turnover rates in key account managers

Source: ClaritasAsia.

tool, but in the context of the survival theme might be particularly important. "The survive theme starts with the creation of an organization specific driver tree from which the key areas with the potential to threaten survival are identified," says Penny. "By creating such a value driver tree for your business it becomes possible to quantify the level of impact, or effect, of various business drivers."

Penny adds that the outputs from the value tree analysis can then be grouped with the Balanced Scorecard's four-perspective framework, as shown in table 4.3.

VALUE CREATION MAP

Penny's Strategy Map builds on the conventional Balanced Scorecard framework, but it is worth highlighting that there are variations to the classic Kaplan and Norton Strategy Map. In chapter 3, we mentioned the U.K. consultancy 2GC's Third-Generation Balanced Scorecard.

Another popular alternative is the Value Creation Map, originated by the Advanced Performance Institute in the U.K. (of which one of the authors of this book is a fellow). We explain how the Value Creation Map works through a case study on GlobeInsure (a fictitious name to protect the anonymity of this company). GlobeInsure is a leading provider of insurance and related risk management services for the international transport and logistics industry. The company has its global headquarters in the City of London, the central hub for insurance firms, but has 20 office locations around the world. Its customers range from the world's largest shipping lines, busiest ports, global freight forwarders, and cargo handling terminals, to smaller companies operating in niche markets. Since its inception, GlobeInsure has grown steadily in terms of premium income, at an average rate of 10 percent per annum for the past 20 years. Customer loyalty has been an essential factor in this growth. Indeed, 90 percent of its customers renew their policies with GlobeInsure each year.

The project to develop a Value Creation Map was part of the strategic planning cycle. GlobeInsure wanted to understand its strategic value drivers better, with an emphasis on the nonfinancial and intangible drivers of performance. The development of the map involved a set of interviews with members of the senior management team, the CEO, and board members. In a facilitated one-day planning workshop with the senior management team, the map was finalized. The Value Creation Map for the GlobeInsure is outlined in figure 4.7.

GlobeInsure decided that its value proposition was to provide sustainable financial security for the global transport industry by offering excellent and customized insurance covers and value added services that people trust. They identified three key competencies: (1) the claims handling and delivery of services such as risk assessments and advice, (2) the deep understanding of the industry and changing client demands and underwriting requirements, and (3) the ability to build and maintain close relationships with the industry that gives GlobeInsure the status of an independent body in the industry.

These competencies are delivered through the structures, processes, and systems in place, together with the reputation and recognition as a specialist and member of the transport industry, as well as the relationships not just with the transport industry, but also with reinsurers and brokers.

At the foundation of the Value Creation Map is the ability to recruit, train, develop, and retain good people, who help to create the knowledge and expertise needed. This knowledge, together with the strong customer care ethos, helps to shape the organization's reputation in the industry. Knowledge also shapes the development of processes, structures, and systems. At the center of the map is capital strength and access to reinsurance, one of the strongest resources in GlobeInsure. There is a dynamic relationship between the relationships with reinsurers and the access to reinsurance. Capital strength is also an important driver of reputation; without appropriate capital strength, the reputation would suffer very quickly. GlobeInsure's global presence helps it to create local relationships, which in turn affect its reputation and recognition in the field positively. The headquarters in London enables GlobeInsure to develop the crucial relationships with brokers who sell its products and with reinsurers to make reinsurance deals.[5]

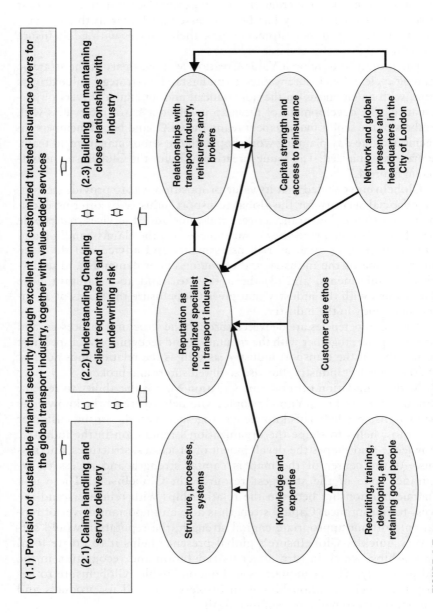

FIGURE 4.7 Value Creation Map for GlobeInsure

RISK MAP

The risk map is a well established tool in the risk management toolbox. Based on the results of a risk assessment, the risk map plots the impact and likelihood of key risks, enabling them to be visualized in relation to each other and enabling clusters of risks to be identified. Based on this information, mitigation plans, priorities, risk treatments, and potential scenarios can be debated and agreed upon.

Risk management expert Andrew Smart of the consultancy Manigent has created a useful risk map that is designed to work with a Balanced Scorecard Strategy Map and has the added benefit of providing an "organizationwide" view and a "perspective" view of risk (see figure 4.8).

This risk map is valuable because it enables organizations to focus on risks in specific perspectives and explore the relationship between

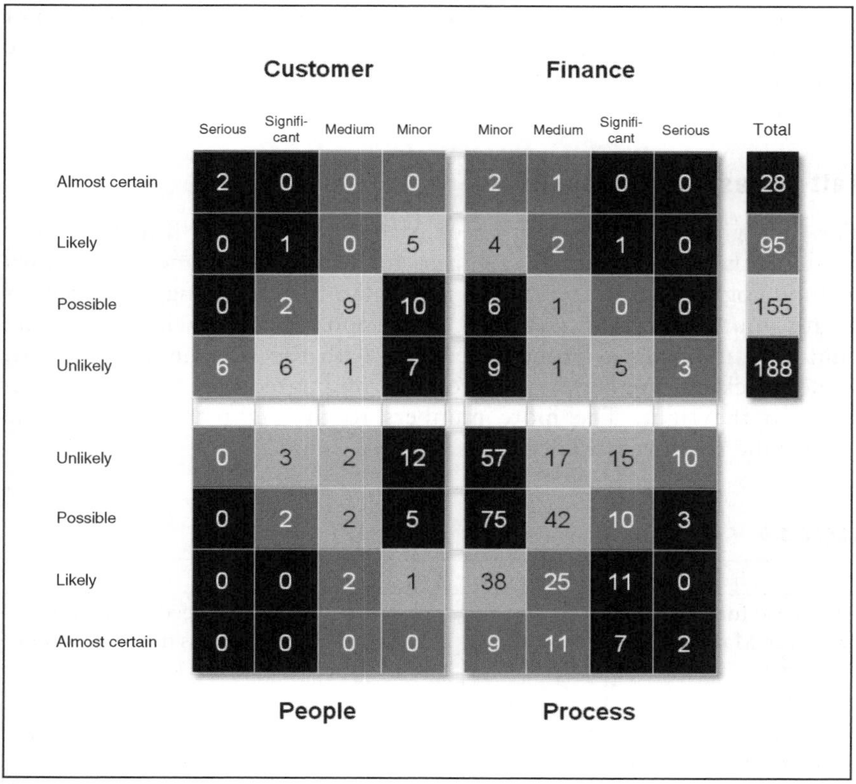

	Customer				**Finance**				Total
	Serious	Signifi-cant	Medium	Minor	Minor	Medium	Signifi-cant	Serious	
Almost certain	2	0	0	0	2	1	0	0	28
Likely	0	1	0	5	4	2	1	0	95
Possible	0	2	9	10	6	1	0	0	155
Unlikely	6	6	1	7	9	1	5	3	188
Unlikely	0	3	2	12	57	17	15	10	
Possible	0	2	2	5	75	42	10	3	
Likely	0	0	2	1	38	25	11	0	
Almost certain	0	0	0	0	9	11	7	2	
	People				**Process**				

FIGURE 4.8 Manigent's risk map

risks across perspectives. For example, one organization that uses the four-perspective risk map focuses attention on the risks within the perspectives as a starting point for its monthly risk review; it explores the causal relationship between objectives, using both the Strategy Map and a risk map. It believes that taking this approach enables it to manage and monitor the delivery of their strategy, while ensuring that it operates within its risk appetite. The work of Manigent in aligning performance management through the Balanced Scorecard with risk management is discussed in chapter 3.

CONCLUSION

This chapter has focused on the creation of strategy maps and the importance of them being built and owned by the senior team—the owner of the strategy. We also stressed the value of strategic theming and the creation of theme teams. With the Strategy Map built, the next step is to select strategic measures, followed by targets. We consider metric selection and target setting in the next chapter.

Self-Assessment Checklist

The following self-assessment checklist (see table 4.4) will help you understand the organizational readiness for using the Balanced Scorecard methodology and framework and the scale of the challenges. Simply indicate your agreement with the two opposing statements. Checking number 1 indicates a strong agreement with the statement to the left, while checking number 7 indicates a strong agreement with the statement to the right. The more numbers to the right are checked, the greater the perceived challenges.

TABLE 4.4   Self-assessment checklist

	1	2	3	4	5	6	7	
The need for a Strategy Map is fully understood by the senior team	✓							The need for a Strategy Map is not understood by the senior team
The senior team will collectively design the Strategy Map	✓							Design of the Strategy Map will be devolved to a lower-level team

Members of the senior team are willing to debate their different takes on what drives success openly	✓							Members of the senior team are not willing to debate their different takes on what drives success openly
The senior team understands the importance of nonfinancial performance	✓							The senior team is only interested in financial performance
We have the capabilities to implement crossfunctional theme teams	✓							We do not have the capabilities to implement crossfunctional theme teams

ENDNOTES

1. James Creelman, *Understanding the Balanced Scorecard: A HR Perspective* (Aurora, Ontario, Canada: HR.Com, 2002).
2. James Creelman and Naresh Makhijani, *Mastering Business in Asia: Succeeding with the Balanced Scorecard* (Singapore: John Wiley Asia, 2005).
3. ibid.
4. Palladium, *Strategy Execution Champions, The Palladium Balanced Scoreboard Hall of Fame Report, 2010* (Cambridge, Mass: Harvard Business Publishing/Palladium, 2010).
5. Bernard Marr, *Strategic Performance Management, Leveraging and Managing your Intangible Value Drivers* (Oxford: Butterworth-Heinemann, 2006).

CHAPTER 5

Selecting Metrics and Targets

EXECUTIVE SUMMARY

1. The function of metrics is to monitor progress toward strategic objectives, and in doing so test the efficacy of the strategy.
2. To apply measures effectively companies must understand at least the basics of this science of measurement. Measurement includes concepts such as precision, accuracy, and bias.
3. Measures should also be limited to the critical few.
4. Key performance questions are a useful innovation for ensuring that appropriate performance metrics (or key performance indicators) are chosen.
5. To be useful for aggregation, comparison, and best-practice sharing, measures should be commonly defined organizationwide.
6. Within the scorecard it is important to include key risk indicators.
7. A list of sample banking metrics is provided.
8. The concept of a Risk Scorecard is introduced.
9. All measures on a Balanced Scorecard should have a corresponding target, just as all objectives require supporting metrics.
10. Targets on the Balanced Scorecard should represent quantum step-changes in performance.
11. In the setting of stretch targets, organizations should, wherever possible, identify comparative performance goals.

INTRODUCTION

To begin this chapter we will make perhaps the most important observation about the Balanced Scorecard framework and methodology. It is one that many organizations fail to take on board, and by doing so fail to secure the

pitfall

greatest benefits from scorecard implementation. That is, that the Balanced Scorecard is not a measurement system. The function of metrics is to monitor progress toward strategic objectives, and in doing so test the efficacy of the strategy. It is for this reason that measures play a crucial role in the scorecard system. Consider these words from Dyah Nastiti Kusumowardani, Bank Indonesia's director, strategy planning. "The Balanced Scorecard should be developed mainly as a strategy execution tool and not as a performance measurement system."

THE CRITICAL FEW MEASURES

The use of metrics is of course widespread within companies across all industries and sectors, and financial services is no exception. However, the usefulness of all the data that is collected to inform the metric is oftentimes questionable. In his research report *Managing Strategic Performance in Banks and Financial Services*, consultant and academic Bernard Marr of the U.K.-based Advanced Performance Institute pointed to a common shortcoming—strategic relevance.[1] Marr stated that his research for the report had found that many organizations were experts at measuring information that is easily collectable, instead of carefully thinking about designing indicators that provide information that they really need. One research respondent noted that:

Book

> It is too easy to get everyone in one room to brainstorm about possible performance indicators. We ended up with a long list of everything we could easily collect and few indicators that really gave us insights. We then put the machinery in place to ensure that we collected all of these indicators—but without ever really questioning them. Last year we conducted a project to assess how much money we were spending on measuring performance and the number we came up with was 3 percent of revenue. That's a huge cost for little value.

Similar "horror stories" about the relevance of data being collected came from other research respondents from the financial services sector, such as: "We are experts at collecting data that nobody needs," and "Our monthly performance report was considered to be our firm's main decision-making instrument, including our key metrics. Yet an IT hiccup meant that, for a period of three months, the reports were not delivered. Not one person asked for the missing information and only after three months did one person mention that he hadn't received the data. That is how useful our data are!"

KEY PERFORMANCE QUESTIONS

However, one bank, one of the world's top 10, implemented a useful step between mapping its strategy and the design of indicators. It identified a series of key performance questions (KPQs), a technique pioneered by the Advanced Performance Institute.[2] Only when these were in place, did the firm allow the development of associated key performance indicators (KPIs).

This process ensured that each indicator was linked to a critical performance question—by default providing evidence that helped to answer relevant questions. Instead of picking any number of possible indicators for a strategic objective, questions would be posed such as *To what extent has our customer satisfaction improved, How well is our brand perceived in our industry*, or *How well are we communicating internally?*

Each of these questions helps to narrow objectives down and identify the aspects of performance that senior management is really interested in. This helps the bank remove purposeless measurement. Indeed, the organization has imposed a rule: if you don't have a question you want to answer, you can't have an indicator.

Although KPIs are well understood, KPQs are not. So as a description, a KPQ is a management question that captures exactly what managers want to know when it comes to reviewing each of their strategic objectives. The rationale for KPQs is that they focus our attention on what actually needs to be discussed when an organization reviews performance and, most importantly, provides guidance for collecting meaningful and relevant performance indicators. Far too often, organizations jump straight to designing indicators before being clear about what they want to know. By first designing KPQs organizational leaders are able to ask themselves: "What is the best data and management information we need to collect to help us answer our key performance questions?" Starting with a KPQ ensures that all subsequently designed performance indicators are relevant. In addition, KPQs put performance data into context and therefore facilitate communication, guide discussion, and direct decision making.

If we might be momentarily permitted to interject a short case illustration from outside the financial services sector that shows how powerful KPQs can be in strategic performance management comes from consider Google—one of today's most successful and admired companies. Google CEO Eric Schmidt says:

> We run the company by questions, not by answers. So in the strategy process we've so far formulated 30 questions that we have to answer . . . You ask it as a question, rather than a pithy answer, and that stimulates conversation. Out of the conversation comes

innovation. Innovation is not something that I just wake up one day and say "I want to innovate." I think you get a better innovative culture if you ask it as a question.[3]

KPQs should be open rather than closed questions. Whereas the latter can be answered by a simple yes/no answer, the former cannot and therefore stimulates a conversation. Sample KPQs used by organizations include:

- How well are we delivering our shareholder requirements?
- To what extent are we responding to the most exciting opportunities that the market is offering?
- How well are we performing in sector X?
- To what extent are we improving our international reputation?
- How well are we meeting our customer needs in segment X?
- To what extent are we keeping our most profitable customers?
- How well are we promoting our services?
- What is our customer's perception of our service?
- To what extent are we effective in our relationship management?
- How well are we innovating?
- How well are we communicating in our organization?
- How well are we continuing to work in teams?
- How well are we sharing our knowledge?
- To what extent are we retaining the talent in our organization?
- How well are we building our new competencies of X?
- To what extent are we continuing to attract the right people?
- Do we have sufficient equipment to meet tomorrow's task?
- How well are we fostering a culture of innovation and continuous improvement?
- How well are we managing our allocated financial resources?
- To what extent do we have the appropriate levels of stock?
- To what extent do we have the appropriate external services?
- To what extent do people feel passionate about working for our organization?
- How well are we helping to develop a coordinated network to perform clinical trials?
- To what extent are our staff motivated?
- How well are we sharing one set of values?[4]

Of course, a raft of KPQs relating to risks can be articulated to align with the strategic objectives captured in the Strategy Map, such as "To what extent are we effectively managing cash-flow risk?" or "How well are we aligning risk appetite with risk exposure?"

A 10-Step Guide to Creating KPQS

The following is a powerful 10-step guide for creating KPQs.

1. Design one-to-three KPQs for each strategic objective on the Strategy Map.
2. Ensure that KPQs are performance related.
3. Engage people in the creation of your KPQs.
4. Create short and clear KPQs.
5. KPQs should be open questions.
6. KPQs should focus on the present and future.
7. Refine and improve your KPQs as you use them.
8. Use your KPQs to design relevant and meaningful performance indicators.
9. Use KPQs to refine and challenge existing performance indicators.
10. Use KPQs to report, communicate, and review performance.

We will now discuss each of these 10 steps in a little more detail and provide more practical advice for creating good KPQs.

1. Design One-to-Three KPQs for Each Strategic Objective on the Strategy Map
Key questions should be based on what matters in your organization—your strategy. Once you have clarified your strategic objectives and captured them within a Strategy Map you can start designing KPQs.

We would recommend that you design one-to-three KPQs for each strategic objective or strategic element on your Strategy Map. As with the logic that it is better to restrict a Strategy Map to a critical few objectives (so to improve focus and clarity on what's really important), the fewer KPQs you have the better—for the same reasons of focus and clarity.

2. Ensure That KPQs Are Performance Related
A KPQ has to be about performance. The aim is to design questions you need to revisit and answer regularly to manage your organization better. Performance-related questions are those that enable an understanding of how well you are implementing your strategic objectives and to what extend you are meeting your objectives and targets.

KPQ - Key performance questions

3. Engage People in the Creation of Your KPQs KPQs should not be designed in the boardroom alone. Designing KPQs is a great opportunity to engage everyone in the organization as well as some external stakeholders. Try to involve people in the process and ask them what question they would see as most relevant. Once you have designed a list of KPQs, take it back to the subject matter experts or different parties within and outside the organization to collect feedback.

4. Create Short and Clear KPQs A good KPQ is relatively short, clear, and unambiguous. It should only contain one question. We often produce a string of questions, which makes it much harder to guide meaningful and focused data collection. The language should be clear and not contain any jargon or abbreviations that external people might not understand. Likewise, try to stay away from management buzzwords, ensure that the question is easy to understand, and use language that people in your organization are comfortable with, understand, and use.

5. KPQs Should Be Open Questions Questions can be divided into two types: closed questions and open questions. Closed questions such as "Have we met our budget?" can be answered by a simple "yes" or "no," without any further discussion or expansion on the issue. However, if we ask an open question such as "How well are we managing our budget?," the question triggers a wider search for answers and seeks more than a "yes" or "no" response. Open questions make us reflect, they engage our brains to a much greater extent, and they invite explanations and ignite discussion and dialog. Whenever possible, KPQs should be phrased as open questions.

6. KPQs Should Focus on the Present and Future Questions should be phrased in a way that talks about the present or future: "To what extent are we increasing our market share?" instead of questions that point into the past, for example, "Has our market share increased?" By focusing on the future we open up a dialog that allows us to "do" something about the future. We then look at data in a different light and try to understand what the data and management information mean for the future. This helps with the interpretation of the data and ensures we collect data that assists our decision making and performance improvement.

7. Refine and Improve Your KPQs As You Use Them Once KPQs have been created, it is worth waiting to see what answers come back—that is, how well the KPQs help people to make better-informed decisions. Once they are in use it is possible to refine them to improve the focus even more. This is a natural process of learning and refinement, and organizations should expect some significant change in the first 12 months of using KPQs. Experience has shown that after about 12 months the changes are less frequent and the KPQs become much better.

8. Use Your KPQs to Design Relevant and Meaningful Performance Indicators
Once you have designed a set of good KPQs linked to your strategic objectives and following the above guidelines, you can use them to guide the design of meaningful and relevant performance indicators.

9. Use KPQs to Refine and Challenge Existing Performance Indicators   KPQs can be used to challenge and refine any existing performance indicators. Linking them to your KPQs can allow you to put them into context and justify their relevance.

10. Use KPQs to Report, Communicate, and Review Performance   KPQs can also be used to improve the reporting, communication, and review of performance information. In our performance reporting and communications, we should always put the KPQs with the performance data we are presenting. This way, the person who looks at the data understands the purpose of the data being collected and is able to put them into context. Furthermore, it enables them to reflect on the answers.

KPIS   *Key performance indicators*

As cited, with KPQs in place, it becomes easier to identify KPIs. Just as objectives should be kept to the critical few that are strategically focused, KPIs should also be limited—to perhaps two per objective; so 30 KPIs should suffice for 15 objectives (two for each).

Where possible, one of the two chosen KPIs should be leading, while the other is lagging. As a simple example, profit is a lagging measure of past performance because it tells us what has happened but it does not provide information on what is likely to happen in the future. A leading measure, on the other hand, provides information on what is happening today that will impact performance tomorrow. For instance, for an organization competing through a strategy based on product leadership, the new product pipeline provides a powerful leading indication of future sales potential.

Case Example: Banking 365

Sample metrics from the Banking 365 scorecard are shown in table 5.1.

TABLE 5.1 Sample objectives and metrics from Banking 365's scorecard

Selected objectives	Selected metrics
Financial	
F1 Increase return on equity	PBT v. target
F2 Grow product volumes and income	Cost income ratio
	Product sales and income v. target
F3 Increase productivity and efficiency	Cost per transaction
Customer	
C1 Increase customer confidence in buying "direct"	Percent products sold "direct"
	Mystery shopper rating
C2 Increase customer satisfaction through superior delivery of day-to-day banking services	Customer satisfaction rating
Internal process	
I1 Drive up sales using both brands	Volume of 365 and Premier sales v. target
I2 Cross sell products	Number of cross sales applications generated
I3 Expand CRM	Number of outbound calls made or converted
I4 Expand worksite sales	
I5 Push payment protection	Number of active schemes
I6 Provide quality sales service	Payment protection take-up
I7 Shift traffic to self-serve device	Percent sales calls answered within 20 seconds
I8 Effectively manage key processes	Percent sales calls abandoned
I9 Effectively manage resources	Number of transactions by self-service device
I10 Effectively manage expenditures	Total call processing time (service)
I11 Outsource noncore activity	Application approval ratio
I12 Deliver quality service	Takeup rate on approval (sales)
I13 Effectively manage customer complaints	Staffing v. request v. budget for services and sales
I14 Migrate customers to Banking 365	Expenditure v. budget
	Status update
	Percent service calls abandoned
	Percent service calls answered within 20 seconds
	Number and type of customer complaints
	Volume of service calls v. target
People	
P1 Develop appropriate culture in services and sales	Staff feedback—survey
P2 Invest in skills training	Percentage of time invested in training

Selected objectives	Selected metrics
P3 Align goals	Staff feedback—survey
P4 Manage staff performance	Staff feedback—survey
P5 Listen and respond to staff concerns	Staff turnover rate
	Staff rotation rate
P6 Retain staff	
Technology	
system performance	
T2 Develop MCA infrastructure	System availability and response times
M1 Introduce KPIs for each function	Project, program updates

Case Example: Bank Universal

Within Bank Universal, there were between 15 and 20 measures for each branch.

- Financial metrics are grouped around revenue and expenses.
- Customer satisfaction metrics include how long customers wait for tellers or service delivery and an annual customer satisfaction survey measures the branch network performance collectively, and branches individually.
- From a process perspective, measures include how long it takes to process a check, to submit a deposit, or to open an account.
- Finally, on the people side, measures include succession planning at branch level and the product knowledge of branch employees.

Case Example: Scotiabank

As a further example, consider the Toronto, Ontario, Canada-headquartered banking giant, Scotiabank. Throughout Canada, the scorecards of the branch managers are identical in that they will consist of the four perspectives of financial, customer, operations, and employee, and will be subjected to a common measurement process. For example, a branch manager's scorecard includes a measure of satisfaction or engagement of branch employees. However, the goals and targets may change from region to region and perhaps branch to branch, depending on local requirements.

Similar scorecards have been created for other levels, such as customer service managers and cashiers. For example, the scorecard for customer service managers, who are responsible for the operations of the branch, includes the objective from the "operational" perspective of "effective facilities management." A KPI for this could be the management of ATM downtimes. Personal banking officer will have a measure of the number of contacts with key customers.

As a useful best practice learning, Scotiabank discovered the limitations of the employee satisfaction measurement. Through experience over the years, the bank concluded that this does not tell the whole employee performance story. Although it will continue to measure and ensure employee satisfaction, the bank would like employees to be engaged and therefore contribute that extra discretionary effort that can bring competitive advantage. The bank has designed a new engagement survey that measures, among other things, the employee's willingness to recommend the bank as a company to work for and willingness to recommend Scotiabank products to potential customers outside working hours.

We should interject here that there are useful employee engagement surveying instruments on the market, which were highlighted in the management white paper *Creating Engaged Employees: The Role of Employee Engagement Surveys* by the authors of this book.[5]

One instrument highlighted was the Infotool Diagnostic Tool (screenshots are shown in figures 5.1 and 5.2). This tool measures employee engagement alongside other culture/climate factors. The tool uses a standard range (often 1–7) for assessing employee engagement. In this instance 1 equals "actively disengaged" and 7 equals "actively engaged," where $1 = 0$ and $7 = 100$, which each score thereafter valued at 16.6. This scale enables the Infotool researchers to use zoom diagnostics and examine each workgroup through lenses of scores and standard deviations.

However, the most famous employee engagement survey is probably the one devised and deployed by the Gallup Organization, which has evolved over more than 30 years and has involved more that 12 million employees. Gallup's survey consists of just 12 questions, although they also suggest adding several that speak to your own organization's unique challenges and circumstances.

In developing the questionnaire, Gallup was not focused on finding out what makes people happy at work, but rather on what most accurately predicts high performance. Gallup was interested in uncovering the behavior or characteristics that will make a quantifiable difference to performance in the workplace. As one example, the Gallup survey does not ask the employee "Are you happy with your work?", rather it asks "At work, do your opinions seem to count?" Gallup's research finds that the latter is significantly predictive of high performance, while the former is not.[6]

Gallup's questions, which are answered through straight yes/no answers are:

- Do you know what is expected of you at work?
- Do you have the materials and equipment you need to do your work right?

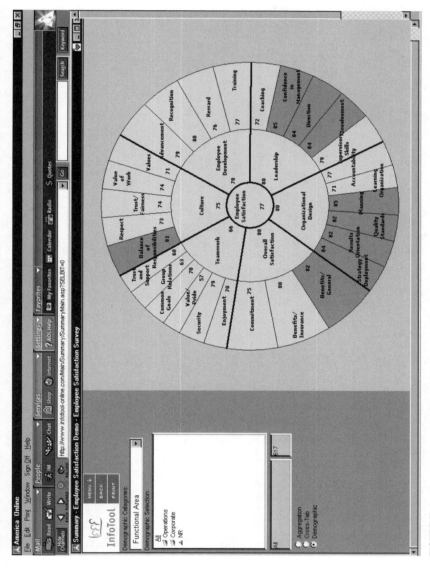

FIGURE 5.1 Screenshot of Infotool Diagnostic Tool

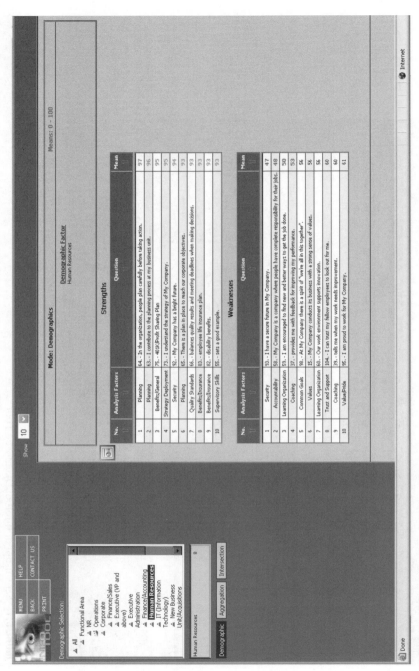

FIGURE 5.2 Screenshot of Infotool Diagnostic Tool

- At work, do you have the opportunity to do what you do best every day?
- In the past seven days, have you received recognition or praise for doing good work?
- Does your supervisor, or someone at work, seem to care about you as a person?
- Is there someone at work who encourages your development?
- At work, do your opinions seem to count?
- Does the mission or purpose of your company make you feel your job is important?
- Are your associates (fellow employees) committed to doing quality work?
- Do you have a best friend at work?
- In the past six months, has someone at work talked to you about your progress?
- In the past year, have you had opportunities at work to learn and grow?

Standard Chartered Bank is one financial institution that runs the Gallup engagement survey each year. By acting on the findings from the survey, Standard Chartered Bank was able to move the ratio of engaged to disengaged employees from 2.8:1 in 2003 to 4.7:1 in 2006. This is a good ratio considering the Gallup employee engagement survey of 2007 found that fully 73 percent of employees are disengaged from the organizations for which they work: this means that they either just turn up at work and go through the motions or, worse, do all they can to do as little as they can. Other research confirms this high level of disengagement.

There are of course many other statements that might appear in an employee engagement questionnaire, such as:

- I believe that I am treated by manager in a manner that is consistent with the organization's values.
- My immediate supervisor keeps me informed of all the things that I need to know to feel part of this organization.
- My immediate supervisor gives me sufficient feedback on how well I am doing my job.
- I believe that the members of the senior management are concerned about the wellbeing of the employees.
- My manager or supervisor has a clear vision of where our workgroup is headed.
- I understand the direct link between what I do and the goals of my workgroup.
- I find my work challenging.
- I have truthful and open communication with my co-workers about job-related issues

COMMON DEFINITIONS

To be useful for aggregation, comparison, and best-practice sharing, measures should be commonly defined and calculated organizationwide. Typically, this is an early and difficult challenge because it is not unusual to find that performance is measured in many different ways across the enterprise. As a nonfinancial services example, a large trucking company might have myriad definitions of what it means by "on-time" delivery. Consequently, performance in one part of the organization cannot be accurately compared with that in another. One unit might claim 95 percent on-time delivery according to its definition and another unit 85 percent based on its own definition. But from the customer's perspective the latter may be more "on time" than the former. Metrics must be commonly agreed, with standard templates documented and circulated.

Ownership

Moreover, as with strategic objectives, ownership and accountability should be assigned to metrics. Objective measure ownership is crucial for the operationalizing of the strategy.

Actionable

But importantly metrics should be actionable. Measures that are nice to know but do not trigger step-change performance improvement typically have no place on a Balanced Scorecard. For instance, if an organization has an objective to retain talent, has clearly defined what constitutes talent, has an agreed common enterprisewide metric, and the measure shows that strategically critical employees are walking out the door, then this should trigger an intervention. Simply put, we have a strategic objective, the measure indicates we are failing to meet that goal, so we do something about it. This represents the most basic, and oldest, premise of the Balanced Scorecard—turning strategy into action.

Performance Indicator Design Template

The Advanced Performance Institute has put together the following 20-point Performance Indicator Design Template, which has been used successfully by many of its clients.[7]

1. *Indicator name*—any KPI needs a name that should clearly explain what the indicator is about.

2. *Strategic element being assessed*—the Strategy Map has identified the different strategic elements, objectives, and priorities. Identify which of those the measure relates to.

3. *Ownership of strategic element*—identify the person or people or function or functions responsible for the management and delivery of the strategic element that is being assessed.

4. *KPQ*—identify the KPQ this indicator is helping to answer.

5. *Decisions supported*—list the decision or decisions this indicator is helping to support.

6. *Data collection method or measurement instrument*—identify and describe the method by which the data are being collected, such as surveys, questionnaires, interviews, focus groups, and collection of archival data.

7. *Source of the data*—identity where the data come from. Think about the access to data and answer questions such as: Are the data readily available? Is it feasible to collect the data?

8. *Formula/scale/assessment*—identify how the data will be captured. Is it possible to create a formula? Is it an aggregated indicator or index that is composed of other indicators?

9. *Date and frequency of data collection*—consider when and how often the data for the indicator should be collected. Some indicators are collected continuously, others hourly, daily, monthly, or even annually. It is important to think about what frequency provides sufficient data to answer the KPQs and helps to support the decisions outline in element 5 of this template.

10. *Who measures and reviews the data?*—identify the person, function, or external agency responsible for the data collection and data updates.

11. *Expiry or revision date*—indicators are sometimes introduced for a specific period only (e.g. for the duration of major projects or to keep an eye on restructuring efforts). Even if indicators don't seem time specific, it makes sense to give all indicators a revision date to ensure that an assessment takes place to see whether they are still needed.

12. *Targets and performance thresholds*—identify the desired level of performance in a specified timeframe and put expected performance levels into context. Targets should be (1) specific and time bound, (2) stretching and aspirational but achievable, and (3) based on good information. Targets can be set as absolute targets (increase by five units), proportional or percentage targets (increase by 5 percent), relative to benchmarks (within the top three hospitals in our area or top quartile), or relative to costs or budgets (increase or reduce by 5 percent same level of budget).

13. *Estimated costs*—consider the costs and efforts required to introduce and maintain a performance indicator. Costs can include the administrative or outsourcing costs for collecting the data, as well as the efforts

needed to analyze and report on the performance. It is important to ensure that the costs and efforts are justified.

14. *Confidence level*—consider the validity of the indicators. For financial performance, the confidence level would normally be high, since established tools are available to measure it. However, when we try to measure our intangibles, the assessment of the confidence level is subjective and forces anyone who designs an indicator to think about how well an indicator is actually "measuring" what it was that it set out to "measure."

15. *Possible dysfunctions*—note down any potential ways this indicator could encourage inappropriate behavior or cheating. Reflecting on possible dysfunctions caused by indicators allows people to consider better ways of collecting and assessing performance. In addition, it helps to raise the awareness of possible cheating behavior, which in turn enables everyone to monitor it much closer.

16. *Audience and access*—identify who will receive the information on this performance indicator, as well as possible access restrictions. Indicators can have different audiences. It might be a good idea to identify primary, secondary, and tertiary audiences. The primary audience will be the people directly involved in the management and decision making related to the strategic element that is being assessed. The secondary audience could be other parts of the organization that would benefit from seeing the data. A possible tertiary audience could be external stakeholders. Also, audience groups have different functions and requirements. For example, some data will be provided to analysts to analyze it further, while a management audience needs data to support its decision making.

17. *Reporting frequency*—identify how often this indicator is reported. If the indicator is to serve a decision-making purpose within the organization, then it needs to provide timely information. The reporting frequency can be different from the measurement frequency. An indicator might be collected hourly, but then reported as part of a quarterly performance meeting. However, it is important to cross-check the reporting and measurement frequency to ensure they are aligned and that data is available.

18. *Reporting channels*—identify the possible outlets or reports that are used to communicate the data. An indicator can for example, be included in the monthly performance report to directors, could be presented in the bimonthly performance review meeting, or included in the quarterly performance report to the board, in the weekly performance reports to heads of service, or could be reported on the organizational intranet or made available to external stakeholders through external reports or the website. It is again a good idea to cross-check

the identified reporting channels with the reporting and measurement frequency to ensure they are aligned and that data are available in time.

19. *Reporting formats*—identify how the data are best presented. The indicator designer should clarify whether the indicator is reported as, for example, a number, a narrative, a table, a graph or a chart. The best results are usually achieved if performance is reported in a mix of numerical, graphical, and narrative formats. More on reporting can be found in the API management white paper: *Best Practice Principles of Performance Reporting*, available on the API website.

20. *Notifications and workflows*—identify proactive notifications and possible workflows. Workflows are predefined and automated business processes in which documents, information, or tasks are passed from one person or group of persons to others. Notifications are predefined and automated messages and involve actively pushing performance data, messages, or alarm notifications to predefined individuals or groups. For example, email notifications or workflows could be automatically triggered if an indicator requires updating, or to tell a specific audience that new data are available or when an indicator has moves over or below a predefined threshold.

KEY RISK INDICATORS

A core focus of this book is that since the credit crunch there has been a heightened importance of capturing risk management as a theme within the Balanced Scorecard. We explained in previous chapters how strategy management and risk management can be more effectively integrated and the value of using a risk map to complement, and indeed inform, the Strategy Map. Out of these processes an organization will be able to identify its key risks (as Andrew Smart of the U.K.-based consultancy Manigent observed in chapter 3, key risks are "the vital few—the critical few that could have the most significant impact on the successful achievement of your strategic objectives."[8])

These vital few key risks can be monitored through key risk indicators (KRIs). By definition KRIs are leading measures, which alert the management team to a potential (and perhaps catastrophic) problem before it happens—or becomes unmanageable. For instance, a bank will likely have a metric that focuses on loan defaults. Simply measuring loan defaults does not, for example, indicate that the bank has enormous exposure to CDOs that will in the near future destroy shareholder wealth. The bank needs to introduce a measure that tracks loans that are delinquent by 30,

60, or 90 days. These metrics will enable the prediction of loans that will go bad in the future. However, as one commentator notes:

> *Of course, most banks do already track delinquencies. The problem is that many banks stop monitoring at this point. Banks that are more successful, however, ensure that they monitor a more complete set of metrics. For instance, if a bank chooses to purchase CDOs that are backed by sub-prime loans, it needs to manage metrics specifically for that segment—default rates of sub-prime loans.*
>
> *Generally speaking, the ability to monitor and manage metrics at the level of a segment, region, product, etc will lead to significantly more meaningful and more accurate performance management. The bank needs to ensure that its set of metrics is complete enough to truly capture its business.*[9]

The author made these useful suggestions on introducing a performance management process to ensure that metric management takes place. This process, he said, should consider several areas, such as:

- Who owns a particular metric?
- At what point does an issue get escalated?
- How often is the scorecard—and each individual metric—reviewed and discussed?
- What is the action a metric owner takes when a metric is tracking poorly?
- Which people analyze a poorly performing metric to ensure that the bank truly understands the underlying business issue?
- How are the metrics evaluated to ensure they are the right metrics to be measuring?
- How often is the scorecard—or other method for managing metrics—compared to the bank's strategy to ensure continued alignment?

He added that: "In the example of the sub-prime mortgage crisis, it is quite likely that a better performance management process could have prevented many of the issues. If the large financial institutions had monitored the risk associated with CDOs when they chose to invest heavily in them, they may have made some very different decisions. If banks had escalated sub-prime delinquency issues more quickly, the crisis may have been significantly lessened."

The paper also provided some sample bank metrics from five perspectives. Four of these strongly align with the traditional four perspectives of the Balanced Scorecard, plus risk management. The five perspectives are: financial performance metrics in banking; operational efficiency metrics in banking; customer-centric metrics in banking; risk management metrics in banking; and workforce metrics in banking.

Financial Performance Metrics in Banking

These include:

- market value or capitalization
- revenue growth
- revenue growth among key growth segments
- earnings per share
- interest revenue
- noninterest revenue
- efficiency ratio
- capital ratios
- net interest margin
- actual versus plan, by location, business line, and so on
- RAROC (risk-adjusted return on capital)
- assets under management
- new account openings
- organic revenue growth (same branch sales).

Operational Efficiency Metrics in Banking

Operational efficiency in banking encompasses all key processes—everything from sales effectiveness to mortgage-loan servicing, from marketing campaign response rates to teller staffing.

Sales and Marketing Effectiveness

- Total product sales
- Product sales per banker per day
- New core DDA accounts opened per day
- Core DDA account and balance retention
- Average cost to acquire a customer
- Response rates per marketing campaign (or marketing campaign ROI)

Customer Service Effectiveness

- Customer satisfaction and delight scores (by survey)
- Customer tenure

- Customer service center: average wait times
- Customer service center: one-time issue resolution
- Complaints

Internal Service Effectiveness (largely IT)

- Service-level agreement achievement percentage
- System Uptime
- Number of employees, assets supported per IT full-time equivalent (FTE; also applicable for audit FTE and so on)

Channel Effectiveness

- Revenue per banking center, Deposits per branch, ATM, and so on
- Transactions per teller, ATM, customer service center, and so on
- Online transactions per month
- Number of bill pay customers

Business Line Effectiveness

- Loan originations per month per FTE (and loans serviced)
- Average loan-processing time (also applicable for item processing)
- Assets under management per FTE (or loans per FTE, or brokerage transactions per FTE—depends on line of business)
- Business line overhead and growth rates

Customer Centricity Metrics in Banking

- Customer profitability
- Revenue per customer
- Cost to serve each customer (ideally based on true costing, not allocations)
- Customer lifetime value
- Customer lifecycle analyses
- Customer risk loss scores
- Behavior propensity scores
- Segment-level profitability (for instance, affluent segment profitability)
- Return on customer management initiatives
- Customer satisfaction
- Customer delight or satisfaction (as measured by surveys)
- Number of customer complaints
- Customer referrals
- Products per customer (also called wallet share)
- Customer service metrics, such as average wait time and per call

- Issue resolution
- Customer loyalty
- Customer tenure
- Retention of core deposits
- Customer acquisition
- New core DDA accounts (often by location or channel)
- New accounts (often by location or channel)
- Cost of acquisition per new DDA account
- Cost of acquisition per new customer

Risk Management Metrics in Banking

Risk management metrics in banking—KRIs—were classified into three categories by the Basel II Committee: credit, market, and operational. In addition, many banks further classify other risks into categories such as strategic risk, compliance risk, liquidity risk, interest rate risk, and reputation risk.

Capital Adequacy and Performance

- RAROC
- Total equity capital
- Total risk-based capital
- Tier 1 leverage capital
- Tier 2 leverage capital

Credit Risk

- Value at Risk
- Nonperforming loans
- Loan loss rates
- Loan past due
- Probability of default (PD)
- Loss given default (LGD)
- Exposure at default (EAD)
- Liquidity and interest rate risk
- Net interest income at risk
- Equity at risk
- Repricing gap
- Available funds as a percent of total assets

Operational Risk

- Expected loss
- Forgery

- Fraud
- Check kiting
- ACH
- ATM
- Bookkeeping
- System downtime
- Money laundering

Workforce Metrics in Banking

Employee Demographics

- Average length of service
- Gender staffing rates
- Diversity staffing rates (by location, if needed)
- Age staffing rates
- Employee experience
- Licensing counts

Team Member Engagement

- Percentage of employees who say they "like work" (by survey)
- Employee turnover rates
- Voluntary termination rate
- Absenteeism

Headcount and Compensation Counts

- Target and actual headcount
- Target and actual compensation
- Counts by region or location
- Recruitment performance and succession management
- Managerial bench strength
- Percentage of executive positions with succession plans
- Promotions
- Open positions
- Net hire rate
- Average compensation rates, per level
- Average applicants per vacancy recruitment source ratio
- Average dollars spent on employee training

As we explained in the previous chapter, when collocated according to Balanced Scorecard framework, the risk metrics here would more probably be captured through objectives that appear within a risk management theme within a Strategy Map. And we should stress that simply identifying a set of KRIs or KPIs for that matter is not sufficient for the successful management of the organization or of its risk component. As we state on several occasions, and as cited by other experts that we have quoted, it is critical to first start with the strategy and then create the strategic objectives, before moving on the metrics. Only then can the organization feel comfortable that is managing the right things, rather than trying to measure everything.

A RISK SCORECARD

It is worrisome that just 37 percent of nearly one hundred senior executives of large U.S.-headquartered multinational organizations surveyed by PricewaterhouseCoopers in 2008 said their organization linked risk indicators with corporate performance indicators.[10] Strategic management and risk management are therefore not being integrated.

Within an article that appeared in the November/December 2009 edition of the *Balanced Scorecard Report*, Professor Kaplan introduced his concept of a "risk scorecard" that would complement the strategy scorecard and that therefore would go a long way to achieving the required integration.[11]

Professor Kaplan noted that, at this time, the development of a risk scorecard is more conjecture and concept than actual fact. So although a working example was not provided, he did consider some general principles for a risk scorecard and its associated initiatives.

In building the Balanced Scorecard for the Strategy Map, an organization would of course formulate metrics for every Strategy Map objective, followed by targets for each metric and, finally, strategic initiatives designed to close the gap between targeted and current performance.

> *Working from the same Strategy Map, we could build a risk scorecard by first identifying for each strategic objective the primary risk events that would prevent the objective from being achieved.*
>
> *For each risk event, we would select metrics that would be early warning or leading indicators of when the risk event might be occurring. Take, for example, the common learning and growth objective "Achieve strategic job readiness," in which all employees in strategic job families have the skills, experience, and knowledge to perform their processes at a high level of*

excellence. This objective would typically have a BSC [Balanced Scorecard] metric "percentage of employees in strategic job families rated as 'very good' or 'excellent' for relevant skills, experience, and knowledge"; a target of 90% or higher; and strategic initiatives involving in-class and on-the-job training, a pay-for-knowledge incentive plan, and planned job rotations.

Kaplan stated that the risk events that could threaten this strategic objective include high turnover or retirements of experienced employees in strategic job families, ineffective training programs, or lack of mobility. Risk metrics would thus reflect each of these potential problems—current turnover rates, number of actual or expected retirements, evaluations of training program relevance and effectiveness, and gaps between the demand and supply of fully qualified employees (such as when some locations have an excess supply of employees, while others, perhaps in different countries or continents, have serious shortages).

For an innovation objective at a pharmaceutical company, the risks could be failed or delayed clinical trials. Supply chain risks could be disruptions in a supplier's plant or bottlenecks at a distribution center. Following this approach, each strategic objective on the strategy map would have one or more risk metrics that would provide an early warning signal about when performance along that strategic objective is in jeopardy.

A rising trend in a risk metric, or even a single observation above a pre-set control limit, would generate a management alert requiring immediate attention.

SELECTING TARGETS

Once measures are agreed, the next step is to identify metric targets. Of course all organizations set targets. However, these are still predominantly financial, with most fixed for an annual, budgeted timeframe. Within the Balanced Scorecard, equal attention must be paid to both financial and non-financial targets, and goals must be synchronized to a longer term, or strategic horizon.

Too often, targets (financial or not) tend to be an outcome of negotiations between, for example, the corporate center and business unit managers. As a result, targets become more about reaching a compromise than beating the competition. Moreover, targets are normally based on an inside-out view of the marketplace (the performance we want to achieve in our chosen markets), rather than an outside-in perspective (what can really be achieved in those markets, and perhaps more importantly what *is* being achieved).

All measures on a Balanced Scorecard should have a corresponding target, just as all objectives require supporting metrics. The target represents a tangible, and quantifiable, vision of desired performance. But targets must not be simply "plucked out of the air," but must be based on a thorough analysis of both required performance and internal capabilities.

As much as anything a Balanced Scorecard implementation is a major change program. The scorecard is about strategy, and strategy is just another word for change. Consequently, targets on the Balanced Scorecard should represent quantum step-changes in performance. A change effort is not about incrementalism, so the same law applies for the scorecard effort. Quantum performance advances require commensurately stretching performance targets. Use of risk frameworks (such as described by Andrew Smart in chapter 3) that enable the alignment of risk appetite with exposure can be powerful for ensuring that appropriate targets appear on the Balanced Scorecard.

Case Example: Bank Indonesia

Consider how target selection fits in with the overall Balanced Scorecard development program at Bank Indonesia.

To begin, it selected metrics based on appropriateness in depicting the strategic objectives and how they might correlate to other measures. Preferably, it could monitor the data quarterly to give early warning on issues that needed to be resolved. It used both quantitative and qualitative measures throughout the four perspectives to create a balance.

It proposed targets based on historical performance, practical experiences, and benchmarking other institutions. To ensure that the target is achievable but stretching, it had not to be lower than the average achievement in the past three periods.

It generated and prioritized initiatives for each measure based on impact and alignment to strategic objectives and themes (see the next chapter for more on strategic initiatives).

The organization formulated the Balanced Scorecard using the following steps:

1. Select measures that most accurately reflect the strategic objectives.
2. Determine the target for each measure based on past performances and desired goals.

3. Prioritize the initiatives needed to achieve the measures.
4. Identify the unit that is accountable to achieve the measures and execute the initiatives.

Dyah Nastiti Kusumowardani says that an ongoing challenge that the bank faces is that work units often try to get measures and targets that are easy to achieve. "But these won't help us achieve our strategic objectives," she says.

Case Example: Investment Bank

The step-by-step process shown in table 5.2 for selecting metrics and targets comes from the investment banking division of a global bank. It drew metrics and targets from the strategic imperatives of the organization (see table 5.3). Although not in support of objectives, the process still provides a useful guide for metric and target selection—simply swap imperatives for objectives.

TABLE 5.2 Process for selecting metrics and targets

To be undertaken	Critical elements
Step 1: Definition of imperatives Examine all sources relating to imperatives: operating plans, presentation by area heads, current reporting priorities. Develop an in-depth understanding of mandatory imperatives. Develop questions for senior managers. Develop key themes around which to summarize interview. Develop a shared understanding of these issues with other team members. Run interviews. Write up interviews linking output to key themes. Circulate for validation. Consolidate all inputs. Extract imperatives. Validate and get signoff for imperatives.	Senior manager of each area must truly engage in the definition of those imperatives as a strategic thinking process. The identification and clarification of strategic imperatives have to be seen as a critical step in their own right, not "jumping into measures." It is essential to focus on the critical few, not the many. The process, timing, and contributors to validation should be clarified and agreed with business area heads in the project planning stage.

To be undertaken	Critical elements
Step 2: Identification of measure areas and measures	
Identify possible measure areas for each imperative.	The decision on whose buyin is needed to agree measures for the business areas, needs to be carefully considered.
Define, refine, and sign off measure areas with senior management.	
Identify possible measures.	It is critical to consider what would we want to know about the imperative, for example measure areas, before coming up with a list of measures.
Reduce measures and get final signoff.	
Identify which quadrant each belongs to and highlight any imbalances.	
Draw up a list of measure definitions to support agreed measures.	The need for old measures to be included should be carefully tested before being accepted.
Note: At this stage you have the opportunity to specify certain measures to be mandated at the next level down. However, it is recommended that no more than 75% of measures are mandated.	Measures must finally be limited to the critical few.
	Ensure that there is a balance between leading and lagging indicators of performance.
Step 3: Setting targets	
Identify who needs to be involved in setting and agreeing targets.	It is important to deal with the sensitivities of setting targets—it may need different people to be involved.
Where no information exists in the current position in relation to a measure, develop "quick and dirty" solutions to allow forward targets to be set (these may be reviewed and refined after six months).	Before beginning the detail, agreement should be reached on whether targets are to be stretching or achievable.
Discuss and agree targets.	The combined contribution of the target must add up to the total target at the higher level.
Get final signoff.	

COMPARATIVE PERFORMANCE GOALS

In setting targets organizations should, wherever possible, identify comparative performance goals. Organizations typically set targets based on what they think they can do. Yet, increasingly, leading companies are less concerned with what they themselves believe they can achieve, but what is actually being accomplished by competitors. For instance, for Company A moving from 75 percent to 85 percent customer satisfaction in nine months might be perceived as a stretch and its achievement a success, but if there are competitors that are already at 85 percent and are aiming for

TABLE 5.3 Example business area alignment with example divisional imperatives

Example divisional imperatives	Example of business area measure	Quadrant
Improve account management to key clients.	Percentage of target clients ranking division or product in top five	Process
	Value of business from key clients	Client
Develop and increase international business.	International business as a percentage of overall business	Financial
	Value of international business	Financial
	Number of international products produced each year	Process
Recruit, retain, and develop high-quality staff.	Percentage of key staff retained and recruited	People
	Percentage of staff meeting or exceeding agreed objectives	People
Ensure that wealth management products are delivered to meet demand from clients.	Income earned from wealth management products and services	Financial
Increase research capability.	Percentage of research teams achieving target output	Process
Develop technology to support the needs of the business.	IT service and development ranking	Process
Achieve positive recognition from clients.	Percentage of derivative-related process problems that have been resolved satisfactorily	Process
	Percentage of target clients ranking division or product in top five	Client

90 percent-plus, then performance for Company A can legitimately still be described as below required standards—despite the "stretch."

Consequently, the management team of Company A must raise the performance bar so that it can beat the competition, rather than meet an internally derived target. This, of course, is easier said than done; organizations often set targets while ignoring what they are actually capable of achieving in light of the present capacity of the organization and the capability of its processes. So if senior management sets a target to be better than the competition by Y percent, but doesn't analyze whether the organization is configured to achieve Y percent, then it's a short-sighted approach that will demotivate the lower-level managers that are being asked to hit targets that they know to be unrealistic. The major steps in selecting strategic measures and targets is shown in table 5.4.

TABLE 5.4 Outlines the major steps in selecting strategic measures and targets

Tasks	Issues
Define measures to track strategic objectives in the scorecard.	As with strategic objectives, the number of measures should be kept to an essential minimum.
Be prepared to be innovative in defining strategic measures.	Most of the nonfinancial measures that are needed for a strategic scorecard are unlikely to be readily available.
Set targets for measures.	Targets convert measures into tools for improving performance.
Ensure that each measure passes the tests of being valid, meaningful, actionable and deliverable.	Measures will need to conform to a number of criteria if they are to be implemented and accepted, particularly in the case of nonfinancial measures.
Measure leading aspects of performance.	Some measures, such as customer and employee satisfaction are unreliable indicators of future behavior, and need further refinement.
Consider the political implication of measures.	Since managers and individuals will be assessed against measures of performance, new measurement frameworks have repercussions for accountability.
Take data accessibility into account in selecting measures.	Be prepared to trade off cost against value since in some cases, the cost of sourcing and collecting the data to populate a measure may exceed their value.
Identify measures that can be subject to benchmarking and relative performance assessment.	Where relevant, measures that compare the organization relative to the competition can help to target strategic performance improvement opportunities.

CONCLUSION

This chapter has highlighted the critical importance of measures, but has stressed that metrics play a supporting role to strategic objectives. That said, we also argued that organizations must make sure that each objective has supporting metrics and that they should take the time to understand how metrics work and to ensure common enterprisewide metrics ownership.

As measures must support objectives, targets must support measures. But targets should be timebound and stretching. With measures and targets selected, the next step is to choose strategic initiatives—which are where the real work of the scorecard gets done. We consider strategic initiatives in the next chapter.

Self-Assessment Checklist

As previously, simply indicate your agreement with the two opposing statements in the checklist in table 5.5. Checking number 1 indicates a strong agreement with the statement to the left, while checking number 7 indicates a strong agreement with the statement to the right. The more numbers to the right are checked, the greater the perceived challenges.

TABLE 5.5 Self-assessment checklist

	1	2	3	4	5	6	7	
It is recognized that the Balanced Scorecard is not a measurement system		✓						The Balanced Scorecard is seen as a measurement system
We have an excellent understanding of the science of measurement		✓						We have a very poor understanding of the science of measurement
Enterprise-wide we have standard definitions of common metrics		✓						Enterprise-wide we have many different definitions of common metrics
In this organization targets are focused on beating the competition		✓						In this organization targets are based on beating internally negotiated targets
Targets are about quantum step-change improvement				✓				Targets are about incremental improvements
We fully understand the difference between a target and a forecast		✓						A target and forecast are essentially perceived as the same thing
We fully understand our capabilities to reach targets		✓						We do not know whether we have the capabilities to reach targets

ENDNOTES

1. Bernard Marr, *Managing Strategic Performance in Banks and Financial Services Firms: from Going Through the Motions to Best Practice,* (Cranfield, U.K.: Cranfield School of Management, 2007).
2. See www.ap-institute.com.
3. Eric Schmidt, CEO, Google Inc. in an interview with Jeremy Caplan for *Time,* October 2, 2006.
4. Bernard Marr, *What is a Key Performance Question?* (Milton Keynes: Advanced Performance Institute, 2008). Available as a free download from www.ap-institute.com.
5. Naresh Makhijani and James Creelman, *Creating Engaged Employees: The Role of Engagement Surveys* (OTI Executive Research Program, OTI Indonesia, 2010. See: www.otiinternational.com).
6. See www.gallup.com/consulting/121535/Employee-Engagement-Overview-Brochure.
7. Bernard Marr, *How to Design Key Performance Indicators* (Advanced Performance Institute, Milton Keynes: Advanced Performance Institute, 2010). Available from www.ap-institute.com.
8. Andrew Smart, *Aligning Risk Management and Exposure: The New Paradigm of Strategic Execution* (London: Manigent, 2009).
9. A paper by Leo Tucker, posted on www.skysolutions.com.
10. Cited in Andrew Smart, op. cit.
11. Harvard Business School Publishing, *Balanced Scorecard Report*, November/December 2009.

CHAPTER 6

Selecting Initiatives

EXECUTIVE SUMMARY

1. Apart from the identification of strategic objectives, the selection of strategic initiatives is the most important component of the Balanced Scorecard framework.
2. Initiatives are where the real work of strategy implementation takes place.
3. It is not unusual that less attention is given to this component of the system than to the other three.
4. Choosing strategic initiatives is often more problematic than the other three scorecard dimensions because once an initiative is chosen it then typically requires funding both financially and in terms of human resources allocation.
5. No initiative should be launched or funded unless the link to strategic objectives is unequivocally proven.
6. Initiatives should be funded through stratex (strategic expenditure), which is a new term in addition to the commonly used capex (capital expenditure) and opex (operating expenditure).
7. The process of initiative selection typically leads to the jettisoning of well-established, and often expensive, projects.
8. Canceling high-profile projects may lead to resistance from the senior executive that sponsors the projects. The CEO must overcome such resistance.

INTRODUCTION

Apart from the identification of strategic objectives, the selection of strategic initiatives is the most important component of the Balanced Scorecard framework. Initiatives are much more important than metrics, which are simply a mechanism for monitoring progress toward strategic goals. Indeed, Kaplan and Norton now speak of strategy maps, balanced scorecards, and action programs (initiatives and budgets) as three separate components.

Viewed sequentially, the Strategy Map describes the logic of the strategy, delineating the critical themes and objectives that create value. The Balanced Scorecard identifies measures and targets for each objective in the Strategy Map. However, objectives and targets are not achieved simply because they have been articulated. For each objective and target on the map or scorecard, managers must identify the strategic initiatives required to deliver the performance outcomes. Indeed, initiatives are "where the rubber hits the road," as Americans would say. Put another way, it is where the real work of strategy implementation takes place.

ORGANIZATIONAL AWARENESS OF THE IMPORTANCE OF INITIATIVES

Some companies that have recognized the full importance of the strategic initiatives now show the initiatives alongside the objectives on the Strategy Map. One Balanced Scorecard practitioner notes that: "Initiatives are the action programs where resources are allocated to drive quantum performance improvements. Therefore to gain a truly accurate crucial overview of how we are progressing strategically we need to capture initiative progress within the red, yellow, and green traffic light system we use on our Strategy Maps."

THE CHALLENGES OF SELECTING INITIATIVES

Despite the absolute importance of identifying strategic initiatives for succeeding with a Balanced Scorecard implementation, it is not unusual that less attention is given to this component of the system than to the other three. This is often because initiative selection is conventionally the last part of the scorecarding process. Because so much energy may have already been expended on objective, metric, and target setting, not enough effort is channeled into the complex challenge of the initiative selection.

Furthermore, choosing strategic initiatives is often more problematic than the other three scorecard dimensions because once an initiative is chosen, it then will typically require—both financially and in terms of human resource allocation. What's more, there are hidden cultural obstacles to overcome. Initiative selection has huge political ramifications as functional and unit leaders seek the funding for their pet projects. De-emphasizing the initiative selection component of the scorecard is often simply the result of a decision to sidestep such battles, preferring initiative resourcing to be left to the more well-established annual budgeting process. Indeed, one of the authors of this book spoke at a conference where another speaker said that in creating the Balanced Scorecard, they had identified a very expensive project that was no longer strategically relevant. However, the organization decided to continue with this project because it was a "pet project" of a senior manager. As much as anything, this points to the importance of the CEO in leading the scorecard from the front. In this organization, the CEO's support could be described as lukewarm at best—therefore the Balanced Scorecard team could not cancel this expensive, but strategically irrelevant, project.

LINKAGE TO THE STRATEGY MAP

However, when done properly, in choosing strategic initiatives the overriding criteria is that they must directly link through the Balanced Scorecard to objectives on the Strategy Map. No initiative should be launched or funded unless this link is unequivocally proven. This is because the purpose of an initiative is to close an identified gap between actual and required levels of performance to achieve a strategic objective. If an initiative is deemed critical for the success of the organization and does not correspond to an objective, then it signals a failing of the Strategy Map. In such cases, the senior team must revisit and reformulate the Strategy Map.

STRATEX

Such is the importance now assigned to strategic initiatives that many organizations are now shaping a financial resource pot known as stratex (strategic expenditure) in addition to the common opex (operating expenditure) and capex (capital expenditure). Experience has shown that if strategic initiatives have to be funded from business or support unit budgets, they will be jeopardized when the unit is faced with a requirement to cut costs in the short term.

Ideally, therefore, the executive team should designate a pool of funds to support the initiative portfolios for all strategic themes—stratex. This is designed to increase the intangible assets that provide organizational capabilities, such as training and customer databases. A formal process to determine the level of stratex enables companies to subject strategic initiatives to rigorous, disciplined reviews just like those conducted for capex spending on tangible assets.

According to Kaplan and Norton this discretionary spending can be guided by a rule of thumb—for example 5 percent of sales. Executives use similar rules of thumb to establish funding levels for categories such as general and administrative expenses and research and development expenditures. If spending falls short of the stratex target, then the organization might be underfunding its future growth. If spending exceeds this number, there might be a question about the adequacy of the controls.

Kaplan and Norton also recommend that stratex should be a separate authorized line item on the company's internal budget or financial forecast.

INITIATIVE PRIORITIZATION

Crucially, the process of initiative selection typically leads to the jettisoning of well-established, and often expensive, projects. It is not unusual that anywhere between 40 percent and 80 percent of existing projects will be canceled as a consequence of a properly architected Balanced Scorecard framework.

Canceling high-profile projects may lead to resistance from the senior executive that sponsors the project, as cited previously. Describing through the scorecard why the initiative is no longer strategically relevant may help overcome this resistance. If not, then it is the responsibility of the CEO to order project cancellation—the political complexities in giving such an order clearly demonstrates why the CEO must not just pay lip service to the scorecard, but demonstrate support with clear action.

Moreover, there is a further bunch of initiatives where several departments are tackling the same issue and are unaware of each other's efforts. The transparency of performance and activities resulting from the scorecard creation enables managers to bring these teams together, so reducing the number of initiatives and cost burden.

Case Example: Wells Fargo Online Banking

As one example, when the U.S.-headquartered Wells Fargo Online Banking launched its scorecard in the late 1990s, its initiative identification process began with an itinerary of the projects already under way. It discovered 600 initiatives organizationwide. Through the scorecarding effort these were reduced to 100, which enabled greater strategic focus and significantly reduced costs.

At Wells Fargo, a comprehensive initiative scoring process was put in place that included percentage weightings (and scores) of the initiative according to strategic importance, business case (including cost and net present value), and implementation (complexity and time).

Canadian Case Example

As a further example, a large Canadian organization created an initiative "funneling" process. This began by setting criteria for a qualifying strategic initiative—as a result it immediately abandoned nonstrategic initiatives.

Next, all qualified initiatives were mapped against strategic objectives and ranked according to priority. Higher-ranking initiatives, but with a need for a stronger business case, were deferred while the highest-ranking initiatives were prioritized and rationalized. Those with the lowest priority have no chance of securing scarce human and financial resources. This ensured that strategically aligned initiatives had the first call on resources.

U.S. Case Example

As a further example, consider this U.S. organization. When building its scorecard, it put in place a three-tiered hierarchical system for initiative prioritization and therefore for resource allocation to initiatives. The three tiers are shown in table 6.1

Within this organization, initiative identification begins with brainstorming in each of its divisions, after which the executive coordinating team, comprising divisional heads, selects initiative candidates. Team members individually sort these candidates into the three-tier order, with the final priorities being agreed to by consensus within the group.

As a result, the organization has created a common understanding of resource priorities amongst the senior team. If budgets need to be scaled back during the year for any reason, it is clear which initiatives will be affected first.

TABLE 6.1 Tiered approach to initiative rationalization

Tier 1: Essential—initiatives with the organization's highest level of commitment, which are certain of funding.
Tier 2: Important—those that are very important, but must be considered against others if funds are limited.
Tier 3: Beneficial—initiatives that are only pursued if they do not infringe upon higher level priorities.

Initiative Selection Templates

As a high-level guide to strategic initiative selection, consider the three elements of prioritization, resource allocation, and accountability. Completing this simple exercise will likely deliver both efficiency and effectiveness dividends.

Prioritization   For each strategic objective, simply order the initiatives (new and existing) in order of perceived importance. This is a relatively straightforward exercise, but one that can deliver immediate benefits as it:

- shows just how many initiatives are under way enterprisewide (the sheer number and aggregate cost might surprise many of the senior leaders)
- enables a first discussion as to "why" these projects are being dispatched (the benefits) and therefore allow senior managers to comment on how they see the programs linking (or not) to strategic goals.

Crucially, therefore, at the corporate level, the initiative prioritization process should involve the senior team and be a key part of the scorecard creation process. Note that just as at the corporate level, the senior team must be responsible for selecting objectives, measures, and targets, they must also do the same for initiatives: especially important because it is only at the initiative level that money is spent. And this takes us to step two.

Resource Allocation   Step two starts with creating a cost breakdown for each of the strategic objectives. As part of this, it is important to map the required resources to the intended initiatives: this ensures that the resources are allocated in the right way. Organizations can use a heat map to get further guidance on resource allocation. A heat map is a powerful tool for the identification of improvement opportunities (as an example of a heat map see figure 6.1). A heat map is a color coded system that highlights current performance levels. Typical colors might be:

- blue: better than expected
- green: everything good
- yellow: some issues
- amber: bigger issues
- red: not good at all.

For initiative selection, the red areas might point to areas where the significant improvement of performance might require the implementation of a strategic initiative. Simply mapping ballpark budgets and human-days to the initiatives will bring out potential imbalances.

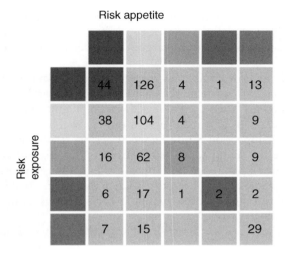

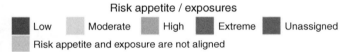

Low   Moderate   High   Extreme   Unassigned

Risk appetite and exposure are not aligned

FIGURE 6.1   Heat Map

As a nonfinancial services example, consider the initiative selection process within the Ministry of Works, Bahrain (another Palladium Hall of Fame inductee. As explained in the book, *More with Less: Maximizing Value in the Public Sector*, which was co-written by one of the authors of this book,[1] it began with generating an inventory of all programs—present and new. These were then mapped against the strategic objectives they would support, to determine their strength of alignment. The initiatives were then scored against importance and difficulty dimensions. Criteria included resource impact, predicted risk, and project benefits. A first filter assessed initiatives on their importance and a second assessed them on their balance between their benefits and their difficulty (costs, risks, and complexity). The final list of initiatives was then prioritized using an automated score as a base for a final judgment-based prioritization. Those selected initiatives appear on the relevant scorecard and are tracked and reported on accordingly.

Project Responsibility

With initiatives selected and funded, responsibilities for project delivery is assigned to appropriate managers (and for high-level initiatives, accountability will lie with a senior manager) with progress monitored against specified milestones. Crucially, as part of "reading" performance to the scorecard, the impact of initiatives to targets or objectives must be closely tracked.

We explain in chapter 11 how companies that get the best from their scorecards tend to use a quarterly strategic review to monitor performance of the strategy. These reviews are often used alongside rolling financial forecasts. The reviews and forecasts give a good overview of how well initiatives are working and their likely impact on future financial performance. These quarterly overviews enable the senior team to kill projects that are either not delivering expected value or that are no longer strategically relevant. Moreover, they enable the reallocation of resources when initiatives are delayed for any reason. This is a much more dynamic process than assessing projects and allocating funding yearly.

Selecting strategic initiatives is the function of workshop 3, which is shown in table 6.2.

TABLE 6.2 Selecting strategic initiatives

Strategic initiative task	Issues
Create a list of all organizational initiatives.	A simple exercise in identifying existing initiatives is a crucial first step in prioritization. Most organizations have far too many initiatives.
Establish criteria for aligning initiatives with scorecard objectives.	Use a weighting, or other explicit scoring system, for comparing the value of initiatives and establishing the business case.
Prioritize strategic initiatives in line with scorecard objectives.	A robust system is required to ensure that the most valuable initiatives are launched and funded first.
Abandon nonstrategic initiatives.	Deal with the political fallout from senior management commitment to abandoned initiatives.
Rationalize, where appropriate, overlapping initiatives within the organization.	Create unitary teams in which staff are working in parallel on the same projects.
Assign responsibility for initiative execution.	Managers must be made accountable for delivering strategic initiatives.
Monitor progress and impact.	Progress must be monitored and close attention be paid to ensure that the initiatives are affecting scorecard targets and objectives.

CONCLUSION

In this chapter we have highlighted the critical importance of strategic initiatives. Indeed, we would argue that in the hierarchy of importance regarding the components of the Balanced Scorecard system, initiatives rank second behind objectives. It is through strategic initiatives that the real work of strategy implementation through the Balanced Scorecard framework gets done. Such is the importance of strategic initiatives that the concept of stratex has evolved as way to protect initiative funding from short–term budget-focused constraints.

Thus far, we have completed the description of the Balanced Scorecard system of a Strategy Map and accompanying scorecard of metrics, targets and initiatives. The next step is implementation, which we begin to discuss in the next chapter.

Self-Assessment Checklist

As previously, simply indicate your agreement with the two opposing statements in table 6.3. Checking number 1 indicates a strong agreement with the statement to the left, while checking number 7 indicates a strong agreement with the statement to the right. The more numbers to the right are checked, the greater the perceived challenges.

TABLE 6.3 Self-assessment checklist

	1	2	3	4	5	6	7	
We fully understand the importance of strategic initiatives								We do not understand the importance of strategic initiatives
In this organization initiatives are chosen based on strategic importance								In this organization initiatives are chosen based on the needs of dominant leaders
We have an excellent process for initiative prioritization								We have a very poor process for initiative prioritization
The concept of stratex is or will be well received by senior management								The concept of stratex is not or will not be well received by senior management

ENDNOTE

1. Bernard Marr and James Creelman, *More with Less: Maximizing Value in the Public Sector* (Basingstoke, U.K.: Palgrave Macmillan, 2010).

CHAPTER 7

Cascading the Balanced Scorecard: The Structural Challenges

EXECUTIVE SUMMARY

1. A scorecard cascade—by which it is devolved from the enterprise level to lower levels of the organization—is intended to ensure that those working in business units and local teams can see how their everyday work is aligned to the strategic goals of the company.

2. Lower-level managers and staff should be involved in creating their local scorecard system.

3. However, lower-level involvement should not be at the expense of setting out clear parameters for objectives and measures that need to be reflected in any devolved strategy maps and accompanying balanced scorecards.

4. An ideal scorecard cascade process would see managers from one level actively involved in leading the creation of the supporting scorecard.

5. In practice, however, this rarely happens. In most cases the first scorecard is put in place at a lower level, which serves as proof of concept for an enterprise-level scorecarding effort. Indeed, such "pilots" should be encouraged.

6. It is our observation that the scorecard is often piloted within a function, such as finance, IT, or human resources.

7. The Bank of England provides a powerful example of building an IT Strategy Map that is a hybrid of the classic Kaplan and Norton map and the requirements of the IT governance framework COBIT.

8. But before all organizations rush to create functional scorecards, there are some who would caution against being overly hasty or enthusiastic. For instance, the benefits of doing so must be well understood.

9. Organizations must honestly assess whether they possess the capability to manage a lot of aligned scorecards.

INTRODUCTION

One of the principles of the strategy-focused organization is to "make strategy everyone's everyday job." It is where the Balanced Scorecard framework takes strategy out of the boardroom and onto the shopfloor or front line. Just as designing and building a scorecard presents a number of obstacles to be overcome, so implementation brings another set of challenges. The fact is that if you want to, (although we certainly would not recommend this) you can build an enterprise-level Strategy Map and Balanced Scorecard in one afternoon session. The more difficult challenge is cascading the scorecard, and securing buyin, deep inside the company.

The greatest implementation challenges are cultural, which we deal with in the next chapter. Here we consider the structural challenges of scorecard implementation.

STRATEGIC LINE-OF-SIGHT

A scorecard cascade, by which it is devolved from the enterprise level to lower levels of the organization, is intended to ensure that those working in business units and local teams can see how their everyday work is aligned to the strategic goals of the company. The aim is to create a strategic line-of-sight from the front line to the center of the organization.

In earlier chapters we described how to build the enterprise-level Strategy Map and Balanced Scorecard and the challenges of doing so. But once created, a similar process of managerial and staff involvement needs to be used in developing scorecards at deeper levels. Just as senior management buyin is best fostered through its active involvement in the Strategy Map and Balanced Scorecard debate and design, this principle applies equally in other cases.

People are naturally more willing to buy in to a change program when they have been involved in its design. This also helps them to understand why they are being asked to change their working practices and objectives. A failure to go through this process is cited by many organizations as a reason their first scorecard attempts failed.

Mahdi Syahbuddin, previously deputy president director at Indonesia's Bank Universal, stressed that although it is fundamentally important to involve senior management in designing the scorecard, it is equally essential for successful devolution to involve branch management, particularly for the identification of branch-level metrics.

"To find the right indicators, you have to involve branch managers because they are the people who really understand what makes their branches perform. If they're not involved, then any performance indicators forced on them stand a good chance of being resisted and inappropriate."

Workshops for branch managers were organized to identify the key indicators that would show branch performance and reveal how branches were working toward corporate strategic goals.[1]

MANDATED OBJECTIVES AND MEASURES

Although the involvement of lower-level managers and staff is a pre-requisite for scorecard success, this should not be at the expense of setting out clear parameters for objectives and measures that need to be reflected in any devolved strategy maps and accompanying balanced scorecards. After all, the point of devolved scorecards is strategic alignment, and the senior team sets the strategy.

Note the investment bank example in chapter 5, where as part of the scorecard design process, there was an identified time to specify certain measures to be mandated at the next level down. However, it was recommended that no more than 75 percent of measures are mandated.

AN IDEAL SCORECARD CASCADE

An ideal scorecard cascade process would see managers from one level actively involved in leading the creation of the supporting scorecard. For example, a global organization's executive committee might comprise divisional heads, each of whom will be involved in creating the corporate scorecard. The divisional head will then lead the scorecard creation process for their direct reports, the business unit leaders. These unit heads will then continue the devolution process by leading the scorecard creation for their direct reports, perhaps function heads, who then may then repeat the process with team leaders. Thus the organization creates a classic family of fully aligned cascaded scorecards (we consider personal scorecards, which might be the deepest level of cascade, in chapter 9).

Case Example: Bank CIMB Niaga

Consider Indonesia's Bank CIMB Niaga. It has created a sequence of scorecards at corporate, directorate, and group or area levels. The corporate scorecard has a mainly strategic focus; the directorate scorecard is strategic and operational within the context of corporate strategy. At the group or area level, scorecards comprise mainly operational targets set within a wider strategic context.

Case Example: Bank Indonesia

Bank Indonesia had devolved the Balanced Scorecard system from the corporate to the individual employee level—a classic cascade. The corporate level Balanced Scorecard is first cascaded to directorate level. "Developing directorate balanced scorecards begins with the identification of relevant corporate level objectives and measures," explains Dyah Nastiti Kusumowardani, Bank Indonesia's director of strategy planning. "The directorate must address these in addition to their own local objectives as defined in their organizational functions." The measures on the directorate scorecard are then assigned to the relevant units, and finally cascaded down to each member of the unit.

The cascade process (which the bank calls "vertical alignment") is facilitated by what is in essence Bank Indonesia's Office of Strategy Management (OSM; see chapter 2). The office assists the directorate's scorecard managers in developing the directorate scorecard. "In this way, we can ensure that the methodology is applied and understood the same way throughout all directorates while at the same time generating the necessary directorate knowledge and expertise from the managers who own the processes," says Dyah Nastiti Kusumowardani. "Local managers responsible for the scorecard are also trained in-house on the scorecard upon their appointment."

She continues that: "This vertical alignment process ensure that lower levels' strategy maps are synergistic with each other and work together toward the same overarching objectives."

Moreover, she says that the process facilitates lower-level work units to understand their role in achieving Bank Indonesia's corporate scorecard objectives and will increase motivation. This is in line with SFO principle four "Make Strategy Everyone's Job," (also see chapter 2).

The role of what is in essence the OSM in the scorecard cascade is noteworthy. Key roles of the OSM include using its expertise to facilitate the rollout of the Balanced Scorecard framework across the enterprise and ensuring that the strategy maps and supporting scorecards are fully aligned.

SCORECARD PILOTS

Although beginning the scorecard program and cascade at the corporate level is theoretically sensible, in practice, the first scorecard is normally put in place at a lower level, which serves as proof of concept for an enterprise-level scorecarding effort. Indeed, such "pilots" should be encouraged. Among the many benefits of a pilot is that it enables the in-house scorecard team (usually directed by an expert external facilitator) to gain practical experience of building and implementing a Balanced Scorecard framework and to get a feel for likely structural, process, or cultural challenges of using the system. It should also be stated that if significant mistakes are made during the pilot, it is always possible to conduct another pilot elsewhere in the organization. Make large mistakes when beginning with the enterprise-level scorecard and it is unlikely that a second chance will be given—at least for considerable time.

Functional Scorecards

It is our observation that the scorecard is often piloted within a function, such as finance, IT, or human resources (HR). Creating scorecards for support functions is an intrinsic component for aligning the enterprise through the Balanced Scorecard system. Indeed, organizations began to grapple with how best to fashion functional scorecards very early on in the scorecard history. By the end of the 1990s, these scorecards were commonplace.

Functions are ideal units for creating scorecard systems because there are typically clear boundaries around their roles and responsibilities. Therefore, it is relatively straightforward to determine the outputs and outcomes of the functions (such as around internal service requirements) and to articulate these as strategic objectives with accompanying measures, and so on.

Case Example: First Union

The U.S.-based First Union Corporation (now merged into Wachovia) built its first scorecard within the HR function in the late 1990s. A scorecard schematic is shown in figure 7.1.

At First Union, scorecard development commenced at the beginning of 2000. Two scorecard teams were formed. First, there was a "core team," comprising two senior HR leaders and two consultants. The core team would provide thought leadership and strategic guidance. Second, a 16-strong cross-functional team from various HR departments would work to ensure that the scorecard captured cross-HR requirements and to investigate the appropriate objectives and measures for each perspective.

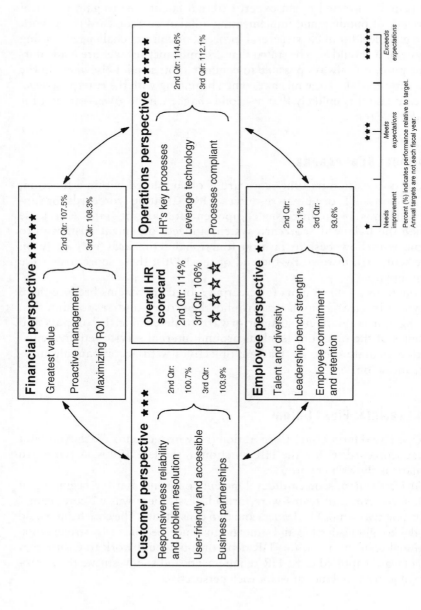

FIGURE 7.1 First Union HR Scorecard
Source: Hewitt Associates

Building the scorecard required the articulation of a process to ensure HR leadership buyin. This new process comprised five aspects:

- building the foundation
- identifying the key questions that the HR scorecard would attempt to answer
- identifying the measurers that would answer these key questions
- establishing targets to measure against
- ensuring data capture and approval.

For "building the foundation," a robust scorecard purpose was articulated. Through consultation with the members of the HR leadership team, the core team clearly delineated how the HR leadership team would use the HR scorecard. This would be for the purpose of:

- reviewing HR divisional performance
- identifying divisional best practices
- identifying potential action plans or interventions to influence performance
- communicating performance to HR leaders and HR employees
- reinforcing HR's strategic priorities by updating key performance indicators (KPIs) to align with the HR scorecard.

Therefore, the scorecard was positioned as a framework that the leadership team would use to manage the division actively, rather than just as a performance-reporting tool.

With input from the leadership team, the core scorecard team and the crossfunctional team, the next step saw the articulation of strategic questions that an HR scorecard would set out to answer through the information that would appear on the scorecard.

First Union identified 12 strategic questions: three for each scorecard perspective. These are outlined in table 7.1.

The next step was to identify the measures that would track First Union's progress against answering the 12 strategic questions. A senior HR leader comments:

We went through a detailed process of analyzing all the metrics we had in the business and choosing the critical few for each perspective. To do this we identified what we called measurement filters. These would help ensure that the measures chosen were really the key ones to drive the HR organization forward.

TABLE 7.1   First Union's 12 strategic questions

Operations
1. How efficient, effective, accurate, timely, and relevant are HR's key processes?
2. How effectively does HR use technology to improve our business processes and customer interactions?
3. Are HR's processes compliant with government and company regulations?

Financials
1. How is the HR division adding the greatest value at the smartest cost?
2. How is the HR division prescriptively managing HR-related financial risk?
3. How is HR maximizing ROI on special projects, initiatives, and so on?

Employees
1. How is HR developing the talent and diversity needed to be successful now and into the future?
2. How is HR developing the leadership bench strength needed to be successful now and into the future?
3. How is HR building a workplace that result in employee commitment and retention?

Customers
1. What is the overall quality of HR's customer responsiveness, reliability, and problem resolution?
2. How user friendly and accessible are HR's tools, products, and processes?
3. How satisfied are HR's clients with their business partnerships?

As shown in First Union's HR scorecard, these questions have become the high-level metrics on the scorecard.

As part of this measure identification process, the HR team actively involved business managers. The manager says:

> *We sent a measurement inventory out to each of our businesses and said that "These are some of the metrics that HR is considering assessing itself against. Do you think these measures focus on your needs and what else would you like to see HR measure itself on?" Their feedback showed that we were looking to measure the right things.*

To illustrate how a measure is aligned with the scorecard 12 questions and objectives, consider an example from the employee perspective.

The question to be answered is, "How is HR developing the talent and diversity needed to be successful now and into the future?"

To work toward showing how HR is answering this question, three objectives have been set, including "develop skills and competencies." This is then supported by a measure of "training use," which in turn is fed by raw data including "training hours per HR employee" and "the percentage of HR employees receiving training."

The senior HR leader emphasizes that setting targets also ensures that HR creates a plan focused on delivering to the critical few KPIs. He also says that they force accountability and therefore influence behavior.

Within First Union's HR scorecard, targets are based on historical data (i.e. what they know has happened) and external best-practice benchmarks.

Case Example: Scotiabank

In the report *Next Generation HR Shared Services, How to Take Customer Service, Efficiency and Savings to a New Level*, which was written by one of the authors of this book,[2] the Canadian banking giant Scotiabank (which as explained elsewhere had been a long-time user of the Balanced Scorecard) provided an example of successfully using the scorecard to the HR Shared Services level, which measures performance against financial, operational, customer, and people targets.

As an example of a finance metric consider cost avoidance. By the end of Q3 2007, C\$8 million in costs had been avoided that year. Fully C\$54 million was avoided in the first three years of shared services implementation.

An operational metric looks at capacity creation. "Part of the value of a shared services organization is around creating capacity to take on further work by, for example, eliminating work that we don't need to do any more," said Kathy Hall, Vice-President, HR.

From the customer perspective there is a Scotiabank satisfaction survey that is distributed twice a year to shared services users and looks at performance dimension such as respect, timeliness, and quality. In the most recent survey, the HR shared services organization achieved an overall score of 4.5 out of 5. There is also a metric of adherence to service level agreements, which is typically set between 95 percent and 97 percent.

For people there is a survey that called ViewPoint that looks at employee engagement against 20 questions, such as willingness to recommend products outside of office time. According to 2007 survey, the aggregate shared services score was 87 percent, with the HR center achieving 91 percent. For more on employee engagement surveys, see chapter 5.

Steps for Building a Functional Scorecard

The six steps shown in table 7.2 might be followed in creating a functional scorecard. Although this is an HR example, the steps can be just as easily configured for creating scorecards for other functions, such as finance, IT, or procurement.

TABLE 7.2   Creating a functional scorecard

---

1. **Understand and internalize the strategy of the enterprise**
   This is the starting point for moving forward. Without this understanding there is little point in creating the scorecard. If the functional leaders are not cognizant of the strategy of the enterprise, they must understand and internalize the strategy before proceeding.

2. **Take the people imperatives from the enterprise-level Strategy Map to deliver that strategy**
   These people imperatives will serve as the steer for the subsequent scorecard creation process.

3. **HR leaders debate and agree on the HR strategic objectives that will appear on the HR Strategy Map**
   These are the objectives that will deliver to the people imperatives.

4. **The objectives are validated through conversations with business leaders and customers**
   The objectives must deliver what the business needs, rather than what HR thinks the business needs, or what HR thinks it can deliver. The objectives must be business focused and ensure that the HR is building the internal capabilities it requires to become and remain business focused.

5. **HR leaders agree on the strategic measures, targets, and initiatives that will deliver to the objectives.**
   These too must be validated with the business.

6. **The HR Scorecard is communicated to the HR departments.**
   If required, aligned departmental and team scorecards are developed.

A HYBRID IT STRATEGY MAP: THE CASE OF THE BANK OF ENGLAND

The Bank of England provides an interesting spin on creating a functional Strategy Map and scorecard. As reported in the case study: *Getting a Handle on IT Governance, Experiences of Using Strategy Maps at the Bank of England,*[3] the organization had implemented an approach based on a Balanced Scorecard Strategy Map and the IT Governance framework COBIT (Control Objectives for Information and Related Technology). Described briefly, the COBIT framework is split into four separate domains, all underpinned by the effective use of IT resources, people, applications, technology, facilities, and data. These four domains are: planning and organization, acquisition and implementation, delivery and support, and monitoring. In total, they cover 34 different processes, which span the entire remit of an IT department, with monitoring covering the performance measurement component. To provide a more coherent mapping between the bank's IT organization, COBIT, and meaningful performance indicators, an IT governance framework was developed to split the COBIT processes into:

- strategy (covers planning and organization processes)
- projects (covers acquisition and implementation processes)
- operations (covers delivery and support processes)
- resources.

Founded in 1694, The Bank of England is the central bank of the U.K. Standing at the center of the U.K.'s financial system, the Bank is committed to promoting and maintaining a stable and efficient monetary and financial framework as its contribution to a healthy economy. A key element of the bank's ability to deliver its overall strategy to support the "core purposes of monetary stability and financial stability" is to "raise business standards across the bank."

In response to this challenge and the need to demonstrate the delivery of value to the business, the bank embarked on an initiative to improve its IT governance in 2004. Ensuring effective IT governance is an industry-recognized approach to improving how IT delivers the desired outcomes for an organization, namely closer strategic alignment, improved value for money, and reduced risk.

With the IT governance framework defined and new decision making structures in place, covering the bank's executive directors (IT executive committee) and senior IT management business representatives (IT steering committee), the next challenge was to define a relevant and succinct set of performance indicators.

The key challenge was providing a closer linkage of IT performance to the strategic needs of the bank as a whole. This resulted in further research into the performance measurement arena and the decision to base the IT performance measurement upon a Strategy Map. However, the standard Strategy Map template covering customer, financial, internal process, and learning and growth dimensions did not prove sufficient to ensure a close relationship with the COBIT framework, which was being used as a basis for the IT governance work within the bank. This led to the development of a hybrid COBIT/Balanced Scorecard Strategy Map, which covered the four COBIT dimensions of strategy, projects, operations, and resources alongside the standard Balanced Scorecard dimensions. In addition to this, the customer and financial dimensions of the scorecard were switched around to reflect that the Bank of England is not a commercial organization in the same way as a retail or investment bank.

The resulting Strategy Map provided a balanced structure around which to define a set of goals and associated indicators across the IT function. The resulting symmetry was deliberate to ensure coverage across the entire IT function of the bank. This is illustrated in the example Strategy Map shown in figure 7.2, which is based upon the same concepts used at the Bank of England.

The COBIT dimensions are shown along the left-hand side and the Balanced Scorecard dimensions along the bottom of the Strategy Map. The arrows illustrate the basic linkages between the different goals shown in the bubbles and the performance indicators are written underneath each goal. The strategy and customer dimensions contain the seven goals that are of primary interest to the Bank's executive directors, who form the IT executive committee as part of the IT governance decision-making process.

The process for developing the IT Strategy Map within the Bank of England was as follows.

- Start with the customer and work backward to identify the goals required to support customer needs. Also check to make sure all the goals support the required IT strategies as well as the overall Bank strategies.
- Identify one goal and one indicator for each element of the matrix. It was acknowledged that future versions may have a greater emphasis on a particular element, but the bank initially wanted a balance across all areas in response to the IT governance improvement initiative.
- Limit the number of goals related to the strategy to the 16 elements, to maintain focus and avoid overcomplication and dilution
- Avoid changing the goals because they are difficult to measure. Once goals had been agreed, it was important to find a way to measure them, regardless how hard this might prove to be.
- Avoid any discussion on numerical information until the Strategy Map was in place to avoid people diving into the detail.
- Ensure that stakeholders were engaged at the right time to balance buyin against progress of the development of the IT performance indicators. Consequently, the initiative was sponsored by the IT executive committee and developed in consultation with the IT steering committee to agree the structure of the Strategy Map and the IT performance indicators.
- Ensure that the Strategy Map could be presented on a single sheet of paper to enable clear and concise communication across both the IT and the user communities.
- Recruit an IT performance analyst to maintain and develop the Strategy Map, along with the performance indicators themselves.

IT Strategy Map

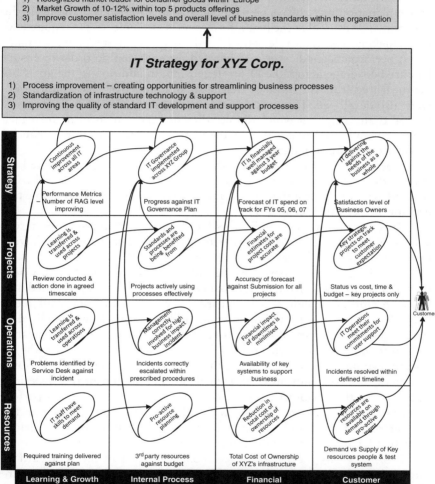

FIGURE 7.2 Example Strategy Map based on the same principles used by the Bank of England

Once the goals for the Strategy Map had been drafted, it was then necessary to work on the development of the actual IT performance indicators, to make it come alive. The decision to refer to performance indicators rather than measures was specifically done to reflect that any measures are not a guarantee, but rather an indicator to the status of a goal. Additional information and explanation will always be required to gain a full understanding of the situation and ensure that the best information is available for the required decision making. This is the role of the IT performance analyst within the bank.

A performance indicator was selected for each goal in order to ensure balanced coverage across the IT Strategy Map. In addition to the goals being measured from the Strategy Map a small number of "base indicators" were also developed. This was done to cover specific areas which the Bank wished to measure, but which did not directly reflect areas of performance improvement work being driven by the Strategy Map, for example financial performance against budget.

A performance measure record sheet (see table 7.3) was completed for each performance indicator to ensure that measures were developed comprehensively, to confirm their applicability, and also to identify suitable targets for the performance indicators.

Once the performance indicators had been identified they were tested against a number of criteria in order to verify whether the measures were considered realistic and practical to use (see table 7.4).

After initial testing, performance indicator data was collected, where immediately available from current data sources, it was then populated into the IT performance indicator scorecard. Where data was not available it was left at 0 percent, to highlight where additional work was required to obtain the data as part of the IT governance initiative. The performance indicator scorecard is grouped into five areas in accordance with the IT governance initiative for the bank, that is, strategy, projects, operations, resources, and base indicators, to provide greater alignment to the desired outcomes of the customer. In this scorecard (see figure 7.3) each performance indicator is shown together with values for the target, status for the measurement period and the change since the last measurement period. Note that the figures are fictional, for reasons of confidentiality.

Table 7.5 lists the performance indicators used in the scorecard of the Bank of England and describes how the performance indicators are obtained at a basic level, along with the example targets.

TO CASCADE OR NOT TO CASCADE?

Generally it is the view of practitioners and advisors within the global scorecard community that functional scorecard systems are a good thing. But too

TABLE 7.3 Performance measure record sheet

Criteria	Description
Area	Area of performance indicators, that is, strategy, projects, operations, or resources.
Perspective	Perspective of Balanced Scorecard, that is, customer, financial, process, learning.
Indicator name	Description of indicator.
Goal from the strategy map	Link to goal as defined in the Strategy Map. Measures may have to change thanks to issues with accuracy or data collection, but the goal should remain fixed.
Purpose	Reason for including this particular measure.
Owner	Individual or group responsible for delivering this measure.
Data source or process	Location of data and summary of process for obtaining the data. In some cases, this will require additional definition as part of the IT governance implementation work.
Frequency	Quarterly or monthly reporting cycle.
Indicator calculation	Formula for calculation of the performance indicator. Final definition will depend on the IT governance implementation, when the formula can be tested.
Target	Target status for the performance indicator.
Weighting	Optional weighting criteria, which may be used if certain indicators require more or less emphasis.
Status red	Status value when a performance indicator will be flagged red.
Status green	Status value when a performance indicator will be flagged green.
Change red	Change value when a performance indicator will be flagged red.
Change green	Change value when a performance indicator will be flagged green.
Action plan or notes	Any additional notes regarding the performance indicators or associated actions that need to be completed for data collection.

TABLE 7.4 Performance measures tests

Test description

Truth test: Is the measure definitely measuring what it's meant to measure?
Focus test: Is the measure only measuring what it's meant to measure?
Consistency test: Is the measure consistent whenever or whoever measures?
Access test: Can the data be readily communicated and easily understood?
Clarity test: Is any ambiguity possible in interpretation of the results?
So what? test: Can and will the data be acted upon?

STRATEGY	Target	Status	Change
Customer			
Satisfaction level of business owners	>60%	75%	5%
Financial			
Forecast of IT spend on track for FYs 05.06.07	>95% & <105%	94%	−2%
Process			
Progress against IT governance plan	<110%	97%	−7%
Learning			
Performance metrics - number of RAG levels improving	>7	12	4

PROJECTS	Target	Status	Change
Customer			
Status vs cost, time & benefit - key projects only	>90%	85%	−5%
Financial			
Accuracy of forecast against submission for all IT projects	>95% & <105%	110%	7%
Process			
Projects actively using processes effectively	>80%	65%	4%
Learning			
Reviews conducted & actions done in agreed timescale	>80%	72%	7%

OPERATIONS	Target	Status	Change
Customer			
Incidents resolved defined timeline	>80%	82%	2%
Financial			
Availability of key systems to support business	>98%	97%	−2%
Process			
Incidents correctly escalated within prescribed procedures	>80%	64%	−11%
Learning			
Problems identified by service desk sgainst incidents	>15%	16%	5%

RESOURCES	Target	Status	Change
Customer			
Demand vs supply of key resources	<80%	93%	5%
Financial			
Total cost of ownership of IT infrastructure	<90%	88%	−2%
Process			
3rd psrty resources against budget - operations	>90% & <110%	84%	−3%
3rd psrty resources against budget - projects	>90% & <110%	119%	4%
Learning			
Required training delivered against plan	>80%	55%	−17%

BASE INDICATORS	Target	Status	Change
Actual cost of operations IT spend Vs forecast	>95% & <105%	94%	−2%
Actual cost of operations IT spend Vs baseline budget	>95% & <105%	88%	−2%
Actual cost of project IT spend Vs forecast	>95% & <105%	88%	−10%
Actual cost of project IT spend Vs baseline budget	>95% & <105%	93%	3%
Workstation compliance - software versions	>90%	85%	3%
Workstation compliance - MS patches	>90%	95%	7%
IT purchasing via procurement system	>95%	94%	5%

FIGURE 7.3   Bank of England Performance Indicator Scorecard

TABLE 7.5   Bank of England IT performance indicators

Area	Performance indicator	Purpose	Data source or process	Target
Strategy	Satisfaction level of business owners	Demonstrates that IT organization is delivering against the needs of the business as a whole	Derived from key questions from the IT satisfaction survey for senior management	> 80%
	Forecast of IT spend on track for FYs '05,'06, '07	Demonstrates that the IT organization is financially well managed against the three-year baseline plans	Derived from financial planning information for three-year business plans	Within 5% of budget
	Progress against IT governance plan	Demonstrates the adoption of IT governance across IT to support the strategy	Derived from the IT governance implementation plan—focused on the processes and procedures area	< 10% over original schedule
	Performance metrics—number of RAG levels improving	Demonstrates continuous improvement across all key measures in the scorecard	Derived from an aggregation of the other 15 performance metrics	Improving two or more
Projects	Status v. cost, time, benefit—key projects only	Demonstrates that key IT projects are on track to meet customer expectations, typically high value and high risk	Derived from Project Support Unit project monitoring reports for selected IT projects	> 90% measures green
	Accuracy of forecast against submission for IT projects	Demonstrates that the estimates for IT projects are being done accurately	Derived from Project Support Unit submissions based against movement from start of project	Within 5% of submission
	Projects actively using processes effectively	Demonstrates that the quality of IT project deliverables is being benefited from and is being managed through the use of the required processes	Requires implementation of relevant processes and procedures and qualitative measures to be applied	80% of all projects
	Reviews conducted and actions done in agreed timescale	Demonstrates that cross project learning is being conducted and acted upon	Requires review process for projects and operations to be in place	80% of all planned reviews

(Continued)

TABLE 7.5 *(Continued)*

Area	Performance indicator	Purpose	Data source or process	Target
Operations	Incidents resolved defined timeline	Demonstrates that IT operations are meeting their commitments for the support of users	Produced from the new service desk database	80% of all incidents
	Availability of key systems to support business	Demonstrates that the impact of service interruptions is kept to a minimum and hence financial impact is kept to a minimum	Produced from service desk database and service catalogue defined availability targets	Within 1% of availability target
	Incidents correctly escalated within prescribed procedures	Escalation process is Correctly followed within the prescribed timescales. This will track involvement of management for high business impact incidents	Produced from the new service desk database	80% escalation in correct timescale
	Problems identified by service desk against incidents	Demonstrates that problem resolution is actively supporting the learning process to reduce the number of recurring incidents	Produced from the new service desk database	> 15%
Resources	Demand v. supply of key resources	Demonstrates that key resource are available when required through proactive management	Derived from resource planning package or from specific planning files for key development resources and test environments	Between 80% and 90%
	Total cost of ownership of IT infrastructure	Demonstrates a reduction on the total cost of ownership of resources for IT infrastructure based against per workstation target	Derived from financial data and procurement inventory information	80%
	Third-party resources against budget— operations	Demonstrates proactive resource planning across IT to ensure that adequate resources are available within the general IT operations resource pool	Derived from financial information and budgets and based against movement for the year	Within 10% of budget

TABLE 7.5   *(Continued)*

Area	Performance indicator	Purpose	Data source or process	Target
	Third-party resources against budget—projects	Demonstrates proactive resource planning across IT to ensure that adequate resources are available within the general IT projects resource pool	Derived from financial information and budgets and based against movement for the year	Within 10% of budget
	Required training delivered against plan	Demonstrates that IT staff have the required skills in order to meet demand and that there is a proactive approach to developing the overall skill base within IT	Based off training budget, since training plan data viewed to be prone to inaccuracy	80%
Base indicators	Actual cost of operations IT spend v. forecast	Demonstrates that the IT organization is financially well managed against annual operations spend	Derived from financial information and budgets and based against movement for the year	Within 5% of budget
	Actual cost of operations IT spend Vs baseline budget	Demonstrates that original expectations set at budget time for operations spend have met needs of business	Derived from financial information and budgets and based against movement for the year	Within 5% of budget
	Actual cost of project IT spend v. forecast	Demonstrates that the IT organization is financially well managed against annual project spend	Derived from financial information and budgets and based against movement for the year	Within 5% of budget
	Actual cost of project IT spend v. baseline budget	Demonstrates that original expectations set at budget time for project spend have met needs of business	Derived from financial information and budgets and based against movement for the year	Within 5% of budget
	Workstation compliance— software versions	Ensures that all workstations are compliant to latest software versions	Derived from Bindview reports, until SMS is online	90% compliant

(Continued)

TABLE 7.5 *(Continued)*

Area	Performance indicator	Purpose	Data source or process	Target
	Workstation compliance—MS patches	Ensures that all workstations are compliant to required MS patch versions	Derived from Bindview reports, until SMS is online	90% compliant
	IT purchasing through procurement system	Ensures that all IT spend is managed through the procurement system	Derived from procurement system and specific ledger account codes from financial planning system	90% compliant

often organizations get so excited by the scorecard idea that they rush to create as many scorecards as possible without thinking through the benefits and cost of doing so.

Organizations must honestly assess whether they possess the capability to manage lots of aligned scorecards. For example, in a fast-moving marketplace, such as financial services, if a market shift requires significant changes to the enterprise-level Strategy Map and Balanced Scorecard, then if the organization has, say, 100 aligned scorecards, how quickly could these scorecards be changed? If they are not changed, then the danger is that the organization stops being strategy focused. However, if they are changed, then there's a danger that the organization becomes focused on managing the scorecard, rather than using the scorecard to manage the business.

CONCLUSION

In this chapter, we have explained that creating devolved scorecards is a powerful way for creating line-of-sight between the work of lower-level units and the strategic goals of the enterprise. But organizations must be clear on the benefits they will gain from creation of a suite of aligned scorecards.

We have also argued the importance of creating functional scorecards, which can be built with or without the existence of a corporate scorecard, and indeed are often built as pilot scorecard efforts. But although building aligned, devolved scorecards is challenging, the greatest challenges in scorecard implementation are cultural, not structural—or even technological. We consider the cultural challenges in the next chapter.

Self-Assessment Checklist

As previously, simply indicate your agreement with the two opposing statements in table 7.6. Checking number 1 indicates a strong agreement with the statement to the left, while checking number 7 indicates a strong agreement with the statement to the right. The more numbers to the right are checked, the greater the perceived challenges.

TABLE 7.6 Self-assessment checklist

	1	2	3	4	5	6	7	
Employees will be involved in creating their own local scorecard system								Lower-level scorecards will be built elsewhere and mandated
In creating devolved scorecards there will be cleat line of sight with enterprise objectives								Devolved scorecards will have little relationship with enterprise level objectives
We fully understand the benefits of cascading the Balanced Scorecard system								We do not understand the benefits of cascading the Balanced Scorecard system
We have the capability to manage a family of scorecards								We do not have the capability to manage a family of scorecards

ENDNOTES

1. James Creelman and Naresh Makhijani, *Mastering Business in Asia: Succeeding with the Balanced Scorecard* (Singapore: John Wiley Asia, 2005).
2. James Creelman, "Next Generation HR Shared Services, How to Take Customer Service, Efficiency and Savings to a New Level," *Business Intelligence*, 2008.
3. Bernard Marr, Chris Piper, Iain Parker, *Getting a Handle on IT Governance: Experience of Using Strategy Maps at the Bank of England* (Milton Keynes: Advanced Performance Institute, June 2007).

CHAPTER 8

Cascading the Balanced Scorecard: The Cultural Challenges

EXECUTIVE SUMMARY

1. Most Balanced Scorecard programs that fail, do so not because the Strategy Maps or accompanying Balanced Scorecards are badly designed (although many are) but during the implementation phase.
2. The cultural bulwarks of resistance are typically erected because a properly implemented scorecard system leads to twin outcomes that can be disconcerting for some and terrifying for others—performance transparency and accountability.
3. Most people in the organization are often not used to having their work regularly measured and are likely to be apprehensive about the consequences.
4. The scorecard must be positioned as a strategic learning tool and a framework for continuous improvement.
5. At all stages of Balanced Scorecard design and implementation, it should be kept in mind that this is a major change effort. Therefore, it is subjected to the same cultural and behavioral hurdles encountered in any change program.
6. It is important to define the kind of culture the company wants to develop to support scorecard implementation.
7. Overcoming cultural obstacles requires the visible support of the senior team.
8. It might be sensible to put in place local "scorecard champions." These are often middle managers who are trained in scorecard

design and implementation techniques—and crucially must be scorecard enthusiasts.
9. A well-developed communications strategy should support scorecard
rollout.

INTRODUCTION

It is interesting that in their five seminal works, scorecard co-creators
Kaplan and Norton pay little attention to the cultural challenges of implementing a Balanced Scorecard. This may be because both being engineers,
they are much less *au fait* with the cultural building blocks of an organization than they are the structural or process components.

Yet most Balanced Scorecard programs that fail do so not because the
strategy maps or accompanying balanced scorecards are badly designed (although many are) but during the implementation phase. And failure during
implementation is typically the result of cultural factors. More than anything else, a Balanced Scorecard program is about creating the right mindset. The "mind" of the organization must "think" Balanced Scorecard, or
rather through the scorecard think strategically. Creating a strategic mindset is not a structural or process challenge—it is a cultural challenge. And
what organizations should be looking for is the inculcation of a performance-based culture. A useful definition of performance-based culture comes
from an article written by Howard Risher, a pay-for-performance expert
and published in *Public Manager*.[1]

> In an organization with a strong performance culture, employees
> know what they are expected to accomplish and are emotionally
> committed to organizational success. They believe in the mission
> and goals and are quick to put their energy into a task without be-
> ing asked or monitored. Informal conversations with coworkers
> frequently focus on performance problems and recent organization
> results. They tend to celebrate successes as a team or group. The
> commitment to performance is a way of life in the organization.

TRANSPARENCY AND ACCOUNTABILITY

A significant challenge in making the Balanced Scorecard "a way of life" is
the bulwark of cultural resistance that is erected. Resistance is forthcoming
because a properly implemented scorecard system leads to twin outcomes
that can be disconcerting for some and terrifying for others—performance

transparency and accountability. However, the Balanced Scorecard cannot be effective without there being transparency and accountability at each level of the organization because by implication the framework makes performance visible. These cultural barriers must be acknowledged and overcome, especially as many organizations implement a scorecard in order to achieve greater performance transparency and accountability.

Indeed Bank CIMB Niaga's head of corporate strategy, Wahyu Edo Wardono, who led the scorecard effort, states that: "Culture was a problem in scorecard rollout due to the transparency and the fact that performance could be monitored. Now everyone can see how the scorecard helps them improve performance and all are motivated to change."

Case Example: Bank Universal

Pak Krisbiyanto, who was head of human capital at Bank Universal, when the organization appeared as a case study in the book, *Managing Business in Asia: Succeeding with the Balanced Scorecard*, which was written by the authors of this book, said that the overriding benefit of using the scorecard has been in transparency and accountability.[2]

> *Through the Balanced Scorecard we can measure the performance of our employees and the organization more clearly. In the past we would blame each other, but now we can see the actual causes of problems that lead to targets being missed and so know where to direct our efforts.*
>
> *The scorecard gives a very clear picture of accountability across the organization.*

He adds that the transparency afforded by the scorecard has also led to better crossfunctional teamwork and understanding. He says:

> *The marketing people can appreciate the service people, and the service people can appreciate the operational and process people, who in turn can appreciate the human resource people. I can now see very effective coordination and communication through the organization.*

FEAR OF MEASUREMENT

With the notable exception of manufacturing (which thanks to Total Quality Management has been subjected to rigorous measurement for decades) people in organizations are often not used to having their work regularly measured and are likely to be apprehensive about the consequences, especially if the results are widely communicated. This holds true for those within financial services.

Front-line employees may be concerned that managers will use the results primarily to identify and punish poor performance. Managers may worry that their units or divisions are held up as poor performers compared to other units: they may not like a bright spotlight shining on their decisions. Indeed Dyah Nastiti Kusumowardani, Bank Indonesia's director of strategy planning, says that an ongoing challenge that they face is that work units often try and get measures and targets that are easy to achieve. "But these won't help us achieve our strategic objectives," she says. In chapter 4 she explained how leadership from the very top was important at the start of the scorecard program to help overcome this and other cultural challenges.

It follows that organizations need to work hard to convince people that the motivation for introducing the scorecard is not for it to be used as a means to merely expose and punish underperformance. Simply put, employees must trust that the organization will not abuse the information and data collected through the scorecard program. Only then will they be prepared to allocate the energy and commitment required to create the "performance-focused" culture required to succeed with the scorecard. A culture that is characterized by fear will not create an organization in which employees readily embrace performance indicators or share performance information that might be construed as negative. A culture based on trust, learning, and improvement will create an organization where employees happily accept performance indicators and share information.

Organizational leaders therefore must emphasize the positive role of the scorecard as an aid to improving performance in line with the firm's strategic objectives. The scorecard must be positioned as a strategic learning tool and a framework for continuous improvement.

Indeed, how the scorecard is used in relation to the traffic light system that is typically used to monitor and report performance will also go some way to deciding whether it is used to galvanize a culture of learning and improvement or is actively resisted (most organizations report scorecard performance using a green (ahead of target), amber (on target), or red (below target) traffic light system). For the scorecard to work effectively and be accepted within the employee base it is absolutely critical that we change the perception that red means bad. One organizational leader said to one of the authors of this book: "I don't care if all the objectives on the Strategy Map are red, as long as I can see stretching targets and performance improvement towards those targets. This is far more useful than a Strategy Map that is 'all green' but represents no improvement whatsoever."

This attitude helps to remove "fear" from the minds of managers and staff and of course remove much of the concerns regarding performance transparency and accountability.

The U.S.-based Pentagon Federal Credit Union's CEO Frank Pollack puts it nicely: "When you eliminate fear from the workplace people begin to think more aggressively, and when people think more aggressively you get closer to your objectives."[3]

Case Example: Adira Finance

Adira Finance, which has about 25,000 people in branches across Indonesia providing financing for cars and motorcycles, also faced early cultural barriers based on a "fear of measurement," when it implemented the Balanced Scorecard in 2003. Falk Archibald Kemur, head of the president's office (that was created to manage the scorecard and other aligned improvement programs) says that initially people were concerned that the scorecard was simply a way to use metrics for monitoring and controlling individuals. "Some employees felt that the use of the scorecard meant that senior management didn't trust them," he says. "It took about a year for us to secure buyin and really get the message across that the scorecard was not intended to control their work, but rather to help them clarify how to achieve their targets and to monitor their development until their targets were achieved," he continues, adding that usage of the scorecard had triggered a culture change. "Pre the scorecard, senior management were the only ones that played a leadership role within Adira Finance," he says. "But now they lead across a system in which people at many levels are taking leadership roles."

A MAJOR CHANGE EFFORT

At all stages of Balanced Scorecard design and implementation, it should be kept in mind that this is a major change effort. Therefore, it is subject to the same cultural and behavioral hurdles encountered in any change program. Many people are quite happy with—and successful within—the status quo (and will likely be the most active resistors of performance transparency and accountability). Convincing them that change is good for them as well as the organization is always a major task. Indeed, when the organization puts together the team that will facilitate the scorecard design and implementation program (typically a mix of internal resource and external consultants) it is usually sensible to give a team member responsibility for managing the change dimension—especially as it relates to measurement and accountability. Indeed, Pak Krisbayanto at Bank Universal was essentially placed as the scorecard leader because being from the HR function, he was thought to be more aware of the change pressures.

Managers should also take time to understand what kinds of changes they intend the scorecard to bring about before the rollout phase begins. Therefore, defining the kind of culture the company wants to develop to support scorecard implementation is also important.

For instance, the senior team might decide that the culture it needs to implement the strategy successfully is one characterized by devolved responsibility, customer-centricity, and teamworking. But once defined, it might be sensible to conduct an audit to ascertain the "as is" of these cultural characteristics. It is then possible to use the scorecard itself to close the gap by putting in place objectives, measures, targets, and initiatives to create the culture.

The U.S.-headquartered Senn–Delaney Management Consulting has created a useful cultural survey instrument, a segment of which is shown in table 8.1. The employee who fills in the profile questionnaire has to state on a scale of 1–7 which of the positive and negative statements most accurately describes the culture of the organization.

A strength of this profiling technique (and there are many similar available in the marketplace) is that it unambiguously points to the cultural strengths and weaknesses of the organization as perceived by the employees themselves. This can serve as a powerful "gap analysis" between the desired organizational culture and the "as is" state. For example, if teamwork is an important scorecard objective but there is a high agreement with the profile statement "narrow focus, turf issues, and we versus they," then considerable work will need to be done to inculcate the teamwork approach and succeed to the objective and will also highlight where strategic initiatives should be prioritized.

Case Example: Bristol & West Consumer Direct

The U.K.-based lending provider Bristol & West Consumer Direct introduced a Balanced Scorecard in 1998, which had four perspectives: financial, competitive (essentially customer), market share, and employer of choice. The organization decided to create a culture based on trust, empowerment, and high performance.

Then division head Denys Rayner explains that both culture and the scorecard had to work together if the business was to succeed.

Culture is the way you do things, not the what. A company can have the best vision and cultural aspirations in the world but if the managers aren't managing against these and employees aren't working towards them they are just worthless words.

TABLE 8.1 Senn-Delaney Cultural Survey Instrument

Positive	Always 7	Mostly 6	Occasionally 5	Sometimes both 4	Occasionally 3	Mostly 2	Always 1	Negative
People clearly understand mission, vision, and goals								People are unclear about mission, vision, and goals
Clear alignment and common focus of leadership at the top								Obvious lack of alignment at the top
Two-way frequent open communications								Top-down inadequate communications
Flexible, fluid, and empowered								Hierarchical or boss driven
High-quality awareness and focus								Quality not a high priority
High service consciousness and focus on the customer								Low service consciousness and low focus on the customer
Teamwork, mutual support, and cooperation								Narrow focus, turf issues, and we versus they
High performance expectations								Low performance expectations
Self starters and high initiative								Need direction and low initiative
Sense of urgency and basis for action								Indecisive, bureaucratic, and slow to respond
People are highly accountable for results and actions								People find excuses, feel victimized, or blame others
Open to change								Resistant to change
Encouraged to innovate and creativity welcomed								Do what is told, risk averse, and poor support for new ideas
High levels of feedback and coaching								Infrequent or no feedback and coaching
High performance is recognized and rewarded								High performance is expected but not rewarded

(Continued)

TABLE 8.1 (*Continued*)

Positive	Always 7	Mostly 6	Occasionally 5	Sometimes both 4	Occasionally 3	Mostly 2	Always 1	Negative
Core values and ethics are very important								Values and ethics nit stressed or tend to be ignored
People are appreciated and valued								People don't feel appreciated and valued
High trust and openness between people								Low trust and lack of openness
Healthy, fast based environment								High stress or burnout pace
Positive, optimistic, and forgiving								Insecure, fearful, or negative environment
Focused, balanced, and effective								Distracted, overwhelmed, and inefficient
Respect for diversity of ideas and people								Lack of respect for diversity of ideas and people

> *Therefore, the best way to make sure "what" happens is to focus the cultural goals through a framework such as the Balanced Scorecard. Through this it is possible to make sure that the performance of management and staff are focused on areas such as customer and staff satisfaction that require the deployment of the new cultural imperatives.*

He also describes the relationship between tracking internal issues and performance results:

> *For example, if we are overly busy then staff may feel overworked so their satisfaction levels will go down. Through the scorecard we can see that when this happens customer satisfaction levels go down. Quite simply, customers are not going to get a great experience if staff feel pressurized and are unhappy.*
>
> *The reduction in customer service correlates with the likelihood to purchase other products, because they are less likely to buy from us if they are unhappy with our service. This of course will eventually negatively affect the financial results.*

Case Example: Banking 365

Creating the right culture is a key strategic objective for Banking 365. The culture is referred to as the "smell of the place," which is fed by "stretch," "support," "discipline," and "trust" performance standards.

SENIOR MANAGEMENT BEHAVIOR

As well as audits, overcoming cultural obstacles also requires something much more immediate—the visible support of the senior team. In short, creating an employee base that is committed, engaged, and willing to go that extra mile for the organization, requires that their leaders demonstrate appropriate behavior and actions.

The role of leadership in creating a "climate for change" has long been recognized as critical for Balanced Scorecard success. Indeed, "mobilize change through executive leadership" is one of the five principles of the strategy-focused organization (see chapter 2). Kaplan and Norton emphasize the make-or-break influence of top management: "If those at the top are not energetic leaders of the process, change will not take place. Simply, if the CEO does not want the scorecard then don't try to do it, the scorecard effort will fail."

As a powerful example of leading from the top, when faced with resistance from a country CEO, one CEO of a global enterprise would reply: "I use the scorecard as the main tool by which I manage the global business. And while using it the organization has delivered exceptional results. Explain to me how you can do a better job without the scorecard."

It is worth bearing in mind that lower-level employees will behave as their leaders behave—so if the scorecard is not placed at the highest level of importance by the senior team then the framework will receive scant attention lower down. Senn–Delaney Leadership Consulting has coined the phrase "shadow of the leader" to describe the fact that how people within the organization behave is a reflection of the behavior of those at the very top. A middle- and supervisory-level manager might abuse power, make unethical decision or even manipulate the data that feeds into the scorecard if the senior team has cast "the shadow" that encourages (or at least turns a blind eye to) misuse. He or she will not do so if the senior team (and most importantly the CEO) is uncompromising in the behavior that must be demonstrated in the day-to-day operations of the enterprise.

As a useful piece of empirical research that demonstrates the role of leadership in creating a performance-oriented culture (whether focused through a Balanced Scorecard or not) consider the HR consultancy Tower Watson's 2007–2008 Global Workforce Study (a worldwide survey of close to 90,000 employees in midsize and large organizations). Tower Watson found that employee engagement rises when people experience a combination of four influences:[4,5]

- effective and caring leadership
- appealing development opportunities
- interesting work
- fulfilling tangible and intangible rewards.

The research identified two elements that have a particularly strong influence: Senior management's sincere interest in employee wellbeing (effective and caring leadership) and the opportunity an employee has for personal development of skills and abilities (appealing development opportunities).

The first element refers to the decisions executives make, communicate, and implement in areas such as company direction, reward programs, and workplace culture and policies. The second speaks to ensuring that an organization has a learning environment, in which valuable training programs and rich opportunities to learn on the job are widely available. Towers Watson reports that when the decisions and actions made by leaders convey that they understand and take employees' concerns into account, engagement goes up. Likewise, when employees have confidence in their growth and development opportunities, engagement also increases. Get both interventions right and engagement will likely rise significantly.

Field observations by the authors of this book would support the findings of Towers Watson. And in the context of a Balanced Scorecard implementation, if an organization fails to engage employees, then no matter how elegantly it formulates the Strategy Map and the accompanying KPQs and KPI, the scorecard will fail. End of story. For more on employee engagement surveys and research, see chapter 5.

Of course, many lower-level managers might be worried about the CEO having the visibility into their performance that the scorecard brings and will attempt to sabotage the scorecard process. Only a CEO has the authority to ensure that the scorecard effort can overcome such attempts to destabilize. Moreover, in chapter 6, we explained that political battles will often erupt when it comes to the funding of initiatives—only the CEO has the power to ensure these battles end and that the more deserving initiatives are funded.

But note that the CEO, and indeed the other members of the senior team, must also demonstrate through behavior that they believe in the scorecard. For instance, nothing will kill a scorecard effort quicker than a CEO loudly proclaiming the importance of nonfinancial performance dimensions, yet punishing people when financials dip even though the nonfinancials are positive and strongly signal a successful future.

When reviewing our scorecard success stories, such as CIGNA P&C, Scotiabank, or Banking 365, it is not coincidence that the CEO was a high-profile champion who "walked the scorecard talk." Note too the comment of Dyah Nastiti Kusumowardani, Bank Indonesia's director of strategy planning in chapter 4 regarding the role leadership played in overcoming strong resistance to the scorecard program from some managers at each management level. "It was through the passionate leadership and commitment of the deputy governor that the necessary buyin from other board members was secured," she says. "With the board of governors onside, systematic and open communications were deployed to secure buyin at each of the other managerial levels and throughout the organization."

Indeed she adds that the first principle of the strategy-focused organization—mobilize change through executive leadership—is the most critical of all scorecard success factors. "It is crucial to get the involvement of the top management level (board of governors), the head of directorates, and Balanced Scorecard managers in each of the working units."

Consider these successes with the following failure. This information was provided by the former scorecard manager at a large Australian bank. In describing why the scorecard failed, the role of the CEO (and indeed other C-level executives) is evident.

"First we wanted to put scorecards in place across all the banking units. But institutional banking was reticent to support any project that tied it to the retail bank," she explains. "They were recalcitrant of the entire process. It ultimately was driven by the fact that the CEO was only interested in overall returns from the institutional bank and did not want to be pegged to the 'how do we achieve it?' There was lack of leadership on this, so the institutional banking scorecard never flew.

"Second, the scorecard was not integrated with the planning process following its establishment, despite many efforts," she adds. "The chief strategy officer wanted the scorecard to 'bed down' before integrating it, which proved counterproductive—if you can't have accepted targets set for the metrics as part of the budgeting and planning process, it is difficult for the metrics to have legitimacy and meaning for management—a circular argument.

"Third, the project was sponsored by the CFO but in light of other more important initiatives going on at the time, we did not seek final CEO signoff, which of course meant it was owned by the CFO and therefore was another reason it never flew."

She continues, "This was one organization where the scorecard effort was tried and failed several times, ultimately due to lack of CEO leadership and desire to break from existing strategy management and monitoring approaches." She makes the powerful observation that: "Lack of leadership means the death of the scorecard."

LOCAL CHAMPIONS

As well as CEO support, it might be sensible to put in place local "scorecard champions." These are often middle managers who are trained in scorecard design and implementation techniques—and must be scorecard enthusiasts. These managers will work with local units to build and manage the scorecard and will continually reinforce the message why the organization is using the Balanced Scorecard. Moreover, they become a powerful community of practice for the sharing of best practices and play an important step in the inculcation of scorecard capabilities into the organization. Of course, in the most advanced scorecard-using organizations such a community will be steered by the Office of Strategy Management (OSM).

COMMUNICATIONS

The constant messaging from local champions and the OSM plays a key part in a wider communication strategy—which is crucial if strategy is to be taken out of the boardroom and onto the shopfloor or front line, as we suggested at the beginning of this chapter. Moreover, as we explained in chapter 2, facilitating the strategic communications process is a key responsibility of the OSM.

The scorecard program has to be underpinned by a communications strategy to reach all parts of the organization. This should involve an integrated, multichannel communications exercise that makes appropriate use of the intranet, paper-based newsletters, brochures, and posters, town-hall type meetings, one-to-one meetings, along with other media.

Case Example: Scotiabank

At Scotiabank, for example, a major communications program supported scorecard rollout. Senior HR Vice President Pat Krajewski comments:

> *Change is all about people. Business planning and strategy is implemented through people. Although we've always been people focused, historically we would tend to undertake technological or process change first and think about people later.*
>
> *Now we've learnt that we have to think about the people issues up front. They have to understand why change is happening, what the change entails, what it means to our customers, what it means to them and how they will be supported through the change.*

Case Example: Pentagon Federal Credit Union

Building trust within Pentagon Federal Credit Union required paying constant attention to regular and honest communication. And communication was an important part of rolling the scorecard out to the organization, especially critical given the stretch required by the scorecard goals. CEO Frank Pollack says: "The single most important success factor is setting the right targets and goals. But these won't be achieved unless you pay heed to the second critical success factor, and that's communication; employees have to understand why we have those goals, that they are meaningful and achievable."

Therefore, the management team spent a considerable amount of time with line employees educating them around the hows and whys of the scorecard. Pollack says: "We walked every employee through every single item on the Balanced Scorecard, being careful to clearly explain what all those ratios and numbers meant and why they were important to the individual employee and the company."

As Pollack points out, most line employees do not usually receive this type of information. One positive output of employees understanding the scorecard is that increasingly they are more proactive in asking for additional knowledge or training to help them better meet their and the company's goals.

At the time this case study was written, as a part of the induction process, each new employee goes through a piece about the Balanced Scorecard, which Pollack said was a powerful way to teach him or her about the company he or she has come to work for.

Continued communication is also secured through quarterly town hall meetings, in which all employees are brought together to learn how the company is progressing towards its strategic objectives, as described in its Balanced Scorecard.

Case Example: CIGNA P&C

At CIGNA Property & Casualty (P&C), alignment was achieved through a formal communication and linkages process, which comprised four key elements:

- business linkage rosters, which pull together people in different processes and operating units so that business rather than functional performance is maximized. A roster is a list of people who support or work in particular businesses
- communication plans and programs
- stakeholder surveys and workshops, including employees, agents, brokers, and policyholders
- incentive compensation (which is outlined in the next chapter).

In addition, our research has found that visual techniques can be a simple yet powerful technique for communicating Balanced Scorecard objectives and measures. At NatWest Bank (now part of the Royal Bank of Scotland) in the early 1990s, simple wall charts, strategically placed throughout the organization, were used effectively to communicate progress against scorecard objectives.

CONCLUSION

This chapter explained that cultural factors provide the greatest challenge to a scorecard effort. If a scorecard fails, it will likely be largely the result of cultural resistance—which might be more covert than overt.

People often resist scorecard implementation efforts because of the performance transparency and accountability that will be engendered. Simply put, many people are afraid of being measured, which is why it is critical that the scorecard is positioned as a tool for continuous improvement and not a way to identify and punish poor performance. Organizations would do well to take the time to understand their culture before launching a scorecard program.

We have now discussed the process for building and implementing the Balanced Scorecard framework. In the next chapter, we consider incentive compensation and personal scorecards, which takes us deeper into grappling with people issues.

Self-Assessment Checklist

As previously, simply indicate your agreement with the two opposing statements in table 8.2. Checking number 1 indicates a strong agreement with the statement to the left, while checking number 7 indicates a strong agreement with the statement to the right. The more numbers to the right are checked, the greater the perceived challenges.

TABLE 8.2   Self-assessment checklist

	1	2	3	4	5	6	7	
We are aware of the cultural barriers that we will face in scorecard rollout								We are not aware of the cultural barriers that we will face in scorecard rollout
In this organization, employees are at ease with performance transparency								In this organization, employees are a not at ease with performance transparency
In this organization, employees are at ease with performance accountability								In this organization, employees are not at ease with performance accountability
We have an excellent understanding of our corporate culture								We have a very poor understanding of our corporate culture
We fully understand the culture that we require to implement strategy								We do not understand the culture that we require to implement strategy
Senior management are excellent role models for using the Balanced Scorecard								Senior management are poor role models for using the Balanced Scorecard
We have an excellent communications strategy to support scorecard rollout								We have an excellent communications strategy to support scorecard rollout

ENDNOTES

1. See www.thepublicmanager.org.
2. James Creelman and Naresh Makhijani, *Mastering Business in Asia: Succeeding with the Balanced Scorecard* (Singapore: John Wiley Asia, 2005).
3. James Creelman, *Understanding the Balanced Scorecard: A HR Perspective* (Aurora, Ontario, Canada: HR.Com, 2002).
4. Towers Watson 2007–2008 Global Workforce study: see www.towerwatson.com.
5. Creelman, op. cit.

CHAPTER 9

Individual Performance Appraisal and Incentive Compensation

EXECUTIVE SUMMARY

1. In a textbook scorecard cascade, personal scorecards serve as the final step in the process from corporate, divisional, business unit, functional, team, and individual levels—or however the organization is structured.
2. At the individual level, the scorecard should impose the same discipline around performance as do higher level scorecards.
3. Personal scorecards are often avoided because of the difficulty in ensuring that they are both aligned to higher-level scorecards and are meaningful to the individual employee.
4. Companies typically create personal scorecards that comprise only the perspectives that the individual can influence.
5. Personal scorecards should also focus on personal competency development, which will be captured in the initiative component of the scorecard.
6. Creating personal scorecards for the CEO is a powerful way to improve corporate governance because it enables the nonexecutive board greater transparency into the performance of the organization's top-ranking officers.
7. Incentive compensation is seen as a key lever for hardwiring the efforts of employees to scorecard objectives.
8. There are arguments for and against the use of incentive compensation in a scorecard implementation, which may have become more heated as a consequence of the credit crunch.
9. Going forward the process and criteria for assessing incentive compensation should be as transparent as possible, with an assessment of risk factors being key to deciding payouts.

INTRODUCTION

In the previous chapter we focused on how to overcome the cultural barriers that might threaten the scorecard effort. Culture is about people. And fully aligning employees to the scorecard brings us to an examination of appraisal systems (or personal scorecards) and incentive compensation. Indeed "balanced paychecks" (compensation) and "personal scorecards" are subcomponents of "make strategy everyone's job," which is principle four of the five principles of the strategy-focused organization, as described by Drs. Robert Kaplan and David Norton and as we outlined in chapter 2.

PERSONAL SCORECARDS

In a textbook scorecard cascade, personal scorecards serve as the final step in the process from corporate, divisional, business unit, functional, team, and individual levels—or however the organization is structured. The belief is that cascading the scorecard to the deepest level of the organization fully aligns the individual's objectives to those of the enterprise; therefore creating the classic "line-of-sight."

Moreover, the argument goes that such a family of cascaded scorecards enables a degree of transparency into organizational performance that would typically have been impossible to achieve previously. We noted in the preceding chapter the importance of, and inherent challenges of, performance transparency.

At the individual level, the scorecard should impose the same discipline on performance as do higher-level scorecards. Simply, the personal scorecard should serve as the only appraisal system used within the organization.

Case Example: Scotiabank

Scotiabank has fully integrated the performance management system with the Balanced Scorecard. Within Scotiabank, scorecards were purposely developed to achieve consistency in performance focus and measurement across the enterprise. For instance, throughout Canada, the scorecards of the branch managers are identical in that they will consist of the four perspectives of financial, customer, operations and employee, and will be subjected to a common measurement process. For example, a branch manager's scorecard includes a measure of satisfaction and engagement of branch employees. However, the goals and targets may change from region to region and perhaps branch to branch, depending on local requirements.

Similar scorecards have been created for other levels, such as for customer service managers and cashiers. For example, the scorecard for customer service managers, who are responsible for the operations of the branch, includes the objective from the "operational" perspective of "effective facilities management." A measure of this could be the management of ATM downtimes. A personal banking officer will have a measure of the number of contacts with key customers. Importantly, managers within Scotiabank have objectives and measures around the coaching and development of their direct reports.

Case Example: J.P. Morgan Investor Services

The report *Corporate Culture: Creating a Customer-Focused Financial Services Organization*, which was written by one of the authors of this book explained how at JP Morgan Investor Services managerial behavior was assessed through a performance scorecard.[1]

The performance scorecard measures the manager against the four dimensions of shareholders, competitors, clients, and employees.

Client measures may include sales and service metrics and whether the client can be referenced to potential clients.

The employee dimension is where such things as employee poll results (which measure leadership, communication, training, diversity, and so on), 360-degree feedback, participation in community programs, and MADPOP (a culture change program) come into play. Examples of the latter may be a team leader ensuring that all his or her staff attended a MADPOP workshop, or the leader committing to opening a number of MADPOP workshops during the year.

The performance scorecard serves as the basis for the manager's annual bonus. Francis Kim, chief of staff, commented: "In the performance scorecard we will look at the manager's performance against the attributes and values and if they fall short it will hit their pockets."

ARGUMENTS AGAINST THE PERSONAL SCORECARD

Yet despite the apparently unarguable advantages of creating fully fledged four-perspective personal scorecards, organizations still do not use them much. They often avoid personal scorecards because of the difficulty in ensuring that they are both aligned to higher-level scorecards and are meaningful to the individual employee.

Personal scorecards can also be demotivating if they comprise objectives and measures that are beyond the control of staff. For example, if tellers in a branch are to be measured against a customer satisfaction score, and this is an aggregate of the speed of service and satisfaction with personal attention, for example, then there is little they can do to influence this scorecard if the regional office has cut teller numbers, forcing irritated customers to spend longer in queues. Simply, personal scorecards can only be effective when the employee can personally influence the measures.

TRUNCATED PERSONAL SCORECARDS

More commonly, companies create personal scorecards that comprise only the perspectives that the individual can influence. For instance, one Indonesia-based organization, a client of the Jakarta-headquartered OTI, first came to the scorecard when seeking a way to motivate employees better and align their performance with the goals of the enterprise. This alignment was made through personal scorecards. On these scorecards, employees have accountability statements that have objectives and measures set against perspectives *that they most affect*, thus enabling line-of-sight from individual performance up through unit and corporate scorecard performance.

COMPETENCY DEVELOPMENT

Another key learning about personal scorecards is that as well as objectives, measures, and targets, they should focus on personal competency development, which will be captured in the initiative component of the scorecard.

Indeed, a key determinant of whether true alignment can be achieved is the extent to which the organization has the appropriate capability to deliver its results. It is important to put in place a system that not only helps individuals understand the targets that they need to achieve but also the capability that they need to demonstrate. From our observations, this tends to be extremely rewarding for both the organization and the individual.

The individual is not only shown "what" he or she must achieve, but also "how" he or she can achieve this. The "what" comes from the creation of an individual scorecard or the selection of key measures and targets from a team scorecard. The "how" is provided by the identification of a set of competencies that are found to be related to the demonstration of "excellent" performance. Encouraging the individual to develop these competencies will also help to improve the organization's capability, which will over time increase its ability to achieve its strategic objectives.

PERSONAL SCORECARDS FOR THE SENIOR TEAM

Although it is difficult to create personal scorecards at the deepest level of organizations, this is not the case for senior managers. Naturally, the higher up the organization a person sits, the greater his or her ability to influence performance—and against all four perspectives. Creating personal scorecards for the CEO is a powerful way to improve corporate governance because it enables the nonexecutive board greater insight into the performance of the organization's top-ranking officers. Indeed it is possible to create a complete Strategy Map for the CEO and for other executive committee members. This executive scorecard describes the strategic contributions of each of the executive committee and is drawn from the objectives within the Enterprise Scorecard, thus ensuring that the executive will take responsibility for the enterprise-level strategic objectives.

The Executive Scorecard becomes the performance contract between the executive and the nonexecutive or supervisory board, and is used to evaluate and reward senior executive performance. Moreover, an Executive Scorecard essentially serves as a job description for a senior role so is equally valuable for selection, or succession-planning purposes. The Strategy Map and Balanced Scorecard that were used several years ago for the CEO of the First Commonwealth Bank of Massachusetts are shown in figure 9.1.

LINKING PERFORMANCE TO PAY

Performance appraisal, whether captured in a personal scorecard or not, is typically linked to incentive compensation.

With regard to the Balanced Scorecard using money, especially through incentive-compensation interventions, is seen by as a key lever for hardwiring the efforts of employees to scorecard objectives. Table 9.1 shows how linking compensation to scorecard performance might look.

Case Example: Bank Indonesia   *Incentive-compensation*

Bank Indonesia, has created personal scorecards at the individual employee level, and has made the incentive-compensation link. In this case example, we consider the compensation link and also expand on why Bank Indonesia firmly believes in cascading the scorecard to individual levels.

The Human Resource Department helps line managers in each directorate to develop their personal scorecards. The line managers are then

• **Strategic role:** The CEO of the bank will grow revenues, transition the organization into a sales-driven culture, and ensure that the Growth Unit has the right management team to execute the FCFC strategy.

Executive Scorecard Framework: Bank CEO

Strategic objectives (from enterprise Strategy Map)	Individual objective	Measure (per enterprise BSC)	Target or targets	Rating
Financial F2- Grow revenues	Enable *key sources of revenue growth:* 1) investment offerings for the affluent segments 2) loan offerings for the commercial market.	Revenue growth	• 2003 10%	
Stakeholder C1-"FCFC provides financial solutions. For life"	Oversee the execution of the "one-name" initiative and new brand image campaign.	Acquisition, development, and retention by segment	• TBD	
Internal I3- Use the preferred way of selling I2- Optimize product and channel opportunities	Identify targeted affluent and commercial relationships. Ensure account profiles are developed.	Sales rate on profiled clients	• 2003 40%	
Learning and growth "We will have employees who contribute to our communities"	Take an active leadership role in high-profile civic organizations.	Personal involvement in civic activities	• 2003	

FIGURE 9.1 Strategy Map and Balanced Scorecard of CEO of First Commonwealth Massachusetts

TABLE 9.1 Linking incentive compensation to scorecard performance

Perspective	Measure	Target	Weight	Actual	Payout
Financial	ROE	15%	30%	16%	3.0%
	Revenue growth	25%	10%	20%	0
Customer	Customer satisfaction	75%	15%	77%	1.5%
	Repeat purchase percentage	80%	5%	75%	0
Internal processes	On-time delivery	90%	10%	85%	0
	Manufacturing efficiency	85%	10%	85%	1.0%
Employee learning and growth	Competency attainment—% of employees gaining 3 new competencies	70%	12%	75%	1.2%
	Employee turnover	5%	8%	4%	0.8%
Total payout					7.5%

responsible for helping their subordinates to develop and approve their scorecards. Dyah Nastiti Kusumowardani, Bank Indonesia's director, strategy planning, explains how their thinking over the incentive-compensation link has changed in recent years.

"Previously, results to the KPI [key performance indicator] part of the Balanced Scorecard was the main factor that we took into consideration when determining employee compensation," she says. "However, problems such as KPI gaming and the fact that there are certain non-KPI factors worth considering such as: the environment (challenging or not) and the business processes (innovation capability, resource utilization, and so on) had shaped the way we think about how to objectively evaluate a person's contribution towards the organization."

In short, today Balanced Scorecard results still remain very important but are no longer the only factors taken into consideration. Non-KPI factors are considered as determined by the senior leaders.

Dyah Nastiti Kusumowardani goes on to provide useful insights as to why the scorecard should be devolved to the lowest levels. "First, the Balanced Scorecard should be developed mainly as a strategy execution tool and not just a performance measurement system. Therefore, more emphasis needs to be placed on reviewing strategy implementation as an organizational learning tool rather then getting caught in a measurement trap that produces unintended and dysfunctional behavior," she says. So the scorecard needs to be cascaded down to individual levels to provide a comprehensive performance management system and benefit from those learnings.

"The organizational Balanced Scorecard is used as the basis to cascade the bank's strategy into strategic work programs in operational levels to be executed by every individual."

Case Example: CIGNA P&C

Early scorecard adopter CIGNA Property & Casualty (P&C) is still one of the best-known examples of an organization that implemented a successful incentive-compensation system. It is also one of the most publicized scorecard stories. The incentive-compensation system that they put in place still provides valuable lessons for today's scorecard users: not least because the division cleverly balanced the requirements to reward both individual and group performance.

CIGNA P&C devised a performance share plan comprising "phantom" shares, which were assigned a standard valuation of $10. At the start of each financial year, each employee was allocated a number of these shares depending on his or her personal responsibilities. The performance of P&C during that year determined the final value of the shares.

Simultaneously, each individual could earn additional shares during the year based on his or her own performance. For example, consider an individual who was awarded 50 $10 shares at the start of the financial year. If the business unit of P&C that he or she worked for performed poorly against scorecard objectives, then at the end of the year the unit's share value may have been $5. However, if at the same time the individual performed well, he or she may have earned 100 additional shares. His or her bonus would be the final share price ($5) multiplied by the total number of individual shares (150). This would have equaled a bonus of $750. Conversely, if the unit performed well and received a share rating of $14, but that same individual gained only 10 extra shares, his bonus would have been $840. However, if the individual had accumulated 150 shares and the business unit's share was $14, then the bonus would be $2,100.

Case Example: Bristol & West

At Bristol & West incentive compensation was group based and based on the Balanced Scorecard. About 5–10 percent of an employee's salary was paid out as a bonus each quarter, depending on the division's performance.

Says Denys Rayner, who was divisional head when the scorecard was implemented in the late 1990s: "Results against the scorecard are openly reported and everyone can see how their work contributes to the scorecard targets and therefore the bonus package." He adds that this also encourages staff to look at the work of the division as a whole, rather than just keeping a narrow focus on their own everyday job. "What we see is that people will typically take ownership of different issues and problems that are not necessarily directly linked to their own work."

He adds that taking this ownership incorporates personal accountability, discretionary effort, and a realization among staff that their actions can have negative or beneficial impacts and consequences.

Performance is based on the scorecard at Scotiabank. At Banking 365 a part of the employee bonus package was ensuring that customer satisfaction levels remained above 90 percent. At Sweden's Nordea Bank (see chapter 11), incentive compensation is linked to Balanced Scorecard targets for all four perspectives of the Balanced Scorecard. Targets being top down avoids any "gaming" to negotiate easier targets.

Case Example: Pentagon Federal Credit Union

An interesting spin comes from Pentagon Federal Credit Union, when it built a scorecard in the late 1990s. The company's annual increase and incentive-compensation system was certainly tied to performance, as measured within its Balanced Scorecard. There were key measures based on member and employee satisfaction, growth and financial results that together calculate employees' compensation package. Pollack says that the company's entire pay system was based on the Balanced Scorecard.

However, Pollack commented that it's critical to decouple the compensation from performance evaluation systems, most notably because evaluation should be about helping an individual grow. In a typical process, he said that once an employee has been told his or her pay increase or bonus, the rest of the conversation fades to the background, especially if the individual is unhappy with his reward.

As Pollack explained, "We're moving traditional ratings to a very different context, where people are evaluated around 'do you create value, or do you take value away from the organization?'"

To do this, and work with the leadership team, the HR function created a performance evaluation system based on three broad categories: technical, interpersonal, and leadership skills. At the line level, 75 percent of the job requires technical skills and 25 percent interpersonal (which is focused on teamwork). At the top of the organization, managers need very heavy conceptual skills, so the evaluation process centers on interpersonal and leadership skills, because the technical skills will already have been garnered.

At each level, skills are assessed against required competencies to deliver to Scorecard objectives.[2]

THE ARGUMENTS AGAINST MAKING THE LINK

In the opening chapter of this book, we detailed a report by the Association of Chartered Certified Accountants (ACCA) on the causes of the credit crunch.[3,4] Among the five areas cited were inappropriate remuneration and incentives. ACCA's Richard Aitken-Davies comments that: "Remuneration and incentive packages have encouraged short-term thinking. We need to ask what inhibited banks' boards from asking the right questions and understanding the risks that were being run by their managements." Existing incentive and career structures that rewarded failure needed to change. "First, we have to question whether the relative share of banks' income paid as remuneration compared with dividends has been in the best interest of long-term shareholders," he said.

"Second, risk management and remuneration and incentive systems must be linked. Executive bonus payments should be deferred until there is incontrovertible evidence that profits have been realized, cash received, and accounting transactions cannot be reversed."

And there is little doubt that much of the anger directed at the banking community as a result of the credit crunch has been focused on the bonuses paid to senior banking executives. Indeed, the "greed" of bankers has been widely touted as a core cause of the global financial meltdown. Clearly, if another such economic catastrophe is to be avoided, then, as ACCA states, the incentive compensation processes used within financial services institutions must be transformed. Applying frameworks, such as the integrated strategic management and risk management framework proposed by Andrew Smart, CEO of the U.K.-based consultancy Manigent in chapter 3 might be a useful place to start. Incentive compensation might then be based on a careful consideration and balancing of strategic objectives and the appropriate risk appetite and exposure for the delivery of these objectives. Personal scorecards might prove useful for monitoring and reporting individual performance towards these objectives. Moreover, this might ensure the inculcation of the performance transparency and accountability that are now being demanded of much of the financial services sector.

Somewhat surprisingly, in their fourth book *Alignment, Using the Balanced Scorecard to Create Corporate Synergies,* Drs. Kaplan and Norton seem to endorse the view that bonuses should not be paid when financial results are weak. "[P]aying bonuses when financial performance is poor is probably not a good idea even if customer, process, and employee performance are excellent . . . bonuses must be paid in cash and such payments may not be desirable when the company is hemorrhaging cash during times of financial distress."

Although this view seems sensible, many might legitimately argue that *not* paying bonuses when nonfinancial performance is excellent yet financial results are poor will do little to increase the reputation of the Balanced Scorecard and will go some distance to discrediting claims by senior management that nonfinancial performance drivers are equally worthy of attention as financial outcomes.

MAKING THE CHOICE

At some point in the scorecard journey, most organizations will consider the incentive-compensation link. Some will attempt to align fully, and equally, all financial and nonfinancial objectives to incentive compensation. Others will be much less ambitious and make the largest part of the bonus based on performance to the annual budget, while taking into account a few nonfinancial metrics. Still others will decide not to make the link at all. One thing is for certain, within financial services (and in particular the banking sector), the criteria by which incentive compensation is decided (and the size of the payouts) will be closely scrutinized by governments, regulators, and the general public over the next few years. Making the process as transparent as possible will go some way to assuaging the concerns of various stakeholders.

CONCLUSION

In this chapter we explained that personal scorecards can be a powerful way for ensuring line-of-sight between the day-to-day activities of employees and the strategic goals of the enterprise. Indeed, personal scorecards are seen as the final step in a full scorecard cascade from the enterprise level down. That said, there are notable challenges in creating personal scorecards.

Most notably it's important that the individual employee can influence the objectives and measures that appear on the scorecard. If not, the personal scorecard will demotivate, which is why full four-perspective scorecards might be used at the most senior level but the number decreases at lower levels of the enterprise.

We have also argued that when deployed personal scorecards should be used as the individual's only appraisal system, which is especially important when incentive compensation is linked to appraisals.

Moreover, we have explained that after the credit crunch, incentive compensation poses particular challenges to financial services institutions. With many stakeholders alleging that "greed" of many senior executives from the sector was a key cause of the credit crunch, it would be sensible that future incentive-compensation processes are as transparent as possible.

Thus far, we have considered the structural and cultural dimensions of scorecard design and rollout. In the next chapter, we turn our attention to technology.

It is through technology that the scorecard can become a real-time strategy management system.

Self-Assessment Checklist

As previously, simply indicate your agreement with the two opposing statements in table 9.2. Checking number 1 indicates a strong agreement with the statement to the left, while checking number 7 indicates a strong agreement with the statement to the right. The more numbers to the right are checked, the greater the perceived challenges.

TABLE 9.2 Self-assessment checklist

	1	2	3	4	5	6	7	
Employees have a great influence over the targets on their appraisal system or scorecard		✓						Employees have little influence over the targets on their appraisal system or scorecard
Appraisal systems or scorecards have a strong focus on competency development		✓						Appraisal systems or scorecards have a weak focus on competency development
Senior management is rewarded for performance to financial and nonfinancial objectives			✓					Senior management is rewarded for performance to financial objectives only
Balancing risk appetite and exposure is key to deciding the incentive-compensation payout			✓					Balancing risk appetite and exposure is not part of deciding the incentive-compensation payout
The general employee base is rewarded for performance to financial and nonfinancial objectives				✓				The general employee base is rewarded for performance to financial objectives only

ENDNOTES

1. James Creelman, *Corporate Culture: Creating a Customer-Focused Financial Services Organization* (London: Lafferty Publications, 2002).
2. James Creelman, *Understanding the Balanced Scorecard: A HR Perspective* (Aurora, Ontario, Canada: HR.Com, 2002).
3. Association of Chartered Certified Accountants, *Climbing Out of the Credit Crunch*, policy paper, 2008.
4. Robert S. Kaplan and David P. Norton, *Alignment: Using the Balanced Scorecard to Create Corporate Synergies* (Cambridge, Mass.: Harvard Business Press, 2005).

CHAPTER 10

Getting the Best from Software

EXECUTIVE SUMMARY

1. In today's fast-moving, global, and unpredictable markets, competitive advantage is secured by getting the right information to the right people at the right time.
2. As scorecard usage grew through the 1990s, it became evident that it is most powerful when technology was used to capture and report performance and, importantly, share best practices and other performance insights.
3. There are myriad benefits of automation, one of the main being that it enables the company to reach every member of the organization with a computer on their desks, or access to the web.
4. Software cannot build the scorecard system for you or overcome change and cultural barriers.
5. Scorecard software should, as a bare minimum:
   - be able to accommodate the basic elements of a scorecard design
   - facilitate strategy education and communication
   - show the relationship between initiatives and objectives
   - be useful for strategic feedback and learning.
6. We provide criteria for selecting software, including a 10-point checklist.
7. Also, we provide an overview of creating an IT strategy to support the scorecard.
8. We introduce a solution for integrating the Balanced Scorecard with risk management.

INTRODUCTION

In today's fast-moving, global, and unpredictable markets, competitive advantage is secured by getting the right information to the right people at the right time. Over the past decade or so, the breathtaking advances in information and communications technology have made it possible to manage and make decisions in near real time.

When the Balanced Scorecard was first developed, the technological revolution was still in its infancy. The internet and web-based technologies were then only known to a few. Yet as scorecard usage grew through the 1990s, it became evident that it is most powerful when technology was used to capture and report performance and, importantly, share best practices and other performance insights.

THE BENEFITS OF AUTOMATION

One of the main benefits of automation is that it enables the company to reach every member of the organization with a computer on their desks, or access to the web.

Organizationwide networks give high visibility to performance to the scorecard objectives, measures, targets, and initiatives. They also enable employees to provide feedback about their experience of implementing the scorecard and help to facilitate the strategic learning process.

Case Example: CIGNA P&C

Early scorecard pioneer CIGNA Property & Casualty (P&C) was one of the first to recognize the potential of IT for scorecard rollout and knowledge sharing. In the mid-1990s, the organization put in place an easy-to-use intranet system, which was accessible through the desktops of all employees (so the organization was as much a pioneer in using an intranet as it was in using the Scorecard and certainly blazed a trail in using both to deliver step-change performance improvements). The intranet housed a CIGNA P&C homepage linked to an overview screen, which lists divisional scorecard objectives, objective statements, key initiatives, and performance assessments. From this page, the employee could access information for a profit center or any of the 16 business units.

At each level, a simple traffic-light system was used to assess current performance against the scorecard objectives. Green indicated adherence to or ahead of plan, yellow meant within plan but with some caution, whereas red meant not on plan.

The employee could then click onto the traffic light and read an assessment by the measure owner on why an objective had been allocated a particular traffic light.

If the employee then wanted to communicate directly with the measure owner (to, for example, provide input based on his or her own experience on how to solve a particular problem), he or she could easily do it through a popup email system.

The system was also invaluable to associates within support functions who may be aligned with a specific business unit. If they were unsure what a specific objective meant for that unit, they could quickly access the objective statement and underlying measures, targets, and so on.

The intranet system also provided other information, such as an analysis of quarterly trends against strategic objectives.

More than a decade on and most organizations still usually begin to work with the scorecard with a paper-based system and spreadsheets alongside PowerPoint presentation tools. However, they inevitably run into some common problems: for instance, they soon discover that compiling information from multiple spreadsheets, from many people, with lots of updates, is not an efficient way to collect or share information. There will also likely be many errors.

Moreover, data collection and performance reporting can become major drains on resources if these tasks have to be carried out with a great deal of human intervention. Managing the scorecard soon becomes more important than using the scorecard to manage performance.

Case Example: Bank Indonesia

To ensure that the organization has the capability to monitor its performance, Bank Indonesia has introduced software that, says Dyah Nastiti Kusumowardani, the bank's director, strategy planning, "is efficient, user friendly, and suitable to the needs of the bank. Bank Indonesia developed a system that is able to help the organization to focus on executing its strategic objectives."

The software is used monthly and quarterly to monitor achievements to key performance indicators (KPIs) on the Balanced Scorecard. "But it cannot be used to create the culture needed to make it a successful implementation," she says. "To be successful, managers must communicate to employees regularly the organizational priorities as depicted on the scorecard." Dyah Nastiti Kusumowardani is stressing the fact that culture, and not structure or technology, is the main barrier to scorecard success.

Case Example: Bank Universal

Indonesia's Bank Universal implemented the software solution from Pbviews (now called BIRT Performance Scorecard[1]) as a way to significantly improving communications and increasing performance transparency.

Former deputy president director, Mahdi Syahbuddin says that through automation it became clear how individual branches were performing against indicators within all four perspectives. Where excellence was identified, then the branch best practices underpinning these scores could be shared throughout the network. So Pbviews also became a knowledge-sharing tool.

Case Example: Bank CIMB Niaga

Wahyu Edo Wardono, head of corporate strategy at Bank CIMB Niaga, a company that is also a BIRT Performance Scorecard user, says: "A benefit of software is that makes decision making fast. Employees can see performance, are aware of their accountabilities, and know what needs to improve."

Case Example: Adira Finance

Adira Finance, which has about 25,000 people in branches across Indonesia providing finance for cars and motorcycles, has been a BIRT Performance Scorecard user since 2004. The organization had introduced the Balanced Scorecard at the corporate and divisional level a year earlier, with the aim of ensuring control and continuous performance improvement during a period of rapid growth.

As with many companies, Adira Finance first managed and reviewed performance through simple Office tools such as Excel. Falk Archibald Kemur, head of the president's office (that was created to manage the scorecard and other aligned improvement programs), explains why they decided to switch from Office tools to BIRT Performance Scorecard: "We found that it was not easy to enter data manually with Microsoft," he says. "Due to the sizable amount of data measured and our large number of branches, we were often not able to complete the calculations in time for our monthly management meeting. It was difficult to use as a review tool because we were not able to obtain a top-down or bottom-up view."

When selecting software, Kemur considered pricing, ease of use, and flexibility in usage, with various computer systems and different types of data feeds, such as Microsoft Excel and Microsoft SQL. "In addition to these capabilities, BIRT Performance Scorecard was chosen because it gave the ability to obtain reports on the performance of all branches throughout the nation and be able to share sensitive information securely across the branch network," he says.

And the scorecard has certainly proven successful within Adira Finance. "In terms of results against KPI targets, we've performed much better than we expected," says Kemur. "Moreover, through BIRT Performance

Scorecard performance is now much more transparent across the organization and we can quickly see which areas of the business require attention and initiate corrective actions."

Case Example: Artesia BC Belgium

While gathering data and reporting to top management, the necessity for professional software tool became more and more obvious to Rob Van Rensbergen, MIS/DSS manager of financial services group Artesia BC Belgium. He also chose Pbviews, because of its:

- extremely user-friendly interface, for the end users as well as for the administrators. This was a very important feature since no one would use the tool if it was too complicated!
- clear visualization, making it easy to compare trends against different comparatives such as budget, targets, and benchmarks
- data connectivity features—Pbviews would be placed on top of existing databases and extract all the necessary data
- web functionality, giving users the opportunity to look at their organizational performance, enter action plans, and give commentaries through the internet, a very important feature for larger companies.

In March 2001, Artesia BC ordered Pbviews after building a "proof of concept" in the software tool, together with a three-day training program. After this limited training, Van Rensbergen started to build the complete Balanced Scorecard in Pbviews with relevant briefing books and reports for top management. The software implementation went very smoothly, but the only thing that was missing was the right way of thinking. For a truly successful implementation, as well as continuing success, the Balanced Scorecard must be a way of thinking and not just a way of reporting! Which leads us to the next section.

WHAT SOFTWARE CANNOT DO

Although automating the scorecard is sensible, the organization must bear in mind that scorecard software does not remove the need for going through the process of managerial discussion and debate that the scorecard requires. Put another way, software cannot create an organization's Strategy Map and Balanced Scorecard. You cannot "plug and play" a scorecard framework. There are no scorecard templates that can be purchased fully loaded with industry-specific objectives, measures, targets, and initiatives.

Similarly, the adoption of software will not on its own solve the many cultural and change management issues that are inevitably raised during a scorecard effort and that we have outlined in previous chapters and are highlighted by Bank Indonesia. What technology can do is support the implementation of a scorecard that is based on a well-structured development program that has gone through all the key steps from Strategy Map definition to scorecard design and rollout.

CERTIFIED VENDORS

In the early part of the last decade, the Balanced Scorecard Collaborative created functional standards to describe the minimum functionality required for a scorecard software support system. There are four elements covered by the standards.

Balanced Scorecard Design

The application should be able to flexibly accommodate the basic elements of a proper Balanced Scorecard design. The application must be able to:

- view the strategy from four perspectives (financial, customer, internal, and learning and growth)
- identify strategic objectives from each perspective
- associate measures with strategic objectives
- link strategic objectives in cause-and-effect relationships
- assign targets to measures
- list strategic initiatives.

Strategic Education and Communication

One of the key reasons for implementing a Balanced Scorecard software solution is the facilitation of strategic education and communication. Therefore, a certified application will enable users to document and communicate descriptions of objectives, measures, targets, and initiatives aligned with the strategy.

Business Execution

Initiatives (discretionary investment programs) are the testing grounds for the strategy expressed in the Balanced Scorecard. Therefore, a certified application must make explicit the relationship between initiatives required and the associated strategic objective.

Feedback and Learning

Through proper system design, the feedback cycle time for management information can be significantly reduced. Analysis of the measure results against targets will allow managers to understand which areas of the organization require further attention. However, the system should not override the judgment of a senior executive; the Balanced Scorecard should rely on objective and subjective judgments, as well as graphical indicators, to report on progress of a particular measure against a target.

CRITERIA FOR CHOOSING SOFTWARE

Kaplan and Norton suggested three criteria for choosing software:

- Select applications that support your own strategic goals, processes, and technical platforms. Make sure the application supports what you currently do and where your organization currently is: it's not necessarily about selecting the coolest application out there.
- Think through what your performance management process is going to be and how this will support you through that process, rather than changing your process to fit the software.
- Focus on strategy management, not data management. Make sure it's focused on managing your strategy and not just collecting data.

Other recommendations in selecting a software vendor include:

- Viability of vendor: Is the company well established? This means determining whether it will be able to maintain product upgrades, new releases, support, and consulting services, and that the organization is likely to remain in business for the long term.
- Scalability, scope of the project: Is the solution scalable enough to grow as the project develops and expands to include additional business units, departments, and so on?
- Openness and flexibility: Is the software able to use existing technology investments (e.g. in ERP) that tie into other corporate technology initiatives (budgeting, planning, and so on) to ensure a viable, long-term solution?
- Features and functionality: Does the solution meet the organization's requirements and can it be deployed in a manner that best suits the client (e.g. over the web)?

■ Domain expertise: does the vendor (and its partner network) offer domain-specific expertise relevant to the organization's industry or sector?

ADVANCED PERFORMANCE INSTITUTE SOFTWARE SELECTION CRITERIA

The U.K.-based Advanced Performance Institute (API), of which one of the authors of this book is a fellow, is a renowned center of expertise for the selection of Balanced Scorecard software. API has put together the following criteria for Balanced Scorecard software selection.[2]

Company and Product

First, it is a good idea to check basic company information about the vendor as well as information about the software product. The main aspect here is the pricing, since prices as well as pricing models vary significantly. Here it is important to check not just license fees but also maintenance fees, which can fluctuate between 10 percent and 25 percent of the license fees. Software pricing is a complex issue and different pricing models might suit one organization better than others, for example pricing per user versus pricing per package. However, software companies are often flexible in their pricing and pricing models are subject to negotiation. It is also important to consider training and implementation costs because they can drastically increase the overall price of solutions, but often are initially hidden.

As for the vendor company, it might be good to understand the background of the company and the product; and how many people work on the strategic performance management solution. Very large software companies might have only a few people working on their strategic performance management application, which might be treated as a byproduct. On the other hand, a small company that specializes in strategic performance management software might have more expertise and a larger client list. The size and global presence of a software vendor might be important if organizations plan to implement the application globally or across countries.

Organizations might want to check the economic viability of the vendor, considering recent collapses and mergers in this market.

Scalability

To assess the required scalability, it is important to consider the final implementation scope. Companies might initially only automate one department or business unit but later plan to roll it out organizationwide. There are three aspects of scalability. The application should be scalable in terms of programming. It should, for example, be easy to add new cascaded strategy maps. The underlying database should be scalable since the amount of data and information accumulates quickly. The communication approach should be scalable so that it is easy to disseminate the information through, for example, a web browser. Language can also be an issue for international organizations and they might want to check whether the application comes in various languages.

Flexibility and Customization

This is an important aspect and nowadays organizations are less willing to invest into applications that are not, for example, able to integrate with other applications. Many tools provide interfaces with reporting packages, activity-based costing solutions, CRM, or planning tools. Flexibility should also be provided in terms of methodology support. Many organizations have multiple performance measurement and reporting needs, besides their balanced scorecard and might also want to use the software for other frameworks (e.g. Malcolm Baldrige National Quality Award, EFQM Award, Deming Prize, or Investors in People). It usually makes sense to use the same application for all the performance measurement and reporting needs.

Communication and Collaboration

The communication aspect of any strategic performance management implementation is key. Organizations have to deal with issues such as: Do you want the software to be web enabled? Or even WAP enabled? Do you want users to be able to comment on any aspect of the strategy? Or do you want to restrict the commentary to any group, for example, managers responsible for certain aspects in the strategy? For most implementations it is important that the application integrates with the existing email system so that alerts, reminders, assessments, and comments can be sent to specific users. Most software solutions are able to trigger automated alerts, emails, or SMS messages, which can be sent to individuals or groups indicating that certain areas of the business are underperforming and action is required. Most applications allow you to assign owners (and persons responsible for data entry) to automate the data collection and remind them if data, comments, or assessments have not been entered. You might want the software to support action and include activity or project management functionality that allows you to track progress against strategic objectives. Some organizations love and fully embrace the data-push concept and workflows, whereas others feel that this approach is too intrusive and doesn't fit with their current culture. Sometimes it is a good idea to start without the automated emails and let people get used to the system and the information first.

Security and Access Control

You need to decide about the level of security needed in the system; some organizations openly share all aspects of their strategic performance with all employees; others require very tight security.

Technical Specifications

The technical requirements depend on the existing information and communication infrastructure in your organization. Any new piece of software should support the existing desktop or network operating system. For a strategic performance management application, it can be important to be able to extract data from existing data sources. This can be a major obstacle for any implementation. It is a good idea to involve the IT department in the discussion about technical requirements.

User Interface and Data Presentation

Here you have to decide about your visualization and data presentation needs.

Applications vary between very graphical to more text and tables based. One of the most important aspects is the display of strategy maps and cause-and-effect relationships. We recommend going for interactive and dynamic visualizations, in which the underlying data are linked to the different elements and the connection means something. Some tools just display graphics without any real data, drill-down, or impact analysis functionality. Dynamic maps allow you to use them as a powerful communication tool with traffic lighting and even the opportunity to test assumed relationships mathematically.

Analysis Functionality

Tools offer different levels of analysis capabilities, stretching from simple drill-down capabilities to multidimensional analysis, complex statistical functionality, forecasting, and even simulations. Organizations that require more complex analysis functionality often have tools for this already in place and have to decide whether to integrate or replace those. Analysis functionality also includes the number of graphical displays (form bar charts to advanced 3-D charts). Requirements in terms of charts and graphs depend on the indicators the organization tracks and their visualization requirements. It is especially important to include the business analysts in this discussion.

Service

Vendors offer different levels of service. Some offer no implementation support and instead partner with consulting companies to provide this. Other vendors offer comprehensive services including their own implementation service, consulting, international service hotlines, and so on. Organizations need to be clear how much support they want and whether the vendor or their partners can deliver this.

Future

Here the organization considers the future developments and release frequency of the product, which might indicate the vendor's attention and commitment to the product. It is also important to understand the future vision of the software vendor, which will influence the direction of any future product development. In an ideal case the future view of strategic performance management would be similar for the vendor and your organization in order to ensure future compatibility. API suggests table 10.1 as a useful two-dimensional matrix for assessing available software products against company requirements.

DEVELOPING AN IT STRATEGY

The following eight key steps might be useful for developing an IT strategy to support a Balanced Scorecard implementation.

1. Understand the Requirements of the Solution Determine who needs to use the scorecard system, who should have access to it, how it will be communicated and reported. This will allow managers to create an initial functional specification for the solution.

2. Identify What Systems Are Available Look at the current reporting mechanisms in the organization and identify how they interrelate and share data. This will provide managers with a view as to what they already have and what additional measures and data would need to be added. This is specifically the case with current reporting systems.

TABLE 10.1   API two-dimensional matrix for assessing software

Criteria	Weight	Product A	Product B	Product ...
Costs and pricing subcriterion I subcriterion II ...	 0–10 0–10			
Company and product subcriterion I subcriterion II ...	 0–10 0–10			
Scalability needs subcriterion I subcriterion II ...	 0–10 0–10			
User interface subcriterion I subcriterion II ...	 0–10 0–10			
Flexibility needs subcriterion I subcriterion II ...	 0–10 0–10			
Communication and collaboration needs subcriterion I subcriterion II ...	 0–10 0–10			
Security and access control subcriterion I subcriterion II ...	 0–10 0–10			
Technical needs subcriterion I subcriterion II ...	 0–10 0–10			
Etc.	0–10 0–10			
Etc.	0–10 0–10			
Score:				

3. Investigate the Market Many options are available, and time spent reviewing these will help managers to answer the questions of what exactly they want and whether they can do it in house.

4. Build a Prototype A pilot system is a valuable way for ensuring that users get a sense of the look and feel of the solution and make changes before a rollout.

5. Agree Timescale and Scope of Solution Outline and agree with the business what can be delivered and when. It may be that a first delivery is just a reporting mechanism with no analytics. The system may still require manual input from various data feeds and may be what the business wants anyway. Test systems design assumptions to ensure deliverability.

6. Put in Place the Appropriate Support Build support into the scorecard systems project from the outset.

This will invariably involve a combination of resources from IT and the business to ensure the right balance between functional scorecard and technical aspects of support. Support staff should be trained in necessary skills and know-how to ensure that the process works correctly. This is an essential element of IT strategy.

7. Prioritize Ease of Use and Add Functionality Over Time Be sure to focus on ease of use and presentation first. These are system features that users rate highly and are essential to gaining their buyin and encouraging use of the system. Keep working on systems functionality.

8. Be Prepared to Evolve the Solution Continually As does the scorecard itself, the solution will need to evolve. This continuing requirement needs to be anticipated because the scorecard is a dynamic framework and systems need to keep pace with its evolution.

STRATEGY AND RISK MANAGEMENT

In earlier chapters of this book (most notably chapter 3), we have made much of the importance of aligning strategy management with risk management: that is, understanding your risk appetite in light of your strategic goals.

We can expect over the coming years that more and more software solutions will be made available to capture the integration of strategy and risk. One such solution already exists and is provided by the U.K.-headquartered Manigent, a specialist performance and risk management consultancy delivering integrated business and technology solutions. The organization has developed a technology solution called StratexPoint, which is an enterprisewide performance and risk management solution. Built on Microsoft's SharePoint platform, StratexPoint is positioned to help organizations to clarify their strategic objectives and determine how much risk they are prepared to accept in the execution of their strategy.

According to Andrew Smart, founder of Manigent, "StratexPoint enables senior executives to effectively manage the risk and reward equation for their organizations, leading to better management discussions, decision making, and action taking."

Some of the activities supported by StratexPoint include:

- defining Strategy Maps and strategic objectives
- defining Balanced Scorecards, with KPIs, initiatives, and actions
- defining and managing key and emerging risks using risk maps
- defining and monitoring risk appetite
- calculating, managing, and monitoring the alignment of risk exposure to appetite
- conducting risk and control self-assessments
- managing and monitoring KPIs, key risk indicators, and key control indicators using organizational and personal dashboards
- defining, managing, and monitoring the initiatives and actions that make up the organizational change agenda
- defining and managing operational processes and systems, and monitoring their performance, risk, and controls.

The StratexPoint solution is an interesting pointer to how technology will develop to support business decision-making processes where strategy and risk are fully integrated.

CONCLUSION

Positioning the scorecard as a fully fledged strategy management system requires automation, and in this chapter we have explained its importance. Automation can make the scorecard a near real-time reporting system, and is particularly powerful as a mechanism for best-practice sharing. It also significantly lessens the amount of effort required to collect and report performance data and overcomes the problems caused by errors in data input.

We also stressed that there is much that automation cannot do, in particular it cannot create the Strategy Map and Balanced Scorecard, and is an aid rather than a replacement for the important managerial discussions around scorecard performance. We look at reviewing performance to the Balanced Scorecard framework in the next chapter, where we also highlight the requirement for a fundamental reappraisal of planning and the alignment of budgets with strategy.

Finally, we pointed to the fact that powerful technology solutions are developing to integrate strategy management with risk management, something we can expect much more of going forward.

Self-Assessment Checklist

As previously, simply indicate your agreement with the two opposing statements in table 10.2. Checking number 1 indicates a strong agreement with the statement to the left, while checking number 7 indicates a strong agreement with the statement to the right. The more numbers to the right are checked, the greater the perceived challenges.

TABLE 10.2 Self-assessment checklist

	1	2	3	4	5	6	7	
In this organization we fully understand the benefits of automation								In this organization we do not understand the benefits of automation
We understand that software cannot build the scorecard system								We expect the software system to build our scorecard for us
We have a well-thought-through criteria for software selection								We have not thought through the criteria for software selection
We have a well-understood IT strategy for supporting scorecard rollout								We do not have an IT strategy for supporting scorecard rollout

ENDNOTES

1. See www.actuate.com.
2. Bernard Marr, *Selecting Balanced Scorecard Software Solutions* (Milton Keynes: Advanced Performance Institute, 2007). See www.ap-institute.com.

CHAPTER 11

Aligning Budgeting and Planning with Strategy Through the Balanced Scorecard

EXECUTIVE SUMMARY

1. Most organizations have difficulty in hardwiring the budgeting process to strategic management through the Balanced Scorecard.
2. There has to be a mechanism for linking the budgeting process to strategy for the scorecard to become part of the fabric of strategic management.
3. Although we can consider how the Balanced Scorecard and budget work best together it is worth noting that although we are confident in the efficacy of the scorecard, we cannot claim the same for the budget.
4. We point to many shortcomings of the conventional budget.
5. One of the fundamental shortcomings of the budgeting process is that it confines the performance horizon to one year. Quite simply, strategy cannot be shoehorned into a financial year.
6. There are many reasons the scorecard should drive the budget. The most compelling reason is that this will help to bring clarity to major investment decisions and the allocation of scarce resources.
7. Managers must understand the connection between financial resource allocation and empowering and encouraging individuals to make strategy happen.
8. An increasingly popular alternative to conventional budgeting is the use of rolling forecasts.
9. A key element of the scorecard concept is the use of quarterly strategic reviews both to monitor how well the strategy is being implemented and to ensure the strategy itself is still relevant to external market conditions.

10. We also describe other forms of meetings that should be deployed to effectively manage performance.

11. It is proposed that a pot called stratex is created to safeguard strategic investments. Stratex therefore has the same importance as the now common opex and capex.

INTRODUCTION

A subcomponent of "make strategy a continual process"—principle four of the five principles of the strategy-focused organization—is "link budgets and strategies," (see chapter 2 for more on the principles of the strategy-focused organization). Yet anyone who has observed the Balanced Scorecard since its inception will have noted the difficulties most organizations have in hardwiring the budgeting process to strategic management through the Balanced Scorecard.

But there has to be a mechanism for linking the budgeting process to strategy for the scorecard to become part of the fabric of strategic management.

Without tying the budget (and indeed other planning processes, such as mid-term planning) to the scorecard process, it will be impossible to create a strategy-focused organization. Organizations need to be aware of the value of linking how budgets are designed to the targeting of scorecard metrics. This can be done by working directly with those involved in creating the budgets throughout the process of creating the scorecard. They need to work together to make sure that the two processes are aligned each year and are reviewed accordingly. This also means that they need to create the reporting mechanisms and timings together.

THE SHORTCOMINGS OF THE BUDGET

However, although we can consider how the Balanced Scorecard and budget work best together, it is worth noting that although we are confident in the efficacy of the scorecard, we cannot claim the same for the budget.

Indeed, we can point to many failings of the typical budgeting process. As just a few examples: it takes up to six months to create, is way too detailed, is typically out of date the day it is published, ties up scarce resources that could be better deployed generating profits, and it is focused on beating internally generated targets, rather than beating the competition. Moreover, within most organizations, once the budget is in place, managers tend to focus on performance to the budget, rather than find ways to improve the performance of the business.

From a sector perspective, the problems with being overly budget focused were highlighted by one participant in the research report: *Managing Strategic Performance in Banks and Financial Services Firms.*[1] "We only use a rear-view-mirror approach—assessing whether people have achieved their budgeted objectives. We rarely look into the future and we rarely put this into the context of our competitors. This means we might all sit there patting ourselves on the back for achieving what we set out to achieve—when we could have done twice as well. The trouble with this introverted approach is that we don't re-forecast our targets or honestly put our performance into relation to our competitors."

One of the fundamental shortcomings of the budgeting process is that it confines the performance horizon to one year. According to the budgeting process, the world begins on January 1 and ends on December 31 (or however the fiscal year is defined), with a brand new world coming into being the next day.

OUT OF STEP WITH STRATEGY

Taking such a restricted view of managing an organization is clearly nonsensical, yet it is precisely how most companies operate. Among the myriad reasons this approach doesn't make sense, perhaps none is more damning than an annualized view of performance being out of step with the multiyear perspective required for the successful execution of strategy. Quite simply, strategy cannot be shoehorned into a financial year. The cul-de-sac where many organizations end up, where performance is kept below its potential, occurs because although they set long-term strategic goals, implementation is stymied by the diktats of delivering to budgetary goals enshrined within the annual performance contract.

One Asia-Pacific practitioner notes: "There is a fairly well-founded belief from most planners that planning is something of a retrofit to the budget. There's a strong view that budgeting is something you do first and then you plan once you've agreed the budget. What happens is that the budget is carved up arbitrarily and then people are told to go and plan with it."

He continues: "This is patently back to front. You should have strategy and planning done first and then figure out what to do with the budget to make the strategy happen. Then you get involved in the tradeoffs around how to service the most important strategies. This is a markedly different approach than slicing up the budget pie and then telling people to go away and plan with the piece they've been given."

Only when strategy and budgeting are accorded their proper hierarchical positions does it become possible to be a strategy-focused organization—the opposite of the budget-focused organization.

THE SCORECARD DRIVING THE BUDGET

Clearly, the next step is to ensure that the budget process supports (and is therefore subservient to) the strategic objectives that are captured within the Strategy Map.

There are many reasons the scorecard should drive the budget. The most compelling is that this will help to bring clarity to major investment decisions and the allocation of scarce resources. This brings us back to the point made in chapter 6 that it is at the level of strategic initiatives that the real work of scorecard implementation takes place. This is where attention is focused on improving performance against those vital few objectives that will make the telling difference to strategy execution. Using the scorecard as a filtering mechanism, companies can decide either to veto projects that fall outside the strategic priorities they have set or to spread them out over a longer period.

Case Example: Bank Indonesia

For instance, consider how Bank Indonesia ensures that strategy drives the budget. Within the bank the internal finance directorate develops a multiyear (long term) budget forecast based on the strategic plan. "To do this, business units especially those with strategic initiatives are required to develop budget projections for several years (or until completion of the initiatives)," explains Dyah Nastiti Kusumowardani, the bank's director, strategy planning, although she adds that this is not always an easy task because it is still a challenge to get all managers to assume a long-term mindset.

Case Example: Depository Trust & Clearing Corporation

As a further example, consider the New York-headquartered Depository Trust & Clearing Corporation (DTCC). A 2009 inductee into the prestigious Palladium Balanced Scorecard Hall of Fame (membership is restricted to those that demonstrate breakthrough performance using the Balanced Scorecard), DTCC is the world's largest security depository, providing custody and asset servicing for 3.5 million securities issued (valued at $33.9 trillion in 2009) from the U.S. and 121 other countries and territories. In 2009, DTCC settled $1.4 quadrillion worth of transactions involving equities, bonds, U.S. Treasuries, mortgage-backed securities, mutual funds, insurance contracts, commercial paper, and other money-market instruments.

As described in the *Palladium Balanced Scorecard Hall of Fame Report 2010*,[2] the Balanced Scorecard (which DTCC calls a Balanced Business Scorecard) was recommended in 2003 by the then chief operating officer (now chairman and CEO) as a way to bring strategic and operational measures together under one framework and to support progress toward common goals.

Developed in 2004, and formally launched enterprisewide in 2006 after successful pilots in 2005, the DTCC corporate scorecard comprises the following four perspectives: stakeholder/financial; customer/service delivery; strategic positioning; employee/enablers. The strategic positioning perspective houses the organization's strategic themes: promote the core franchise; broaden scope geographically; broaden the public suite; broaden the client base.

The *Hall of Fame Report* states that: "Strategic initiatives for each theme are assigned to the appropriate business unit or functional area within a specified subsidiary and are given an investment level and a target completion date. For example, 2009 initiatives associated with the Product Suite theme included implementation of an over-the-counter (OTC) derivatives confirmation partnership with Markit, a leading global financial institution. The service was launched in September 2009 as MarkitServ."

DTCC's planning cycle begins in the second quarter with strategic planning, business planning takes place in Q3, and target setting and budgeting unfold over Q3 and Q4. Planning oversight is conducted year round.

Each one of five groups: the management committee, strategy council, business planning committee, service delivery policy and planning committee, and BBS steering committee, plays a specific role in planning and execution. For instance, the management committee's responsibilities include aligning the values, strategies, plans, and budgets endorsed by the board of directors. The strategy council identifies emerging market opportunities and threats, and develops strategy. The BBS committee defines measures and targets with the help of measure owners.

Since launching the scorecard DTCC has recorded many impressive results. As examples, product revenue has grown fivefold and customer satisfaction has risen from 73 percent to 91 percent (against an industry average of 87 percent). Moreover, the number of new clients brought on board and prepared for full production has skyrocketed from 10 per year to 332—an increase of more than 3,000 percent. Employee engagement (as measured by the per cent of employees who see DTCC as a good place to work) has increased from 55 percent to 70 percent, against a financial services industry average of 63 percent.

DEVOLVED RESPONSIBILITY

At a deeper level, the scorecard makes fundamental assumptions about the role of the budget and resource allocation, which have not yet been made explicit enough in the scorecard literature thus far. These assumptions, though, are critically important to getting the most from the scorecard. Simply, organizations have to devolve responsibility through the organization, giving people the opportunity to discuss and debate what their targets should be. These should not be fixed for the year, because flexibility is a key strength of the scorecard. There should then be a rich discussion on which resources are required to meet those targets and people must be held accountable for their performance.

Managers must understand the connection between financial resource allocation and empowering and encouraging individuals to make strategy happen. You cannot make "strategy everyone's everyday job" without empowerment.

ALTERNATIVES TO CONVENTIONAL BUDGETING

Having become increasingly frustrated with the budget as a constraint of strategy, some companies are abandoning conventional budgeting altogether in favor of a more dynamic approach.

Rolling Forecasts

An increasingly popular alternative to conventional budgeting is the use of rolling forecasts whereby the company typically forecasts six-to-eight quarters into the future while operating through the first quarter in the sequence. In this way, there is always a timely multiquarter future forecast available for reference, irrespective of the time of year. The advantage of this approach is that corporate planners and business unit managers can, based on current experience, revise their future quarter prediction (already forecasted). This can be done quickly, and results, so users report, in more realistic forecasts because managers are not evaluated on their performance to a fixed annual budget. They will also have less reason to play the budgeting game of setting readily achievable targets, a common complaint in most organizations.

The rolling forecast approach can be used to link financial allocation directly to identified strategic requirements. One of the key goals of using the Balanced Scorecard is to respond rapidly to a sudden change in the competitive or economic environment. An annual budgeting process that is separate from strategic planning makes rapid realignment extraordinarily difficult. However, being able to reshape organizational resource allocation frequently, yet within a controlled financial framework (i.e., the rolling forecast) gives an opportunity to create a more effective strategy-focused organization.

It should be noted that the use of rolling forecasts does not require the abandoning of the budget (which is a nonstarter for most organizations—especially in the U.S., where companies are driven by the reporting of quarterly results). Many companies are creating a "de-emphasized" budget—less detail, less time to create—which they use as a "stick in the ground," relying on the rolling forecast and strategic review as the primary method for managing the business. And when quarterly rolling forecasts are deployed, there is always a forecast to the end of the year—as well as to the subsequent quarters.

Strategic Reviews

Furthermore, by monitoring performance through the Balanced Scorecard, organizations receive continual updates on how effectively their strategy is being implemented and can identify where rapid change is required. A key element of the scorecard concept is the use of strategic reviews both to monitor how well the strategy is being implemented and to ensure the strategy itself is still relevant to external market conditions, and to either tweak objectives or measures accordingly, stop or start strategic initiatives (with the implications for resource allocation), or signal a more fundamental strategic shift.

Case Example: Bank Indonesia

As a case example, to review performance continually, Bank Indonesia conducts strategy review meeting quarterly and twice-yearly. For the quarterly reviews, what is essentially the bank's Office of Strategy Management (OSM) meets with KPI managers to review its performance.

For the twice-yearly meetings, the office facilitates a review between the deputy governors and the heads of each business unit. "In the review, the office identifies issues and their implications for the achievement of the strategy," says Dyah Nastiti Kusumowardani, director, strategy planning. "Then we discuss the required action plans and assign accountability. This is done to monitor and manage performance so to achieve our ultimate goals."

Case Example: Nordea Bank

Sweden-headquartered Nordea Bank provides one of the world's best examples of integrating the scorecard with performance reviews and rolling forecasts—while also jettisoning the budget.[3]

In 2000, the new senior team (of what was then a new company born from a merger) wanted a planning and performance management process that was more action and future oriented, was more flexible, and gave them a continuous view of performance.

"Our then CEO was particularly keen on change because he felt a calendar-year-driven process made it difficult for him to clearly communicate to the market what this new company was trying to achieve," says senior vice president, head of group planning, Sven Edvinsson:

In 2001, the organization launched an integrated Planning and Performance Management Model (PPMM), see figure 11.1. So let's explain how PPMM works in practice. We will begin with the Balanced Scorecard, which is Nordea's core tool to drive strategy into business targets and actions.

As demonstrated in figure 11.2, Nordea's Strategy Map comprises the four perspectives of financial, customer, internal process, and learning. These perspectives set out to deliver the ultimate objective of "sustainable growth in economic profit" through the three themes of:

- ensure growth of income
- ensure operational excellence, strict cost management and reduced complexity
- ensure capital efficiency and high credit portfolio quality.

Within the Balanced Scorecard system, each focus area (as Nordea calls strategic objectives) is supported by a focus area description, KPI, target, and strategic initiative.

So, as an example, the focus area: "reduce complexity" has the description: "We need to simplify, unify and consolidate internal processes in all service and support units in order to reduce complexity and become One Bank." The KPI is "percentage of transformation and structural cost initiatives on track." A percentage target is supported by a strategic initiative to "identify major processes for best practice implementation."

A key factor of the PPMM is that the Balanced Scorecard is the only process for annual target setting within Nordea. Targets are set during an annual strategic review and update in which the economic, market and competitive situation is analyzed, with the appropriate revision to the group-level Strategy Map and Balanced Scorecard.

The targets are stretching, so, crucially, they are based on what is possible, not on what is forecasted.

"The Balanced Scorecard system is a logical process for target setting. It is based on a thorough assessment of what is possible in the markets we serve," explains Edvinsson.

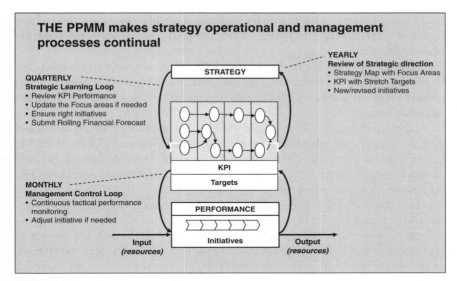

FIGURE 11.1   The PPMM Model

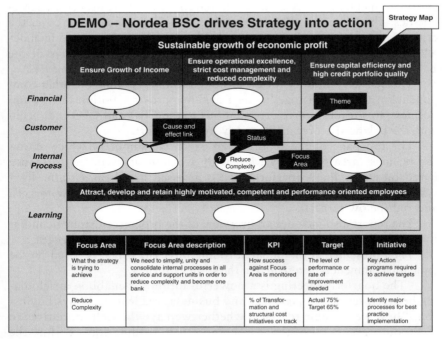

FIGURE 11.2   Nordea's Strategy Map

The targets are also aligned to a three-year planning horizon, which forms a better linkage between long-term goals and short-term strategic objectives.

Nordea's confidence in the Balanced Scorecard is demonstrated through it having about 1,700 scorecards organizationwide, with about 1,200 almost identical scorecards within the essentially homogenous retail banking branches.

Edvinsson believes that to get the best out of the balanced scorecard process requires the adoption of a rolling financial forecast (RFF). The RFF, he says, serves as a powerful mechanism to review how Balanced Scorecard initiatives and objectives are affecting financial performance regularly. The RFF is the second component of Nordea's PPMM.

Nordea works to a five-quarter RFF. The forecast is updated each quarter and is based on the latest possible information from the business. This information includes performance to the Balanced Scorecard, the impact of corrective actions taken in the previous quarters, and managers' assessment of the market and trading conditions. RFFs are created at division, business area, and group levels.

Crucially, the RFF is remarkably simple. It is essentially an income statement including specifications tailored to business area-specific characteristics. The RFF typically comprises less than 10 line items that cover the critical drivers of revenues, costs, and volumes. The forecast also includes KPIs that are aligned to the KPIs within the financial perspective of the Balanced Scorecard.

The quarterly strategy review meeting facilitates pulling the other components of the PPMM together as a dynamic process. Within this forum, business area leaders make presentations to the CEO and CFO that begin with the Balanced Scorecard quarterly strategy report.

The top page of the report is an executive summary which shows the business area's Strategy Map with a commentary on performance based on traffic lights (performance is assessed based on a traffic light system of green (on or ahead of target), amber (slightly below target), and red (below target)).

The report also includes an overview of the progress of strategic initiatives and an assessment of market, competitive, and internal challenges.

Then presented is the updated rolling forecast, which is based on the data and commentary presented in the strategy review.

"The quarterly meeting is a powerful forum for enabling a rich dialog between senior management and business area leaders," says Edvinsson. "In it we are able to assess whether we have the right initiatives to meet our targets, test the cause-and-effect assumptions within the

Strategy Map, and launch corrective actions to close any identified performance gaps."

Nordea also has monthly management meetings in which costs can be analyzed to a greater level of detail than in the quarterly meeting. The organization calls this "continual tactical performance monitoring," and essentially serves as an added or fourth dimension to the PPMM. How yearly, quarterly and monthly meetings work together is shown in figure 11.3.

Types of Meetings

Strategic reviews represent one of three different meeting types that are implemented to align operational and strategic activities fully, according to Kaplan and Norton: the other two being operational reviews and strategy testing and adapting. As shown in table 11.1, these meetings have different information requirements, frequency, attendees, focus, and goals. For example, the goal of an operational review is to respond to short-term problems and promote continuous improvement; the goal of the strategic review is to fine-tune strategy and make midterm adjustments; the goal of the strategy testing and adapting meeting is to improve or transform strategy.

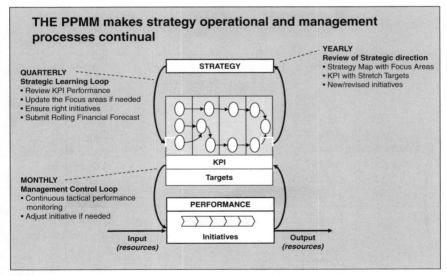

FIGURE 11.3 How Nordea's meetings work together

TABLE 11.1 Kaplan and Norton suggested meetings

	Meeting type		
	Operational review	Strategy review	Strategy testing and adapting
Information requirements	Dashboards for KPIs; weekly and monthly financial summaries	Strategy Map and Balanced Scorecard reports	Strategy map, Balanced Scorecard, ABC profitability reports, analytic studies of strategic hypotheses, external and competitive analyses
Frequency	Daily, twice weekly, weekly, or monthly, depending on business cycle	Monthly	Annually (perhaps quarterly for fast-moving industries)
Attendees	Departmental and functional personnel; senior management for financial reviews	Senior management team, strategic theme owners, strategy management officer	Senior management team, strategic theme owners, functional and planning specialists, business unit heads
Focus	Identify and solve operational problems	Manage strategy implementation issues Assess progress of strategic initiatives	Test and adapt strategy based on causal analytics; Use scenario planning to evaluate tail risk events; War games to test against competitors' strategies
Goal	Respond to short-term problems and promote continuous improvements	Fine tune strategy; make midcourse adaptations	Improve or transform strategy

Advanced Performance Institute Suggested Meetings

Strategy review or revision meetings are also part of a suite of performance improvement meetings suggested by Bernard Marr and James Creelman in their book *More with Less: Maximizing Value in the Public Sector*,[4] the others being strategic performance improvement meetings, operational performance improvement meetings, and personal performance improvement meetings (see table 11.2). These meetings are interdependent and the content and outputs influence each other. However, each of these meetings has its own clear purpose and each of them differ in terms of time horizon, frequency, outputs, focus, and supporting performance information.

Strategy Review Meetings   These meetings are used to revise and renew the strategy. The time horizon of these meetings is to look one-to-three years ahead (although this is dependent on the volatility of the market). The objective of these meetings is to agree on a new or revised Balanced Scorecard.

The meeting is the opportunity for the executive team and the directors to get together and agree on their new or revised strategy. The executive team would take the insights from various strategic analyses and performance data to firm up their strategy. It is usually recommended to also have the leader of the corporate performance management team, or OSM, and relevant performance management analysts in the meeting. These individuals can provide answers to any data queries and analyses. Strategy revision meetings tend to be held offsite and usually last one or two days. As with all these meetings proposed here, the emphasis is not on data presentation, but on decision making and reaching strategic agreement.

Strategic Performance Improvement Meetings   These meetings have the purpose of discussing the execution of the existing strategy. Here, the overall strategic assumptions are not questioned, instead, the meetings take place to fine tune elements of the strategy and to revise the strategy execution plans. These meetings revise the operational activities of the strategic objectives on the scorecard. This would involve decisions about reallocating resources and refocusing projects. The time horizon of these discussions is medium term, meaning between one and six months ahead.

Usually, these meetings would take place monthly and are attended by the executive team together with directors and head of departments. Similarly to the strategy revision meetings, Marr and Creelman recommend that members of the corporate performance management or OSM team and relevant performance management analysts attend the meeting to provide answers to any data queries and analyses. Strategic performance

TABLE 11.2 Four types of meetings as suggested by the Advanced Performance Institute

	Type of meeting			
	Strategy revision meeting	Strategy performance review meeting	Operational performance review meeting	Personal performance improvement meeting
Purpose	To review and revise the strategy and to agree the content of the Balanced Scorecard	To discuss the execution of the existing strategy To fine-tune the strategy and review and revise the existing strategy and execution plans	To discuss and respond to short-term operational issues To discuss and find solutions to "burning issues"	Forums in which employees and their line managers can discuss the strategic priorities for the next year
Frequency	Annually	Monthly	Daily, twice-weekly, or weekly, as required	Annually or twice-yearly
Time horizon	One-to-three years ahead	One-to-six months ahead	One week to a month	One year
Information requirements	Insight from various strategic analyses and performance data	Insights from various strategic analyses with performance data. Updates from strategy execution programs	Operational analytics, performance to operational targets. Operational performance feedback from various employees	Personal objectives and development plans along with departmental and enterprise balanced scorecards (to ensure alignment between individual objectives and those of the department and enterprise
Attendees	Senior team and the leader of the corporate performance management team (or OSM) and relevant performance management analyst	Executive team together with directors and heads of departments as well as members of corporate performance management team (or OSM) and relevant performance management analyst	Departmental managers, functional supervisors and relevant employees	Individual employee and line manager

improvement meetings can also be used to model and test assumed causal relationships among different strategic objectives.

Operational Performance Improvement Meetings　These are meetings to discuss and respond to short-term operational issues. Often called "performance clinics," they represent the frequent forums in which departmental managers and functional supervisors and personnel get together to talk about the "burning issues." In some organizations these meetings take place daily, in others weekly or twice weekly. The discussions and decisions that take place in these meetings have a short time horizon (a week to one month). The meetings can focus on specific operational performance issues or can focus on project performance. Operational performance improvement meetings are the engine rooms of an organization in which the operational decisions take place and in which any short-term operational issues are discussed and resolved.

Personal Performance Improvement Meetings　Most of the dreaded personal performance and development reviews that take place in organizations are purely administrative human resources (HR) tickbox exercises. The atmosphere is cringeworthy and the outcomes are not very constructive and tend to demotivate much more than they motivate. At most they tend to produce records of suggested training needs, which are sent to the HR department and only ever see the light of day again at the next round of meetings.

Here, Marr and Creelman suggest a different kind of meeting: personal performance improvement meetings. There should be forums in which employees and their line managers can discuss the strategic priorities for the next year. The time horizon for these meetings tends to be between six and 12 months and they usually take place annually. More recently, we have seen organizations that have successfully introduced six-monthly personal performance improvement meetings. These meetings are a great opportunity to engage everybody in the organization in a strategic discussion and ensure that any personal objectives, performance plans, and development plans are aligned with the overall priorities of the organization.

REPORTING RISK

As cited in chapter 3, Andrew Smart, CEO of the U.K.-headquartered management consultancy Manigent, states that a key step in integrating strategic management (for which he recommends using a Strategy Map) and risk management is the completion of a risk assessment. "Risk assessments at this strategic level are often conducted on a quarterly, biannual or even annual basis. Between assessments indicators can be used to monitor changes in risk profiles (key risk indicators) and changes in control effectiveness (key control indicators)." He adds that he is seeing organizations accelerating risk assessments from "relatively setpiece events to more continuous, rolling processes that may be conducted on a monthly basis."[5]

As Smart suggests, risk assessments play a crucial role in ensuring a financial services institution successfully implements sustainable strategies, and should certainly be used alongside other performance review meetings.

STRATEX ~~strategy + operations~~

As cited in chapter 6, a new idea that has emerged from Kaplan and Norton's fifth book: *The Execution Premium: Linking Strategy to Operations for Competitive Advantage*[6] is that of strategic expenditure, or stratex. They argue that such is the importance now assigned to strategic initiatives that organizations now require a resource pot known as stratex in addition to the common opex (operating expenditure) and capex (capital expenditure). More than anything, the idea of stratex has emerged as a powerful mechanism for protecting investments into long-term strategic initiatives from being cut to meet short-term budget targets. A formal process to determine the level of stratex enables companies to subject strategic initiatives to rigorous, disciplined reviews, just like those conducted for capex spending on tangible assets.

According to Kaplan and Norton this discretionary spending can be guided by rule of thumb—for example 5 percent of sales. Executives use similar rules of thumb to establish funding levels for categories such as general and administrative expenses and research and development expenditures. If spending falls short of the stratex target, then the organization might be underfunding its future growth. If spending exceeds this number, there might be a question about the adequacy of the controls.

Kaplan and Norton also recommend that stratex should be a separate authorized line item on the company's internal budget or financial forecast.

They write: "Executing strategy requires that the portfolio of initiatives be executed simultaneously in a co-ordinated manner. This requires explicit funding for the portfolio of strategic initiatives. The traditional budgeting system focuses on the resources provided to existing organizational functions and business units, and the accountability and performance of these units. The strategic investments, for initiatives that cross functions and business units, must be removed from operational budgets and managed separately by the executive team. The creation of a special budget category called stratex . . . facilitates this process." See figure 11.4 for the stratex model.

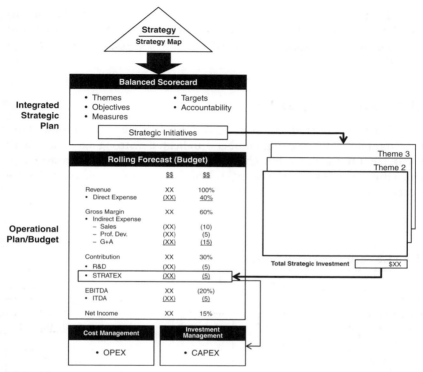

FIGURE 11.4   Stratex model

CONCLUSION

This chapter has explained that the traditional budgeting process often stymies attempts to manage strategy execution through the Balanced Scorecard. We have argued that the scorecard should drive the budget, rather than goals on the scorecard being constrained by the budget. Many organizations are looking to break the budget shackles by implementing either a new, improved budgeting process (de-emphasized), while placing more emphasis on the use of forecasting and in better allocating or reallocating resources through a quarterly strategic review. We also outlined other performance-focused meetings that should, or might, be conducted, such as for risk assessments.

Moreover, we explained that the idea of stratex has emerged as a way to protect the funding of long-term strategic investments from pressures to meet short-term budgetary goals.

In the next, concluding chapter, we pull together all the key learnings of this book and provide an action roadmap for building and implementing a Balanced Scorecard framework—or turning strategy into action.

Self-Assessment Checklist

As previously, simply indicate your agreement with the two opposing statements in table 11.3. Checking number 1 indicated a strong agreement with the statement to the left, while checking number 7 indicated a strong agreement with the statement to the right. The more numbers to the right are checked, the greater the perceived challenges.

TABLE 11.3 Self-assessment checklist

	1	2	3	4	5	6	7	
In this organization budgeting and strategy are fully aligned			✓					In this organization budgeting and strategy are not at all aligned
In this organization the budgeting process is efficient			✓					In this organization the budgeting process is inefficient
We place performance to the strategy above that to the budget				✓				We place performance to the budget above that to the strategy
We make excellent use of rolling forecasts				✓				We do not use rolling forecasts
In this organization we make excellent use of strategic reviews			✓					This organization does not use strategic reviews
We conduct formal risk assessments regarding the delivery of strategic objectives		✓						We do not conduct formal risk assessments regarding the delivery of strategic objectives

ENDNOTES

1. Bernard Marr, *Managing Strategic Performance in Banks and Financial Services Firms: from Going Through the Motions to Best Practice* (Cranfield, U.K.: Cranfield School of Management, 2007).
2. Palladium, *Strategy Execution Champions, The Palladium Balanced Scorecard Hall of Fame Report, 2010* (Cambridge, Mass: Harvard Business Publishing/Palladium, 2010).
3. James Creelman, *Reinventing Planning and Budgeting for the Adaptive Organization* (London: Business Intelligence, 2006).
4. Bernard Marr and James Creelman, *More with Less: Maximizing Value in the Public Sector* (Basingstoke, U.K.: Palgrave Macmillan, 2010).
5. Andrew Smart, *Aligning Risk Management and Exposure: The New Paradigm of Strategic Execution* (London: Manigent, 2009).
6. Robert S. Kaplan and David P. Norton, *The Execution Premium: Linking Strategy to Operations for Competitive Advantage* (Cambridge, Mass.: Harvard Business Press, 2008).

CHAPTER 12

Conclusion and Action Roadmap

EXECUTIVE SUMMARY

1. This concluding chapter is organized into two parts. Part one considers the future of the Balanced Scorecard within financial services organizations, while part two provides a six-phase roadmap to help the reader plan his or her Balanced Scorecard journey.
2. To ensure that the credit crunch does not happen again, there must be better oversight and control of decision-making processes and greater insights into what is driving them.
3. Without question, financial institutions must be much better at integrating strategic management with risk management.
4. Corporate boards must do their oversight duties much more effectively in the future. A well-architected Strategy Map and Balanced Scorecard can be a powerful framework for achieving this.
5. The roadmap for planning the Balanced Scorecard journey is:
   - defining the scope and relevance of the scorecard for your organization
   - winning support and assessing readiness for a scorecard program
   - building the capabilities and resources to implement a program
   - managing the strategy mapping and scorecard process
   - managing the scorecard implementation process
   - making strategy a continual process.
6. In the final analysis, financial institutions must do a much better job in balancing the "short term" with the "long term." Hopefully, usage of the Balanced Scorecard within financial institutions (most notably banks) will evolve to ensure that the decisions that led to the global financial meltdown will not be repeated.

PART ONE: THE FUTURE OF THE BALANCED SCORECARD WITHIN FINANCIAL SERVICES ORGANIZATIONS

Introduction

Within the introductory chapter of this book, we described how the so-called "credit crunch" of 2008 uncovered critical failings in how banks, and other financial institutions were being managed. As the report *Climbing Out of the Credit Crunch*,[1] by the Association of Certified Chartered Accountants, noted, a lack of proper corporate governance oversight had led to a culture of short-term thinking (fueled by inappropriate remuneration and incentive systems) and a blindness to the extraordinary risks that were being taken (and that led to catastrophic consequences for banks and for national economies).

Clearly—and for the benefit of all sectors and industries—it is critical that the credit crunch does not happen again. Such an assurance relies on two key interventions:

- Substantially better oversight and control have to be inculcated to ensure that banks are being managed appropriately for the benefit of shareholders (and consequently the wider community).
- There must be much greater insight into what is driving the decisions that should lead to sustainable financial performance; with particular regard with the potential impact of the risks that are being taken.

Learning from Past Mistakes: Balancing Strategic Goals with Risk Management

This book has explained that the Balanced Scorecard offers financial services organizations a framework for ensuring that these requirements are being met. But as we have explained in this book, since the Balanced Scorecard was first introduced back in the early 1990s, the financial services industry has been among its heaviest users—but they *still* didn't see the credit crunch coming. In short, their Balanced Scorecard failed to provide early warning signals of the potential impact of present activities on future outcomes, most notably financial. It perhaps took the credit crunch to point up that many organizations (and one would suspect just about all in the financial services industry) needed to make risk much more transparent on their scorecards. As Professor Robert Kaplan said in chapter 3:

The high-level objective in a Balanced Scorecard's financial perspective is growing and sustaining shareholder value. Traditionally, we have advocated two methods to drive shareholder value: revenue growth and productivity improvements. The third method for sustaining shareholder value, missing in many companies' strategies, should be risk management.

Kaplan is presently leading the efforts of the Palladium Group (founded by Dr. David Norton, his co-creator of the Balanced Scorecard system) in better integrating the management of risk in the Balanced Scorecard system. Indeed, also in chapter 3, we quoted this from Kaplan:

Defining a risk management strategic theme highlights risk management as a key component of the company's strategy and makes it visible for resource allocation, monitoring, and discussion at strategy review meetings. I have tentatively concluded, however, that measuring and managing risk differs so substantially from measuring and managing strategy that it may be preferable to develop a completely separate risk scorecard. Strategy is about moving the company forward toward achieving breakthrough performance. The Strategy Map and scorecard provide the roadmap to guide this strategic journey. Risk management, in contrast, is about identifying, avoiding, and overcoming the hurdles that the strategy may encounter along the way. Avoiding risk does not advance the strategy; but risk management can reduce obstacles and barriers that would otherwise prevent the organization from progressing to its strategic destination.[2,3]

But there are others doing innovative and useful work in better marrying risk management and strategy management and using strategy maps and balanced scorecards as central tools in its achievement. We point to the excellent work by the U.K.-based strategy and risk management consultant Manigent. Its work in this field is documented throughout this book. And note the words of CEO Andrew Smart in his white paper, *Aligning Risk Appetite and Exposure. The New Paradigm of Strategic Execution*:

[S]uccessful strategy execution, in a post credit crunch world, will be built on the foundation of balancing risk appetite and exposure within the context of clear strategic objectives. Embracing the new paradigm will enable organizations to answer three critical questions:

1. *What are we trying to achieve, i.e., what are our strategic objectives.*
2. *What level of risk is acceptable to achieve those objectives, i.e., what is our risk appetite?*
3. *What is our current level of risk, i.e., what is our risk exposure?*

In chapter 5, we made much of the importance of identifying key risk indicators (KRIs) and capturing and reporting these within a Balanced Scorecard. When KRIs are part of a well-focused risk management theme in the scorecard system, it will provide all in the organization, from the corporate board through the executive committee to lower-level managers and employees with insight into how risk is being managed within the organization and how staff are being trained to manage risk (as described within the learning and growth perspective). This will help ensure that the decisions made are appropriate and based on a thorough understanding of the inherent risks.

Better Board Oversight in the Future

It should also be noted that a properly architected enterprise Strategy Map and Balanced Scorecard can also serve as a powerful governance tool for corporate boards of directors, therefore providing much better performance management and the management of risk. The board will receive an excellent and concise view of corporate financial performance and the non-financial drivers of that performance and, of course, with a risk theme incorporated. As a governance tool, this is clearly much more useful to corporate boards than the weighty, opaque, and overly detailed board packs that they typically receive before board meetings. Clearly, these board packs were of little value in the runup to the credit crunch.

Moreover, strategy maps and balanced scorecards can be created for the board itself (and constituent committees). This provides clarity into how the board is dispatching its own duties (as a failure of boards was a significant contributor to the credit crunch). We described the Board Scorecard system in detail in chapter 2.

PART TWO: ACTION-ORIENTED ROADMAP

Within part two of this chapter, we provide an action-oriented roadmap to help readers steer, and succeed with, their scorecard effort.

The following six-phase template outlines a roadmap for planning a Balanced Scorecard journey. More specifically, it takes you to the point where the scorecard has been established as a performance management process. Thereafter, the scorecard needs to evolve and develop in line with changing organizational needs.

You can use this to identify action points, responsibilities and deadlines and create a plan for developing and delivering your own scorecard development program. The actions can form the basis of your own roadmap for managing all the phases of building and implementing a strategic scorecard. Among other things, the planner can be used to identify:

- people and other resource requirements for developing a scorecard
- training needs
- the business case for the scorecard
- a timetable for each phase of the scorecard program
- the potential benefits of introducing a scorecard
- the political, organizational, and practical roadblocks to be cleared
- implications for corporate performance management.

Although there are no hard and fast rules governing the time it takes to develop a scorecard, most companies find that it takes up to three months to agree a high-level scorecard and significantly longer to achieve an organizationwide rollout. But much will depend on the size and scale of the organization, geographical spread, and, not least, the amount of energy and drive dedicated to the program. The book reveals what individual organizations have achieved and under what circumstances and conditions. Combined with the book, this planner should enable you to negotiate the main requirements for getting a scorecard up and running:

- Phase one: Defining the scope and relevance of the scorecard for your organization (see table 12.1)
- Phase two: Winning support and assessing readiness for a scorecard program (see table 12.2)
- Phase three: Building the capabilities and resources to implement a program (see table 12.3)
- Phase four: Managing the strategy-mapping and scorecard process (see table 12.4)
- Phase five: Managing the scorecard implementation process (see table 12.5)
- Phase six: Make strategy a continual process (see table 12.6).

TABLE 12.1 Phase one: Defining the scope and relevance of the scorecard for your organization

Tasks	Actions, responsibility, deadlines
1. Determine the potential scope and advantages that the scorecard could bring (e.g. in terms of improved strategy focus and performance improvement, better balance of strategic objectives and risk management). Define the goals and objectives for introducing a scorecard program.	
2. Assess the state of senior management awareness of the Balanced Scorecard.	
3. Assess the status of the organization's strategy: is it well defined? Does it need to be clarified? How would the Balanced Scorecard help?	
4. Assess the organization's vision, mission, and value statements. Do they need to be revised, made meaningful and actionable?	

TABLE 12.2 Phase two: Winning support and assessing readiness for a scorecard program

Tasks	Actions, responsibility, deadlines
1. Develop a compelling business case to justify allocating scarce resources to the scorecard program.	
2. Identify sponsors and champions with the enthusiasm and authority to carry the program forward.	
3. Assess the scorecard's implications for any existing performance management system in use.	
4. Assess the likely cultural resistance to a Balanced Scorecard program. Consider conducting a cultural audit.	

TABLE 12.3   Phase three: Building the capabilities and resources to implement a program

Tasks	Actions, responsibility, deadlines
1. Develop a two-tier approach to building your scorecard with a steering group of senior managers and a development team from one level down.	
2. Appoint a program manager with the capability to manage the scorecard long term.	
3. Consider the value of using consultants. Especially consider whether the organization has the knowledge, experience, and requisite skills to do this on its own.	
4. Build in scorecard training and awareness building from the outset of the program.	
5. Consider the creation of a dedicated Office of Strategy Management to manage the strategy management process.	

TABLE 12.4   Phase four: Managing the strategy mapping and scorecard process

Tasks	Actions, responsibility, deadlines
1. Plan a series of workshops to create and implement the enterprise-level Strategy Map and scorecard.	
2. Start with a series of one-to-one and anonymous interviews with senior managers to get their views on strategic priorities.	
3. Consider whether lower-level staff and other stakeholders should be involved in the highest-level Strategy Map and scorecard creation process. Balance likely benefits with time and resource issues.	
4. Identify senior managers as theme team, and objective, measure, and initiative owners.	
5. Consider using Key Performance Questions as a bridge between strategic objectives and KPIs.	

TABLE 12.5   Phase five: Managing the scorecard implementation process

Tasks	Actions, responsibility, deadlines
1. Plan on a two-year rollout to implement the scorecard organizationwide.	
2. Develop a cascade program that involves managers and staff at every level.	
3. Establish ways of aligning departmental and personal behavior and performance with scorecard objectives throughout the organization.	
4. Evaluate the case for personal scorecards.	
5. Consider the value of aligning incentive compensation with Balanced Scorecard results.	
6. Determine how IT will support the scorecard program for data collection, reporting and communicating results, as well as its value for strategic feedback and knowledge management.	

TABLE 12.6   Phase six: Make strategy a continual process

Tasks	Actions, responsibility, deadlines
1. Make the scorecard the focus of management meetings.	
2. Set up separate strategic reviews meetings to analyze scorecard results and review the efficacy of the strategy.	
3. Ensure that budgeting and planning are linked to the scorecard.	
4. Consider the potential advantages of replacing, or at least augmenting the budgeting process with rolling forecasts to improve the responsiveness and agility of the organization.	
5. Assess the value of deploying stratex (strategic expenditure) as a mechanism for safeguarding strategic investments.	

PARTING REMARKS

In the final analysis, financial institutions must do a much better job in balancing the "short term" with the "long term." Being able to achieve this has been a core promise of the Balanced Scorecard since its inception in 1992. So too has been the promise of being able to understand the underlying drivers of "sustainable" financial performance.

Hopefully, usage of the Balanced Scorecard within financial institutions (most notably, perhaps banks) will evolve to ensure that the decisions that that led to the global financial meltdown will not be repeated. But that said, the Balanced Scorecard has always been primarily about ensuring that an inappropriate focus on chasing short-term dollars is not allowed to dominate an organization's decision-making processes or infiltrate its culture. It is interesting that some long-term scorecard users from the banking sector— such as Scotiabank—which had long understood these facts, fared better than most of their competitors during the downturn and well understood the integrating strategic management with risk management. Best practices have been around for some time.

ENDNOTES

1. Association of Chartered Certified Accountants, *Climbing Out of the Credit Crunch*, policy paper, 2008.
2. Harvard Business School Publishing, *Balanced Scorecard Report*, November/ December 2009.
3. Andrew Smart, *Aligning Risk Management and Exposure: The New Paradigm of Strategic Execution* (London: Manigent, 2009).

Index

2GC, 30, 32, 45, 46, 88

A

Adira Finance, 10, 163, 192
Advanced Performance Institute,
47, 88, 96, 97, 108, 196, 218
Aitken-Davies, Richard, 184
Alignment, 19, 23, 25–27, 38, 42,
55, 61, 63, 70, 86, 119, 122, 133,
139, 140, 147, 150, 172, 178,
184, 203, 210
Analog Device, 14
Annual budgeting process, 129, 210
Artesia BC Belgium, 193
Asian Currency Crisis, 68
Association of Chartered Certified
Accountants (ACCA), 1, 3,
4, 184

B

Bain & Company, 14
Balanced Scorecard, 3, 4, 7–10,
14–16, 18–21, 23–26, 29, 33, 34,
36, 37, 38, 40, 41, 43, 44, 46,
48–51, 53, 55–60, 61, 62, 68, 69,
72, 73, 74, 76, 78, 80, 82, 83,
85–88, 91, 92, 96, 108, 113,
116–119, 127–129, 138, 140,
141, 145–147, 148, 156, 160,
161, 163, 164, 167–173, 176,
179–184, 185, 190–197, 199,
203, 206, 208–212, 214, 217,
222, 226–229, 233

Balanced Scorecard Collaborative,
46, 57, 194
Bank CIMB Niaga, 5, 70, 71, 139,
161, 192
Bank Indonesia, 5, 36, 41, 68–70,
96, 119, 140, 162, 169, 179, 181,
191, 194, 208, 211
Bank Niaga, 70, 71
Bank of England, 146–150, 152,
153
Bank Universal, 73, 74, 82, 103,
138, 161, 163, 191
Banking 365, 6, 7, 73, 76–77, 80,
101, 102, 167, 169, 183
BIRT Performance Scorecard, 191,
192
Board Balanced Scorecard, 29
Bristol & West Consumer Direct,
164
BS31100, 54
Business Unit, 10, 18, 19, 21–23,
25, 31, 33, 35, 40, 63, 83, 118,
138, 139, 176, 182, 190, 191,
197, 208–211, 220

C

Cascade, 23, 34, 138–140, 150,
181, 182, 197
Certified Vendors, 194–195
Change Management, 194
Change Program, 119, 138, 163,
177
Chemical Bank, 1, 9, 10

235